Emerging & Women

**ALSO BY JULIE KEENE
AND
IONE JENSON**

Women Alone: Creating a Joyous and Fulfilling Life

Available at your local bookstore, or call Hay House at:
(800) 654-5126

Please visit the Hay House Website at:
http://www.hayhouse.com

Emerging & Women

THE WIDENING STREAM

JULIE KEENE
and
IONE JENSON

Hay House, Inc.
Carlsbad, CA

Published and distributed in the United States by:
Hay House, Inc., P.O. Box 5100, Carlsbad, CA 92018-5100 • (800) 654-5126
(800) 650-5115 (fax)

Edited by: Jill Kramer
Designed by: Jenny Richards

*Masil Hulse, the artist who painted the lovely work on the front cover, is available
for private commissions, and she also sells prints of her existing works. You may contact her by calling The Holo Center in Idaho: (208) 772-2816.*

Library of Congress Cataloging-in-Publication Data

Keene, Julie.
     Emerging women : the widening stream / Julie Keene and Ione
Jenson.
        p.   cm.
     ISBN 1-56170-356-7
1. Women—Biography. 2. Women civic leaders—Biography.
3. Women in the professions—Biography. 4. Self-actualization
(Psychology)—Case studies. I. Jenson, Ione. II. Title.
HQ1123.K44   1997
920.72—dc20   96-46155
                                   CIP

ISBN 1-56170-356-7

00 99 98 97   4 3 2 1
First Printing, April 1997

Printed in the United States of America

*We lovingly dedicate this book to all of the
Emerging Women of planet Earth who are allowing
the feminine spirit to rise and who are creating new
paradigms for the 21st century.*

CONTENTS

PART II: WEAVING NEW PATTERNS OF EMERGENCE

APPENDIX

ACKNOWLEDGMENTS

We would sincerely like to thank Louise Hay for supporting our emergence as writers and giving us the opportunity to be associated with such a tremendous publishing staff! A special thanks to our editor, Jill Kramer, who always lends such consistent encouragement and good advice—we appreciate her beyond words. We are so grateful to all of the women who have lovingly and willingly shared their stories and given so much of themselves to help make this book a reality. Thanks to Sunny Stone, minister of Unity in Tallahassee; to Jean Houston; and to Barbara Marx Hubbard for their "beyond-the-call-of-duty" help in connecting us with some of the outstanding women we interviewed in these pages. We have been wonderfully supported by women everywhere who are finding the value in networking and the collective wisdom and power we possess in our unity. God Bless you all!

PART I

Models,
Motivators,
and
Mentors

INTRODUCTION:
Individual Patterns of Emergence

The words *emerging women* mean, simply stated, that we are giving birth to a new kind of feminine maturity. In previous generations, women played out predetermined roles and often felt helpless and unable to change things. Often they remained in these cultural prisons and never realized that, at least to some degree, those prisons were of their own making. The male population remained the captors because women cooperated with them by playing out the assigned scripts. There have always been, of course, a few brave women who refused to accept their assignments.

They Dared to Challenge!

Historically, it seems that there have always been a small number of brave women throughout the generations who have, individually and collectively, demanded a greater voice in their lives and who have been willing to strive for the advancement of all women. Women such as Carry Nation and Susan B. Anthony, along with other suffragettes, began to demand the right to vote in the early 1900s. Still others, such as Margaret Sanger, struggled to have access to information regarding the practice of birth control. Eventually, women began to push for the right to enter the workplace, and then for equality in the job market. However, until the 1960s, when the number of feminists, led by women such as Betty Freidan and Gloria Steinem, began to swell the ranks through modern-day consciousness-raising groups and more overt demands for equality and the passage of the Equal Rights Amendment, the number of women demanding more freedom and the right to be heard was extremely limited. Most women, too frightened to rock the boat of male authority, remained subservient to the other half of the population, and either played out the traditional roles or gained a certain amount of power and control through the long-practiced art of subtle feminine manipulations.

Emerging Values for the Emerging Woman

However, today we do see a new kind of woman emerging—a woman who is not always as radical, perhaps, as in the early days of feminism, but who is, nonetheless, independent and assertive. A new woman is emerging who does not necessarily need to be aggressive in the same way that males do, but she *does* come from a place of power and self-respect. She is a woman who has often recognized her own, as well as the culture's, co-dependent attitudes and patterns and has moved to break free of these constraints. Nonetheless, her freedom has usually come not from the spirit of rebellion after long repression, but rather as a slow and methodical movement forward, and is oftentimes the result of her efforts to attain wholeness through personal and spiritual growth. The new emerging woman has often worked with a therapist or has taken part in self-help or support groups. She has come to recognize that in order to attain a healthy lifestyle, she needs to surrender her victim mentality and replace it with an increasing awareness that she—and she alone—is responsible for her own life and ultimate happiness. While she does not deny the outer realities, she has come to rely on a greater truth, and she has come to understand that by changing her attitudes and mental thought patterns, she can literally recreate her life!

In reclaiming personal responsibility, this emerging woman has, in fact, also reclaimed her power. She does not need to bulldoze her way through life in the old male model, but she can, through connection to her own creative nature, access unlimited ideas and opportunities. Step-by-step, she has been able to release old programming and let go of old guilts and fears. By learning to take responsibility for herself, she is also learning to hand the responsibility back to others to do likewise. She is no longer willing to accept the role of simply making others happy or being the constant caretaker of everyone else's needs!

The new emerging woman is—in brief—liberating herself from the inside out. In the early forms of feminism, the struggle was to raise the cultural awareness level and to attempt to change the traditional roles a woman was expected to play by modifying only the outer forms and circumstances. However, the woman we now see emerging is the one who realizes that she must also change the inner world as well. From these inner changes, she develops the confidence and courage to simultaneously change the outer forms of her existence. She is beginning to do so from a place of both wisdom and clarity. The end result is that the emerging woman we see is very sensitive and caring, but she is also strong and determined.

The emerging woman is learning to balance the yin and yang energies, and she is finding the inner marriage of both the masculine and feminine principles to be the perfect union. She realizes that only from this place of inner perfection will it be possible to become a whole human being. Capable of giving—without giving herself away; capable of caring—without bearing the burden of caretaker; and capable of sensitivity to inner guidance—while immune to outer criticism, she can now chart her own course.

Unwilling Beginnings

The emerging woman is often forced, unwillingly, into her new birth. Sometimes divorce and death are the birth pangs that push her into a new life, and she suddenly finds herself thrust into a world in which she is both unfamiliar and uncomfortable—a place where she gasps for breath, kicking and flailing, and then is forced to fight for her survival. This very struggle for existence, difficult and painful though it may be, is the same experience that makes her strong and becomes the catalyst for her new emergence. These events may not be what she would have consciously chosen; however, she will look back in retrospect and seldom will she choose to go back and surrender the new strength she has gained.

A Season of Discontent

In other cases, the emerging woman has sprung forth with a creeping sense of uneasiness. Perhaps married and not wanting to change that status, she nonetheless begins to feel a vague discomfort with her current life, and it may take her quite some time to figure out why she is uncomfortable. She may seek a counselor or a support group to aid her in discovering the reasons behind her season of discontent. For the first time, she may uncover deep longings that have been repressed in order to play out her more traditional role, but bit by bit, she discovers the many facets of herself that have remained largely unexplored. As these long-repressed shadows are given glimpses of light, they began to surface and clamor for expression, and in time they become impossible to silence. Eventually, the need for new and expanded forms of expression becomes so intense that the emerging woman's fears give way—first to deep exploration, and then to a changing set of values that includes honoring her unique gifts and a new way of conveying that uniqueness!

Living Solo

At times, the emerging woman chooses to remain single, but at other times, she is forced into a solo life, stemming from the lack of a suitable committed relationship. In either case, she learns to create a life that encompasses nontraditional ways of filling her basic emotional and physical survival needs. As she finds herself alone, she learns to dance to her own music and take responsibility for creating a rich and fulfilling life. As she becomes stronger and more confident that she is able to rely on her own resourcefulness—thus feeling increasingly empowered—she begins to form either loosely or tightly knit support systems that allow for autonomy and interdependence. As these highly satisfactory models evolve, the emerging woman is no longer willing to settle for just anyone or anything. Her standards are far above the norm that was often accepted in earlier decades, and she determines that partnering must provide a distinct opportunity for both members of the relationship. If it does not, she knows she is far better off in her solo flight pattern.

Womanspirit Rising

Although true cultural equality is not yet in existence, the emerging woman has still benefited greatly from the feminist movement and from the new information regarding co-dependency in relationships. Through the availability of self-help or psychospiritual groups that encourage her to seek and find personal power and to create new opportunities for herself, she is, in fact, reconnecting with her own soul, and she sees and understands her own divinity.

Finally, the emerging woman is beginning to access the positive strengths that come from bonding with other women. Instead of viewing other females as rivals for available males or good jobs, she is coming into a greater awareness of just how much can be accomplished through cooperation and mutual support systems with her sisters. She is discovering how much simpler it is to find true communication and mutual growth opportunities, and how much easier it is to hone spiritual qualities and the gifts and talents within herself when she enters into a community of women. It is, in essence, a return to the tribal spirit of women with one added advantage: She no longer needs to be a caretaker of men (as is the case in some tribal systems). And while she is capable of expressing tremendous amounts of love and encourages individual empowerment in others, she knows that each of us, ultimately, can only be the true guardians of *our own soul.*

ABOUT THE PROFILES

> *"Sharing our story can open our eyes to*
> *the ambushes we share with others and*
> *open paths to freedom."*
> — Marion Woodman

The following profiles are reflections and examples of the transformative energy bursting forth from an ever-increasing number of women. Many we spoke with are reaching out to their emerging sisters all over the globe and becoming catalysts for positive changes in every area of human endeavor. We realize that there are many thousands of emerging women all over the world who are currently making potent contributions, so these profiles are only a brief sampling.

Some of the women you will meet here are well known. Others are well known only in a more limited sphere of influence. Many are relatively unknown. As you discover the challenges and ambushes they have dealt with, we hope the path to your own freedom and fulfillment will be made wider and smoother. We have been audacious enough to include our own stories, and we hope you will find those valuable to you as well.

We have made an effort to include women from a variety of geographical areas who have divergent occupations, backgrounds, and lifestyles. Their ages range from 15 to 95. May these profiles inspire you to motivate and mentor women in your own life if you're not doing so already. If you are, we offer our congratulations and honor your efforts. We all have tremendous power to make a positive difference, and we are not alone in our efforts! As dynamic model, motivator, and mentor Jean Houston says: "The emergence of women is one of the most critical movements in human history, the biggest in 5,000 years." Let's seize this opportunity and make the most of it!

CAROL AMOS
A Minister Living Her Dream

---

*"Guided by my heritage of a love of beauty
and a respect for strength, in search of
my mother's garden, I found my own."*
— Alice Walker

She wore her hair "natural" for the first time in the sixties when she was a teenager. It was her symbol of freedom, self-acceptance, and hope. "For the first time, I realized I just might be acceptable just the way I was," Carol Amos recalls. "Maybe I could break out of my family's pattern."

Carol's parents were from the South and lived in fear of white people, and Carol grew up in Black Bottom, a part of the inner city of Detroit, with her ten brothers and sisters. "We were poor," she says, "and being the oldest, I took a great deal of responsibility for my siblings and for my mother, who was sick much of the time. My father wasn't always around."

Carol's mother had no faith in herself, and she lived in fear and poverty, but she did have faith in Carol. She always said, "*I* can't do it, but you can, Carol," and somehow her daughter believed her. However, Carol's dreams were deferred for several years. She married young and had seven children of her own. It wasn't until after her divorce that a new life seemed possible. At the time, her youngest child was 9 and the oldest was 18. Carol was employed by the state of Michigan in the food stamp program, and she started college part time, working toward a degree in sociology. Carol recalls:

> About that same time, I began working with a counselor. She happened to be a licensed Unity teacher who introduced me to West Side Unity and Rev. Ruth Mosely, who would prove to be a major model, motivator, and mentor for me. I remember talking to her and making the statement, "Things are really going to be hard for me." Ruth's answer was, "Why should they be?" She taught and lived the principle that life is what we make of it, and it doesn't have to be hard once we begin to take spiritual charge of our own lives. She's a simple woman, but a strong and eloquent one who lives what she teaches. From that time on, I began to take charge of my life in a new way. Of course, there were challenges; one can't raise seven children without them, but I knew I wasn't really alone because I was working with the Christ Spirit in a supportive church environment.

After Carol had attended her church for a few years, Rev. Ruth started an outreach urban ministerial program. Students could study with her for a year and do local outreach work and then finish their studies at Unity Village in Missouri the next year. Carol applied and was accepted for this program, but then began to have self-doubts. "Can I really do this?" she asked herself. Rev. Ruth's response to her was, "You can't afford *not* to do this." She believed in Carol so much that Carol began to believe in herself again. "And of course, Rev. Ruth was right," Carol declares. "My ministry has meant everything to me, and changed my life completely. I thank God for Ruth; I'll always be grateful to her. She looked past my limitations to my potential."

Other women have been models and mentors for Carol as well. A friend and fellow ministerial student, Mercedes Hill, worked with

Carol for several years before they entered the ministry. "She loving-ly corrected every bit of incorrect English that happened to flow from my mouth," Carol says. "It amazes me that she never let up, yet she always left my dignity intact."

After Carol was ordained in 1983, she co-ministered for eight years with Etta Farrior in Asbury Park, New Jersey, and in Arlington, Texas. From different backgrounds and lifestyles, they met in minis-terial school, learned from each other, and encouraged and supported each other. Etta is white, had been a practicing lawyer, and she came from a more privileged environment. However, the two women dis-covered that the Unity teachings transcended their race and back-ground. "As a biracial ministerial team, we symbolized the insignifi-cance of color by operating from the spiritual level," Carol affirms. "We became motivators for people in our congregations and for each other."

Carol is now minister of Unity Church in Kalamazoo, Michigan, a comm-UNITY of Love where, according to Carol, "we notice that all of us are not of the same color. We appreciate each unique indi-vidual, and as loving brothers and sisters in Christ, color is not an issue."

Carol also mentors at-risk students in the Kalamazoo Academic Achievement program who need a caring adult outside their family who will give them quality time. She often goes into the school to eat lunch with students; at other times Carol takes a group of students to museums, plays, or movies—things they don't normally do. Carol says:

> They remind me so much of myself at that age, and I want them to know that someone cares. I want to infuse them with hope and to inspire them to open their minds and hearts to new possibilities. When I think about it, that's my mission at the church as well. Every one of us needs hope and inspiration, and I'm grateful for the oppor-tunity to dedicate my life to the work that Rev. Ruth Mosely would not stop believing I could do. It has changed my life. It *is* my life.

ALICIA APPLEMAN-JURMAN
Triumph Beyond the Holocaust

"However confused the scene of our life appears,
however torn we may be when we do face that scene,
it can be faced, and we can go on to be whole."
                                            — Muriel Ruckeyser

---

A s the attractive, smiling woman in red walked to the podium
after her introduction, the nearly 1,200 high school students in
the auditorium clapped and cheered. They had read her book, and
they were eager to hear more from her personally. With a warm and
open demeanor and obvious affection for her audience, Alicia
Appleman-Jurman began to speak.

We too had read her book, *Alicia: My Story*, and had been deeply
moved by the account of how a courageous young Jewish girl managed to survive the Holocaust and save many others. However, the
most inspiring element of her story was that Alicia, in the midst of
unspeakable horrors, which included the murders of her father, mother, and three brothers, never gave up her spunk, her spirit, her will to
live, and her desire to be a complete human being. Alicia herself

came close to annihilation a total of six times, "but they never touched my soul," she passionately testifies.

Alicia wrote her book and now speaks to students for two reasons. First, she swore on her brother Zackery's grave that she would tell the story so that her family and other silenced young people might live through the pages. Secondly, Alicia loves and respects students and wants them to know the truth of what happened and what could happen again if people allow hatred or scapegoating to take over their lives.

She makes it clear both by her words and by her loving actions that she refuses to *hate*. She wants her work to serve as a stimulus for humankind to be more humane. "I tell the story of individuals," she says, "because it is difficult for people to relate to six million corpses, but they *can* relate to individuals." Perhaps that is why *Alicia: My Story* is being approved by an ever-increasing number of Boards of Education in the United States and Canada for use as a textbook in history and Holocaust-study classes.

Alicia's dedication and sincerity is illustrated by the fact that she does not accept fees of any kind for her work in the schools. Alicia's passion to tell the story drove her to write 6 days a week, up to 13 hours a day for 3 years. She believes that the angels kissed her book, because five publishers wanted it, and then during the editing process, the only changes or corrections were for grammar and punctuation.

In the course of her writing, Alicia traveled back into her past, becoming the little girl whose sheltered and serene life with her family was shattered. The reader sees how the strength and values she gained from her early childhood carried her through the grueling ordeals of her teen years. Alicia now recalls:

> I was a proud Jewish girl. When the oppressors called the Jews terrible names, I didn't believe them. I had studied Jewish history and knew that we had built an advanced civilization while our persecutors were still living in caves.

Alicia's strong will and sense of self-worth led her to defy first the Russian and then the German occupiers of her Polish hometown. The Russians began by taking all Jewish civil rights away, including the right of children to attend school. But Alicia loved school and her teacher, and she was determined to continue learning. A tree outside her former classroom window overlooked the teacher and the blackboard. For several days, Alicia walked to the school before daylight, climbed the tree, and then made herself as comfortable as possible in its branches. Through the open window, she heard the day's lessons, then climbed down the tree after everyone had gone home. Alicia laughs as she remembers the day the teacher wrote a math problem on the board and asked for answers. Alicia forgot herself, raised her hand, and slipped down the tree. The teacher came outside and made it clear that she must stay away from the school.

"Maybe that's why I love being in schools now," she tells her audience. "You students need to know that one of your greatest gifts is to be able to enter a classroom and to say 'here' when the teacher calls your name. Sometimes people ask me how I can stand being in noisy schools, and I answer, 'What noise?' The voices of the children are beautiful to me; they are the voices of children with a future."

As Alicia speaks to the adults and students in the auditorium, everyone is spellbound, and many quietly cry. After the presentation, Alicia receives a standing ovation and the gift of a bronzed apple from the students. The next day we are invited to spend time with her as she talks with groups of students at one of the local high schools. In these small and informal sessions, Alicia sits on the desk, relaxed and obviously delighted to be here. In turn, the students show interest and respect as they ask thoughtful questions. Because they've read her book, many want to know what eventually happened to some of the specific people whose stories she so eloquently recounted. The students sound more than just curious; they seem to care. A student asks why more of the Jews didn't fight back. Alicia makes it clear that the Jews did not all submit like sheep to slaughter.

Many Jews fought back; my brother Zackery was hanged for fighting back after they killed the girl he loved and her two little sisters. Children can be brave and maintain values in the midst of horrors. We fought the murderers by building and digging hiding places in order to save as many people as we could. Wearing an apron with hidden pockets, I took dirt far away from our yard so it wouldn't reveal our secret activity.

Once while bathing in a creek with my mother, I became aware of my pitifully skinny body and asked, "Will I ever be a woman?" She replied, "You are a woman already." She taught me to make decisions and to be responsible, and her teaching was an important element in my survival. I loved her with all my heart and protected her and my brothers in every way I could.

However, there was no way that Alicia could stem the tide of horrors. She saw soldiers shoot off the faces of babies and young children. She herself was stomped on by a soldier, thrown in prison, given drinking water laced with typhus germs, stomped on once again, and left for dead. She was buried while the Germans watched, but was then miraculously dug up again by a Jewish gravedigger who had felt her feverish body and realized she was still alive. He hid her under the straw of his wagon, took her home, and nursed her back to health.

A student asks Alicia how she deals with people who deny that the Holocaust ever happened, and she responds:

I don't even bother to answer adults who are so foolish. But a 14-year-old boy in another school told me his uncle believes the Holocaust never happened. I asked the boy if he had a mother and father, sisters or brothers, grandparents. He said. "Yes." I replied, "They don't exist, you don't have them, never had them." He burst out, "That's crazy!" That's right! I said. And people who deny the Holocaust are telling me that my father, mother, brothers, neighbors, friends, and countless others never existed. The boy then exclaimed, "That IS really crazy! I'd better have another talk with my uncle."

Another student asks about hate groups such as skinheads, and Alicia answers:

> Not long ago two of them sat in the front row, ready to mock me. I spoke directly to them. "I understand your loneliness, but this group is not the answer. You will destroy yourself with hatred. Don't let these hatemongers use and abuse you." One of the boys walked out, but the other stayed and listened. This is also what I say to gang members. "Why allow anyone to destroy you with hatred?" Once after a talk, a young German came up to me sobbing, asking for my forgiveness. I held him in my arms and told him there was nothing to forgive, that I didn't hold him responsible for what his ancestors did.

After the war, Alicia continued her work, again risking her life to save Jews by helping to smuggle them into Israel. Later, she herself emigrated and served two years in the Israeli navy. In 1950 she married an American construction engineer who had come to Israel to help build the country. They later moved to the United States and became the parents of three children.

Between 1982 and 1985, Alicia recorded her experiences in the book her children asked her to write. During the process, she often found herself reliving the horror, many times laying her head down on her typewriter and crying bitter tears. But the catharsis was important. The pain needed to be drained. Alicia now talks to other Holocaust survivors before they interview with Steven Spielberg, who is preserving their stories for history. She gently draws them out and helps them to deal with their pain in such a way that they are then able to coherently speak about their experiences.

When a student asks Alicia why, after all she'd seen, she still decided to bring children into the world, she replies:

> I had to have two major surgeries in order to get pregnant for the children I so desperately wanted. I trusted in the goodness of God, of the people in this country—I trusted life. I don't hate. I believe in God. People let God down when they decide to kill each other. I don't

blame God; it's a human disgrace. I decided not to hate because I wanted to do something that could cause God to believe in us.

It is coming close to the end of the period, and a student asks, "What is the most important thing you'd like us to remember?" Alicia replies:

> You young people possess strengths within yourselves in times of need. You can be brave and resourceful and hang on to your dignity, no matter what, even when the world seems to be withholding it from you. I trust that you will not forget what we learn from each other here today. Hatred can destroy a human being, a group of people, a country. It is important to face ourselves, to not blame and scapegoat each other. To do so is to put our country in danger. You have your page in history yet to write. You are the children of the future. Please make a pledge to work for the freedom of everyone. Love, be happy, celebrate life.

The session ends with hugs and time for autographing books. We are amazed at the energy of this vivacious woman in her sixties who doesn't look a day over 50. She invites us to sit and chat awhile. We learn that in December of 1994 she had a serious heart attack and then complications from surgery. The doctors had given up hope. What was supposed to be a five-day hospital stay extended into seven weeks. But her work on earth was not finished. "The good Lord has always made the decisions about my life." She says:

> When I was in school in Israel after the war, we didn't pick the oranges in the orchard during the day because Arab snipers would shoot at us. One day, I couldn't wait for the taste of a juicy orange and went outside to pick one. An Arab bullet went through a branch, burned a path across my blouse, and fell at my feet. That bullet is in my jewelry box now. It reminds me that as long as God has work for me to do, I'll be around to do it.

JUDITH BILLINGS, J.D.
Living Victoriously with AIDS

---

*"I believe that the co-creative feminine energy must
rise to leadership now—taking the initiative to
transform our political and social dialogue."*
— Barbara Marx Hubbard

It has been said that a crisis neither makes a coward nor a heroine, instead, it merely shows what one has gradually become. Judith Billings, Washington State Superintendent of Schools, emerged as a heroine when she stood before a microphone during a press conference in January of 1996 and announced to the public that she has AIDS. With grace and dignity, despite the emotional content of the message, she displayed no self-pity. Instead, she assured the viewing audience that she feels fine and promised to continue giving her best to the job she was elected to do.

Her statement is indicative of the mettle of Judith Billings: "I am certainly not going to allow what may happen tomorrow to sidetrack me, derail me, depress me, or defeat me in any way today. Life was never meant to be lived through fear." Her decision in the early 1980s to attempt motherhood through artificial insemination has proven to be a choice that defines her AIDS battle today. However, as the epitome of an emerging woman, she remains in control of her responses to this current challenge. She is determined to live her life, not her death.

Judith does not easily fold under challenges. In July of 1993, she found herself being threatened and stalked by a disgruntled employee whom she had laid off due to budget cuts. For a year, she was harassed. Among other things, bullets arrived in the mail with notes that said: "You don't deserve to live." She went public with her story and refused to allow the stalker to intimidate her. While taking reasonable precautions and sometimes wearing a bulletproof vest, she continued to do her job and live her life. But why should anyone be surprised? She has, almost from the beginning, thrived on challenge and has insisted on meeting life on her own terms. Judith Billings has not become the courageous lady she is today simply because either a stalker or AIDS has come into her life. As is the case with just about all emerging women, many events have helped to forge and create her.

Born into the warm embrace of an unconditionally loving, nurturing, and supportive nuclear and extended family unit, Judith always felt encouraged to do or be whatever she wanted. As a child, she admired Amelia Earhart for her independence and ability to take risks, and Judith wanted to emulate her.

> I wanted more than to just stay at home, I wanted to go into the foreign service or be a flyer. One summer while walking with my Uncle Winton, whom I deeply admired and always held in the highest regard for his credibility—a man of unquestioned integrity and someone I really wanted to be like—I can remember saying that someday I was going to be the first woman president.
>
> Other family members, like an aunt who was a very independent woman, all became terrific role models for me as I grew up. This kind of family makes you secure in whatever you do. If you fail in some-

thing, they're still there, and they are not disappointed in you. They provide the encouragement to step out one more time. My dad has always been so proud of his daughters. To this day, he clips out newspaper articles about me and sends Xeroxed copies to his relatives!

Involved in the yearbook and the student newspaper in high school, Judith remembers that her journalism advisor, Marvin Evans, was the motivator who pushed, encouraged, and supported her in maximizing her potential. Her participation in college forensics taught thinking processes that were the most important part of her education. Professor Theodore Karl, head of the speech communication department, inspired and challenged her to become a skilled speaker and to expand her interests.

When I was in school and took the tests geared to explore interests, the only careers available to women were secretaries, nurses, or teachers. I resented that. That wasn't what I wanted to be, and it ended up being a challenge, a clarion call. I thought, You're not going to put me in that box. It spurred in me the determination to step into some arenas that were not traditional.

Judith continued her education and remained involved in the varied aspects of public education. She has been a classroom teacher, earned a master's degree in communications, administered federally funded programs for disadvantaged children, and supervised Washington's Remediation Assistance Program. Each role expanded her expertise, and eventually she served as national legislative committee chair for the National Association of Title I Coordinators. This piqued her interest in the legal aspects of education, and she began attending evening classes at the University of Puget Sound Law School. She completed law school, graduating with a Juris Doctorate, cum laude, and spent the next year as a staff member of the Education and Labor Committee of the House of Representatives in Washington, D.C.

In 1988 she was elected Washington State Superintendent of Public Instruction, defeating an opponent who had been in the legislature and was thought to be a certain winner. She was only the third woman to be elected to that office, and the first since 1945. While running for her first term, it took awhile to convince people she was credible and knew what she was doing—that she could effectively manage a state education agency.

> Somebody in one of the organizations was quoted as saying, "I wonder if she can handle the superintendents in this state." I thought, Man, you talk about the good old boys' network! What they're admitting right up front is that most of the school superintendents are males, and then they're making this incredibly sexist remark that a woman isn't capable of handling men. It was interesting on a number of levels. I remember saying at a press luncheon here in Olympia, "Look, I'm not some brunette bimbo stepping into this. I've got experience behind me." I think at that point, people began to realize that I was a person who knew what she was doing.

Indeed, she did, and she was not afraid to ask the tough questions nor afraid to challenge anyone not serving the best interests of education.

Judith is now completing her second term in that office but will not run for reelection in 1996. This decision has nothing to do with having AIDS; she has always known she would only serve two terms and then move on to her next challenge. She has not decided exactly what that will be. "Boy, am I having a hard time deciding that one," she laughs. But whatever she decides to do next, it will definitely include speaking out honestly and passionately about a number of things dear to her heart.

As we approached the topic that she discussed in January of 1996 with such openness and honesty that it had endeared her to the hearts of so many, we asked where she had found the inner strength and the sustenance to meet this challenge with such courage. She again opened her heart willingly and shared deeply.

> I have always known there was a Higher Power I could talk to personally, and my family has been extremely supportive. They have

been just incredible all the way through. For the first ten months after the diagnosis, our family didn't share the AIDS diagnosis. This gave us the necessary time to think about it, to work through our processes, to be together, and to gather strength and support.

My family members were like rocks for me and sent me cards and notes and didn't change at all. When HIV/AIDS was first around, there was so much fear connected with it in terms of personal contact, but our relationships never changed—with the single exception that they're very careful not to bring the grandchildren over if they have the flu or a cold or something they think might be harmful to me, so that is tremendously helpful. (Judith and her husband, Donald, have four grown children from his previous marriage.)

∾ ∾

Jean Houston, renowned scientist, philosopher, and pioneer in human development, finds in her work with AIDS patients that many of them have access to depths of their psyche and to spiritual "sourcing" that many healthy people simply do not have. Certainly, Judith touches her inner depths and connects with that "source." She's had a lifelong relationship with a Spiritual Being she knows is always in her corner, and this has become her sustaining power.

I must admit it has heightened my awareness of how important it is to talk daily with "whoever" that is. In fact, there was a particular time just about a month after my diagnosis when we were at a conference in Portland, and one of the evening events was a dinner trip to Timberline Lodge on Mt. Hood. I was riding up in the front of the bus and looking out the window and thinking how beautiful it was, how great it was. Then, all of a sudden, and I believe this was a DIVINE message, a wonderful mantle of total peace and contentment settled over me, and I knew, "Okay—it's going to be okay. I've been talking to you, God, and now I know you're here and you are taking care of me, and so I'm not going to worry about anything." And now, that understanding is a daily satisfaction.

Since publicly acknowledging she has AIDS, the response from people has been beyond any of her expectations. She receives cards,

letters, phone calls, books, and information about alternative therapies, most of it from people she doesn't even know but who just want
to lend their support. "It's such a reaffirmation of the basic goodness
of people, and that's needed so much now. Regardless of what sometimes seems an overwhelming cynicism about life, there are hundreds
and hundreds of people who don't believe that way. We've got to find
a way to make those positive attitudes more visible."

As Judith mulls over her choices and gets ready to move on to
whatever she decides to do next, she is determined to speak forthrightly and passionately about her concerns. She wants to see a society that builds people up, restores trust, and treats others courteously
and respectfully. She strongly wants to be involved in the process of
helping to create a healthier society. But there is also another message
she wants to convey.

> There are many, many wonderful people out there who have
> AIDS and who are still living full and joyous lives and have not suc-
> cumbed to the idea that once you get the news that's the end of every-
> thing. It's been a terrific experience to meet those positive people liv-
> ing with HIV/AIDS here in the state, as well as nationally, and to see
> the level of caring and the level of joy in people's lives regardless of
> what they're facing.
>
> One of the first things I said to my doctors, once I knew the diag-
> nosis, was, "I'm going to learn to live with this, not die from it." This
> message of positive thinking and hope is definitely the motivator for
> the National Organization of People Living with Aids—it's a whole
> different way to look at it.

Prior to her own diagnosis, Judith had always been an advocate
for AIDS education. A national leader in the HIV/AIDS curriculum
for grades 5 to 12, Washington State mandates HIV/AIDS education
in its schools. Actively working with the National Association of
People Living with AIDS, the Northwest AIDS Foundation, and other
organizations working in the area of AIDS education, prevention, and
services, Judith will continue making a difference in this whole arena.

A healthy blend of tenacity and strength mixed with honesty, warmth, and inner depth, Judith is an excellent role model. She does not allow herself to become a victim of her challenges, but has instead become a responder to life in both its ebb and flow. Determined to make the most of her life, she states simply and succinctly, "No one of us can predict what our futures are going to be. The only thing we know for sure when we are born is that someday we are going to die. What I want people to know is I can forge ahead and be positive. I have to treasure every moment."

Believing in the interpenetrative weave of the body, mind, and spirit connection, we are certain that Judith Billings has the inner and outer resources necessary for living a *long* time and for continuing to create a life filled with richness, meaning, and beauty. Let's all affirm it with her.

JOAN BORYSENKO, Ph.D.
Medical and Spiritual Pioneer

---

*"I tore myself away from the safe comfort of certainty
through my love for truth; and truth rewarded me."*
— Simone de Beauvoir

Medical researcher, cell biologist, psychologist, author of several bestselling books, speaker, and retreat leader, Joan Borysenko is, above all, a warm human being who cares about people. Her messages about the importance of spiritual awakening, body-mind medicine, and healing are the gifts she presents from her unique background and perspective. "My priority," she says, "is to reach as many people as possible, so my focus now is writing, speaking, and retreats. I do about 80 events a year, and I do an increasing number of women's spiritual retreats in partnership with some beautiful and incredibly talented women."

Joan's awakening to the importance of women in her life came late. She entered early into a predominantly male profession, married, and became the mother of two sons. "Even the dog was male," she laughs. She worked for a number of years at Tufts Medical School and Harvard Medical School. "I was taught and socialized," Joan says, "to act like a 'junior male,' an apt term invented by my good friend Dr. Christiane Northrup." Finding this predominantly male environment isolating, Joan became involved in the mid-'80s with a women's group that focused on prayer, meditation, and intuition. These women soon became enormously important in her life, and she realized how much she'd missed the company of women. "Ever since then," she says, "I've been involved with a women's group."

Joan continues, "One of the problems in the world today is that there aren't enough role models and mentors for young women. Your *Emerging Women* book sounds like a fabulous project for motivating women to become more aware of what we can offer each other, and I'm happy to be a part of it." Joan regrets that she never had a personal woman mentor, "although I've surely searched," she says.

"My mother provided negative mentoring in a certain sense," Joan muses, "because she was the catalyst that caused me to search for another way of being." Joan grew up questioning life at every turn, while her mother believed it was safer and better to not question. When Joan was 15, she came home with information about the Unitarian church, which her nonbelieving Jewish mother promptly threw in the trash, forbidding any further religious questing or any study of psychology.

"Since I grew up to be a scientist and psychologist with a major interest in religion and philosophy, I can truly say that I owe my mother all that I am," Joan says with a touch of irony in her voice. "She was the perfect foil for my rebellious nature. She played her part in the drama of my life perfectly, contributing the precise energy required to spur my quest for meaning!"

Joan feels fortunate to have been a student at Bryn Mawr College in the '60s, where she came of age in an atmosphere where intellectual pursuits for women were considered the norm. However, as a student in the hard sciences with a double major in biology and psychology, she didn't have the opportunity to connect with a female mentor. Although there were some women on staff, Joan ended up working almost exclusively in the laboratories of men.

"Because my awareness of the importance of women in my life

has come to me later, I especially value the sense of kinship and sisterhood I now share with women," Joan declares. In her extensive travels, she observes that women comprise about 85 percent of her audiences as she talks about consciousness, healing, and global awakening. Many women return year after year to the women's spiritual retreats, so a solid kinship is building. "There is the feeling that we're all growing together throughout the year," Joan adds, "and this is extremely important to me."

Working with women partners to co-create retreats that incorporate spirituality, music, and humor is another joyous element of Joan's work. Her voice reflects warmth and affection as she talks about these women. Elizabeth Lawrence is an energy healer who has a master's degree in pastoral counseling. Formerly Joan's neighbor in suburban Boston, Elizabeth called one day because she was familiar with Joan's work, offering to do a healing session. "My first reaction, was—never mind!" Joan laughs. Over the next year, they got to know each other, and Joan discovered that Elizabeth was a superb healer. "Earlier in life she'd been a nun and then married and raised four sons," Joan says. "We now jokingly refer to ourselves as Mother Superior and the Jewish Mother!"

Their retreats, called *A Gathering of Women*, focus upon the healing of memories, centering prayer, body prayers, music, and humor. They strive to incorporate many traditions, including Native American, Buddhist, Tibetan, Hindu, and Judeo-Christian. Musician Jan Maier, who has "a voice like an angel," and Annie DeSarcina, a nurse who specializes in humor, are also part of the core of presenters.

Joan feels so rewarded by this cooperative work that she is developing two more women's retreats. The first is with Janet Quinn, who is currently writing a book about "recycled" Catholics. "Janet is a dear friend, a Ph.D. researcher, and nurse who has focused upon therapeutic touch." Joan explains:

> Our retreat brings together common roots of the Judeo-Christian spiritual path. Our aim is to reconstruct rituals from a time before rituals became dogmatized by organized religion. The roots of both

Judaism and Christianity come from earth-centered feminine traditions, so we incorporate these ancient traditions that offer a variety of ways to restore interconnectedness. We find that when women recognize all the similarities and connections, a depth is added to their spiritual lives.

Joan's partners in another set of retreats are Loretta LaRoche and Mona Lisa Schultz. Loretta, "the funniest lady on the face of the earth" according to Joan, will help women see themselves in a new light through humor. Joan calls this process "cognitive restructuring." Mona Lisa, a brilliant and witty physician, psychiatrist, neuroscientist, and medical intuitive, will teach women how to develop their own intuition. "I'm excited about all these retreats," Joan reiterates. "It's satisfying to be working with women in such a variety of ways."

As we spoke with Joan, she was just finishing her latest book entitled *The Woman's Book of Life: The Biology, Psychology, and Spirituality of the Feminine Life Cycle.* "It moves through the life cycle in seven-year segments," Joan explains, "and incorporates neurobiological development and sociological and psychological theories. It will highlight the intrinsic spirituality of women."

Currently, Joan is receiving many letters from women who are responding well to *Pocketful of Miracles*, a daily spiritual practice book containing nurturing affirmations, meditations, and prayers from several different traditions. The 15 varieties of meditation from around the world are keyed to the seasons and earth holidays and designed to provide year-round support for the reader dedicated to spiritual growth.

Joan's dedication to spiritual growth shines forth clearly in her impressive body of work. She often shares her own challenges and processes while encouraging others on the path. In *The Power of the Mind to Heal,* Joan and her ex-husband, Miron Borysenko, display their incredible talent for making complex medical concepts not only clear, but actually fascinating, to the general reading public. They are open and authentic as they share their own challenges and processes, and then they skillfully and lovingly provide readers with specific ways to heal their own lives.

As we end our conversation with Joan, we ask her to give our *Emerging Women* readers her parting thoughts. She says:

Be gentle with yourself. Don't deny your pain. Learn from it and move forward. When you pray, don't ask for a perfect life, ask for an authentic sense of longing for the Divine, ask to come home to God. Peace of mind is our birthright, the inner radiance of our own true nature, the Higher or Wisdom Self. To find it, we need only part the clouds of fear and illusion that obscure the wholeness that we already are. It is truly time for our emergence.

PAT BRADDOCK
A Banker with Heart

---

*"Failure promotes the examined life. We may choose
to go on as before, but we cannot do so blindly.
Failure is a marker, a turning point."*
— Carole Hyatt and Linda Gottlieb

Pat Braddock is a bank loan officer who has found a compassionate niche in an arena normally known for its inflexibility and lack of heart. "I find ways to help customers make their dreams come true, and as a supervisor, I encourage the people who work for me, mostly women, to learn everything I know, to advance as far as they wish, and to manifest their own dreams." Since she was 19, Pat has been employed in both small and large banks. From nearly 30 years of experience, she has learned much about banking, human relationships in that world, and about herself and other women who strive to make progress beyond entry-level positions in a male-dominated sphere.

"I was fascinated with banking right from the start," Pat says enthusiastically. "I married twice, but always kept working and never had children. I was the first and youngest female bank officer in

Coeur d'Alene, Idaho, and one of the first in the state."

Her first difficult experience came when a male supervisor became verbally and sexually abusive. "Not knowing what else to do at the time," she recalls, "I just took it. Of course, I wouldn't do that now." After a period of time, she was able to join forces with another female employee who was in a position to take the problem to corporate headquarters. After much soul-searching, Pat put her complaint in writing, and the man was fired. "At the time," Pat says, "it took a lot of courage."

As the mentors who had helped further her early career began to retire, younger and more aggressive male leaders began to take over. "I made the mistake," Pat explains, "of trying to imitate them. My behavior was threatening to them, and I lost my job as a consequence. Devastated because my 'hot shot' record would then be blemished, my ego was so damaged I became immobilized for months. Unable to even begin looking for another job, I feared I was a failure, and it felt like the end of the world."

However, Pat's intelligence, strength of character, and underlying spunk and courage came to the surface as loving friends supported her. She discovered a book written from a woman's viewpoint that dealt with exactly the kind of situation she was experiencing. *When Smart People Fail: Rebuilding Yourself for Success,* by Carole Hyatt and Linda Gottlieb, inspired Pat to learn from her experience, to explore her options, and to move on with her life.

Pat had previously taught management classes to several women at her former bank who ultimately became managers themselves. Pat explained her plight to one of those former students who had become a bank manager, and she was sympathetic and wanted to help. However, she could offer only an entry-level teller position, which meant that Pat would be starting over. "I was just happy for another chance," Pat says. "I made the most of it and shortly became a branch night supervisor, and was later promoted to an even higher managerial level."

Pat has made several moves and gained additional expertise since that time. In the process she has developed her own style and philosophy.

I feel strongly that women cannot simply try to imitate male strengths and characteristics. We must develop and utilize our own unique approach. Trying to be good ol' boys won't do it for us. I learned that the hard way.

As part of my own career development, I teach a class about human behavior in business, and will be doing more consulting in the future. I advise students not to think they must adopt either an aggressive style or a meek style. "Your ultimate strength will come from developing your natural self," I tell them. I believe that men and women can learn to work together and create a humane workplace without sacrificing excellence and productivity.

The trust Pat establishes with the people—mostly women—who work for her is the key to her success as a supervisor and manager. She describes her philosophy.

People work with me, not for me. I treat them with the utmost respect and show appreciation for jobs well done. I take time to discover their personal and professional interests and then strive to match their assignments with their interests. I never forget a birthday or a work anniversary. I'm in a powerful position, and I know it, but I don't flaunt it because I never forget that I can't function without them. As a result, I've received many awards and accolades over the years because the people I've worked with have been part of a team.

Currently, Pat is head of the loan department in a small community bank in Kennewick, Washington, where her mission is to help local people acquire what they need. She is outspoken in her criticism of the banking conglomerates.

Cold-hearted banking institutions have little regard for individual employees and customers, and I don't believe they'll survive in the long run. I see people turning to small community banks that stay in tune with local people and are flexible enough to meet their unique needs.

I'm not required to answer to a huge home office; I'm already in the home office, and I'm expected to make decisions on my own. If a customer needs something that is reasonable but not in our policy, I consult with the computer people and those who do the paperwork, and we figure out a way to help that customer. We are truly working for the community.

A recent event illustrates that more humane approach. Not long ago, an older woman walked into the bank in tears. Her husband had recently died, and they'd used all their money for medical bills. She had bill collectors at her door and no money for food, utilities, or desperately needed dental care. She was a proud woman who hadn't sought help from any local social agencies.

Pat invited the woman to sit down and brought her a cup of coffee. Then they began to explore the woman's alternatives. After making calls to agencies that agreed to help with her immediate needs, Pat directed her to an agency that provides free legal aid, and she encouraged her to declare bankruptcy, "which is not the usual banker's advice!" Pat laughs. "By the time this woman left, she was no longer feeling desperate, and we gave each other a big hug. She's doing better now and occassionally stops in to say hello. Not a single bank executive suggested I might be wasting valuable time counseling with this woman. Our philosophy is to be helpful to each person who walks through our doors."

Pat works with people who have gravitated to this area of central Washington state from all around the country; they've had successful banking experiences elsewhere, but became disillusioned with the corporate world. "We're a different breed," Pat says, "because we're not afraid to let a tear drop or to give a hug. I feel fortunate indeed to be a part of this unique team."

ELLEN BURSTYN
Academy Award-Winning Actress

"Art is the method of levitation that separates one's self from enslavement by the earth."

— Anaïs Nin

A woman who has enjoyed an illustrious career on the stage, in films, and on television, Ellen Burstyn is still going strong, even though depending upon others for creative opportunities is often an occupational hazard for actors. "If we are not offered parts, our creative outlet is blocked," Ellen explains to us in her rich and distinctive voice. "However, I find it absolutely necessary to find a way to express my creativity, because if it gets bottled up, I become neurotic." Fortunately, Ellen's creativity continues to flow unimpeded, and her graceful aging process has not threatened her prolific career.

Her strong and unique talents were recently displayed in such films as *How to Make an American Quilt*, *The Cemetery Club,* and *The Spitfire Grill*, which won the top prize at the Sundance Film Festival. *The Spitfire Grill* has a strong but subtle spiritual theme that bucks the Hollywood trend toward explicit sex and violence. Those closely involved with the film see it as a redemption story that deals with hospitality, respect for creation, and love for one another. Ellen is proud to be a part of such a quality film.

One thing seems certain. Regardless of how many or how few roles she may be offered, she refuses to stagnate in her country home in New York State, passively waiting for opportunities. "I am committed to continuous expression of my creativity, and fortunately, I've found a way, through writing, that's not dependent upon age or circumstance," she declares.

"I write every day whenever I'm not out 'earning a living' as an actress, but this is not a new thing for me. I've kept a journal all my life, and over the years I've been an active participant in sculpting the screenplays for the films in which I've appeared. Currently, I'm working on a screenplay for John Calley of United Artists, and his faith in me and his support are very much appreciated," Ellen emphasizes.

Resurrection, one of Ellen Burstyn's most memorable films, was originally presented to her with a very different story line than what finally emerged. "The first plot just didn't feel right," she says. "Jesus Christ came back to earth in the form of a woman who discovered this identity after she made a trip to Jerusalem and began to experience stigmata. I suggested changes, but the directors didn't want to make them, so I refused the part. Later, the producers called and said they liked my story better than their own, so with my permission, they went back to the studio and started over with a new writer and director."

Released in 1979, *Resurrection* is the story of an ordinary woman who has a near-death experience and returns to the earth plane with the power to physically heal people. The film deals with how pure healing energy can move through people open to the experience, regardless of their theology. The difficulty fundamentalist religions often have with such free expression of healing power is an integral part of the plot. "This is the role that most fully expresses the essence of what I believe," Ellen says. "Extensive research and study with healers helped me absorb the character. Because the film was before its time, the studio didn't have a category for it and didn't know how to effectively promote it, so it didn't turn out to be a big money maker, but I'm proud of the film and that I received an Oscar nomination for my role."

We asked Ellen if she had always wanted to act and how she got started in show business. "I was in the high school plays," she recalls, "but I wanted to be many things. I love animals, so I wanted to be a veterinarian; I love plants, so I wanted to be a farmer. I also wanted to be a lawyer, a fashion designer, a photographer, and a dancer. As an actress, I eventually got to play all those parts and many others as well. I feel fortunate that I've had the opportunity to express so many facets of myself." Ellen began modeling in high school and continued with that career until she was 24, when she decided she wanted to be in a Broadway play and began enthusiastically announcing this desire to everyone around her. Finally, after someone introduced her to an agent who believed she had talent, Ellen made her debut on Broadway in 1957 in a play entitled *Fair Game.*

She soon became a student of Lee Strasberg at the Actors Studio and went on to star in other Broadway productions, as well as appearing in films and on television. At ease with her role as an actor, and masterful in each sphere, she won numerous awards. Ellen's portrait of an ex-housewife turned waitress/singer trying to support herself and her 12-year-old son in *Alice Doesn't Live Here Anymore* won her the Oscar for best actress in 1974 as well as a Golden Globe and the British Academy Award. "It was one of the first films to tell a story from the woman's point of view," she declares, "and I'm proud of the example it set." We ask Ellen if she believes it will be easier in the future for older women to obtain starring roles. "Not unless women take an active part and start creating them," she answers. "I'd like to see even more actresses developing their own projects, and more women producers and directors."

Ellen's childhood, which included a stepfather, was not a particularly happy one. She remembers being sent to a Catholic church where she received comfort and inspiration, but she also remembers being wounded by its teachings of guilt and sin.

I left the church when I was 18, and for the next 15 years, I looked for answers in science. I did a lot of exploring, but as Sartre so accurately described it, I felt like I had a "God-shaped hole in my heart." I yearned for answers. Then I found the work of Gurdjieff, the philosopher and mystic who traveled the world seeking the meaning of life. He brought "The Work," an ancient esoteric oral tradition handed down from teacher to pupil for thousands of years, to the West. His philosophy helped me see profound spiritual and psychological ways we can work with ourselves outside an organized church.

Eventually, Ellen discovered the Sufi system, which embraces all religions and all people with love and forgiveness. "Spirituality is not separate from any part of my life," Ellen explains. "Every interaction with a person, an animal, a plant, a tree, is my spirituality. Except," she adds, "when I forget myself and lose connection with my source and become angry or fearful."

Introspection, a yearning to create, and a desire to express her essence have been essential for her, and she relates to Jean Houston's description of the dynamic drive to unfold our Essential self—*entelechy*. In *A Mythic Life*, Jean says: "It is the entelechy of an acorn to become an oak tree, the entelechy of a popcorn kernel to be a fully popped entity, and it is the entelechy of a human being to be—God knows what!" Jean also states that she knows only a handful of people who live out of a potent sense of their own Essence, but that her neighbor and friend, actress Ellen Burstyn, is one of those rare people.

Always seeking richer layers of life and expression, Ellen continues to go deeper into her writing, and she has dramatically transformed an earlier script she wrote. "I've created new stories and events that better illustrate the true spirit and essence of my life. A kind of alchemy happened when I went back and revisited from a more experienced and expanded viewpoint and added fictitious events that reflect more truth than the 'real' ones."

Single for over 20 years and the mother of an adult son, Ellen explains why she chooses not to live in New York City or Hollywood.

I love life on my two-and-a-half acres in the country. This makes me an outcast in certain ways, but it's more important to spend time in my garden, to have time for solitude and introspection. The seasons of the year are important. I believe trees are supposed to lose their leaves! I love the textures of the plants and life forms here in the Northeast.

During the hours I spend working with the earth in my garden, I feel closer to nature and to the feminine energy of Mother Earth. I've studied the earlier religions where the godhead was thought of as feminine and when the natural elements of the earth were more respected. It's satisfying to be in touch with these ancient philosophies and to incorporate them into my life.

Although Ellen enjoys the country, she is by no means a recluse. In addition to her many acting stints and her involvement in writing screenplays and stories, she is an active member of the Executive Board of the Actors Studio, where she studied with Lee Strasberg and where she was the Artistic Director for six years. She is also a very caring person who was the first woman to be elected as president of the Actors Equity Association in 1982.

Perhaps because she is living from her Essence self, Ellen refuses to allow her creativity or her philosophy to be in any way diminished by uncertainty about the future. A multitalented model and motivator, she contributes to the universe through her continuing involvement in issues and concerns that matter. Finding it impossible to place limits around her expansive heart and inquisitive mind, she lives life on her own terms, empowered and fully alive.

CONNIE CHEREN, R.N.
Champion of the Aged

"Create a dream and give it everything you have. You could be surprised by just how much you are capable of achieving. If you don't have a dream—borrow one! Any which way, you must have a dream!"
— Sara Henderson

Connie Cheren's passion is to ensure the well-being of nursing-home residents, and she works toward her goal with focused high energy and missionary zeal. "The end of life should be as much a celebration as the beginning of life," she declares. Owner and president of Quality Care Assurance in Alpharetta, Georgia, Connie is a national expert in her field. Before beginning her own company, she was in charge of licensing all nursing homes in the state of Florida. Before that, she administered a program for the state of Illinois that provided financial incentives for nursing homes that provided care and programs above the minimum standards. She now works diligently to help nursing homes implement restorative programs that encourage resident function at the highest possible level of independence.

As a nursing-home consultant, she has visited over 2,000 of them in 32 states. Connie teaches the difference between a body-work facility and a restorative-care facility. She explains the difference.

> Body-work facilities feed people who can't feed themselves and dress people who can't dress themselves. Residents are placed in wheelchairs or gerichairs and assisted around the facility by staff. The pervading feeling in these homes is often hopelessness. Restorative-care facilities respect their residents as whole people and help them stay as independent as possible for as long as possible. If residents can't feed or dress themselves, time is taken to teach them, using cuing or reminder programs, perhaps putting staff hands over residents' hands to guide them through the process. There is an atmosphere of hope and possibility in these facilities.

A "can do" attitude was a gift that Connie received from her parents who always told her she could do or be anything as long as she was willing to do the necessary work. "At 17, I thought I could marry and create a happy home even if I had to do it singlehandedly," she laughs. "I worked in a General Electric factory packing flashbulbs on the midnight shift so my husband could attend college. I took a few classes as I could and finally finished up a year's work by the time he graduated. Soon after that, our first son was born."

It was around this time that a seemingly minor incident changed the course of Connie's life. It was Christmas, and Connie's women's group had a decorated tree to give away. It was suggested that a nursing home would be an appropriate place. Connie took the tree to the front desk of the home and started to walk away. "Wait a minute," the receptionist said. "We don't do things that way. If you want the residents to have this, you'll have to walk back and take it to them yourselves. After spending only a brief time with the residents, Connie became hooked and agreed to come back once a week for Bingo. She soon became a regular volunteer.

After a move to Champaign, Illinois, she continued to do volunteer work with the elderly through an organization called TeleCare.

Connie and her close friend, Diane Joy, who also shared the love of the elderly, started a coffee group with seven older people. They met weekly for several years, helping, loving, and supporting each other. The day Connie graduated from nursing school, Diane surprised her by bringing the entire coffee group to share in the capping ceremony. "I never knew my own grandparents," Connie laughs, "so I guess I went out and found some for myself."

One cold and snowy day not long after her graduation, Connie was at the grocery store when she overheard a distinguished elderly gentleman asking the store manager if he could push his grocery cart to the far end of the lot toward his apartment. A voice inside Connie's head said, "Offer to help him." She asked if he'd like a ride home, and he accepted. Two weeks later she saw the same man in the parking lot and again offered him a ride, which he accepted. The third time it happened, Connie asked him to join her coffee group, and again he accepted.

The man was Dr. Victor A. Hirsh, an 80-year-old retired University of Illinois professor of mathematics. He had nursed his wife, who suffered from multiple sclerosis, until she died. They had no children or close relatives nearby. "He was a charming and delightful man, and we became good friends, often attending the Unitarian church together," Connie recalls. "He spent holidays in our home, and my children grew up with him as a grandfather figure. Eventually, he went into a nursing home, but our friendship continued, and our family stayed involved with his life. I promised him that he wouldn't die alone, if there was any way I could prevent it, and I was able to keep that promise. The night he died, I stayed through the night with him in the nursing home."

Victor left Connie two legacies. One was the inspiration to help other elders the way she'd helped him. "He could see that was my calling and encouraged me," she says. The second legacy was a gift of enough money to pay for the remainder of her graduate school education. After finishing her undergraduate degree in psychology, she went on to get a master's in social work with a focus on policy planning and administration. The gold coin on the chain around her neck was Victor's. "It reminds me of his special gift of love and friendship," she says.

Connie's dedication to her calling never wavered as Connie tended to her family of five children, held a job, and completed her education. While still a graduate student, she gave testimony before the Illinois State Legislature, speaking as an advocate for the elderly in nursing homes. As a result, she was offered a position in state government after graduation that provided an opportunity for her to work with nursing homes.

Connie's job was to go into nursing homes, analyze their systems, and then come up with better ways to accomplish tasks. Her natural affinity for the residents was evident in her work from the beginning. A major change she instituted, which is still a large part of her teaching today, is the concept of resident teams. Instead of aides being assigned to different patients each day, residents are put into small family-size groups who then have the same nurses and nursing assistants every day. This creates a bonding and caring as well as an in-depth understanding of each resident's needs. Resident satisfaction and well-being increase immensely as a result. "Such things as personalized rooms, plants, and community integration are also very helpful," Connie explains, "but it's imperative that we stop treating these residents like children and that we give them the respect they deserve. I have always taken time to talk with these individuals to find out directly how we can make their lives better."

It's gratifying for Connie to go into facilities that are eager to make the kind of positive changes she advocates. Her vision for the future is to set up a nursing home in a central area that will serve as a training facility for those who want to come to her. That way she will have more time to focus her energy upon what she does best.

"I want to stop getting on and off so many airplanes each year," she declares. "I want to spend more time at home with my husband and children." If past patterns repeat themselves, Connie will find a way to create her dream, a teaching home that will serve as a model facility of new and innovative ideas for improving the lives of nursing-home residents. There can be no doubt that whatever Connie does, she will do it zealously, continuing to motivate and to mentor and to be a model of compassionate caring for those who want to join with her in a new vision of human dignity for the aging.

CAROLYN CORNELISON, Ph.D.
Crusader Against Addictions

---

*"Dependence on the creator within is really freedom
from all other dependencies."*
— Julia Cameron

With her full-bore enthusiasm and unremitting zest for life, Carolyn Cornelison is a model and motivator whom college students flock to hear. Her message inspires them to delve deeply into themselves to find a guiding philosophy. "I know how easy it is to become sidetracked with addictions in the collegiate atmosphere because I did that myself, so in my travels throughout the United States, I talk with students about early warning signs of addiction and urge them to seek help in those early stages."

By the time Carolyn enrolled in a Ph.D. program at Florida State University in Tallahassee, her alcohol addiction was behind her. While she was a graduate assistant, she became the part-time director of the campus Alcohol and Drug Information Center. At that time, she expanded an existing program that now has a national reputation, the BACCHUS and GAMMA Peer Education Network. The only national collegiate peer-education movement, it has over 700 campus affiliates. Its purpose is to encourage students to make wise decisions about alcohol and drugs and to provide strategies to help them be more skilled in influencing their friends to make the right choices. "In our programs and special events, we don't make moral judgments," Carolyn explains.

Students listen to Carolyn because she doesn't preach as she shares her own story of slipping into alcoholism and its consequences. No one in her stable and loving family ever used alcohol, but just before her 18th birthday, she was introduced by friends into the drinking scene. Outgoing already, she enjoyed being a party girl. Despite the fact that she drank heavily, she was a good student in college, played intercollegiate softball, belonged to a sorority, and managed to graduate with honors, even winning the senior award.

"However, I graduated with something else," she says. "By that time I was a substance abuser, an alcoholic." Before she could admit that to herself or anyone else, she was arrested for drunk driving three times. Finally, her father set up an appointment with a judge who told her, "You have three offenses; you are an alcoholic and you caused a serious accident that could easily have killed someone. You are a menace to society." Still unable to admit her problem, she promised she wouldn't drink for six months just to prove to everyone that she wasn't an alcoholic.

Everything was going well until New Year's Eve, when she thought she probably could have just one drink to celebrate.

That led to nine Kamikazes (27 shots of alcohol). After that episode, I realized I couldn't control myself, that once I started drinking, I couldn't stop. However, I kept on drinking through my master's program and then as Assistant Director of Student Activities at Louisiana State University. I drank and smoked pot with the students. On one road trip where I was accompanying students to the Sugar Bowl, I blacked out for seven hours. I'd purchased a new black sports car, and I knew in my heart that I might well kill myself or someone else while driving it under the influence. I also knew it would only be a matter of time before I'd lose my job, and then all the years of school and work would be lost.

Unable to control her drinking, afraid, despairing, and finally ready to acknowledge the seriousness of her situation, Carolyn visited 16 different churches in 16 weeks in a desperate search for answers. A campus minister finally directed her to a 12-step program, which she eagerly embraced.

Here's to Sister Carolyn is a teaching video for college students where Carolyn explains how proud she was of herself because she could drink more and faster than anyone else. "I tend to bring my competitive athletic nature into everything I do, so I nearly destroyed myself," Carolyn explains. Students now salute her with the words *Here's to Sister Carolyn* because she sought help for herself, and she helps others by telling her story. She still gives her all to what she's doing, only this time she's using her zest and energy for a productive purpose. She wrote part of a Life Skills program for the National Collegiate Athletic Association that focuses on health issues, especially substance abuse, as they affect young women and men college athletes.

Carolyn is grateful for the positive and supportive people in her life. She explains:

> Models of love, excellence, and achievement were all around me to see, even as I struggled with the alcohol addiction. My parents, teachers, and coaches have always been there for me. My mentor in graduate school, Dr. Melvene Hardee, taught a class about the role of the woman administrator; she called me "coach" and always encouraged me not to settle for vice-president when I could be president. However, I must emphasize that in spite of all that outer support, I was forced to learn that the ultimate support must come from within, from a higher power.

"The Pied Piper" became Carolyn's nickname at Florida State because students followed her around, eager and willing to do anything for her. That's not surprising, because she's one of those rare people who seems to be everybody's friend—down to earth, natural, and fun-loving. Yet she is also focused, serious, and philosophical. In her thirties, she is older than many college students, but still very much attuned to their issues and perspectives.

As she delivers motivational speeches on campuses all over the country, Carolyn talks about love, integrity, forgiveness, enthusiasm, and the importance of finding a personal philosophy and then living it every day in every situation. "I tell the truth about my life and the lessons I've learned in the hope that others will avoid the kind of mistakes I made. I'm grateful for the opportunity to minister to students in this unique way, and I love what I do."

ROBERTA TAYLOR CUTSHALL
Moving Beyond Abuse

"...women's resourcefulness and resolve increase as circumstances become more difficult."

— Margaret Mead

Bobie Cutshall has never been happier, and with a heart as big as the great outdoors, she is bringing love and compassionate caring into the lives of many elderly people. Following her heart, she quit a lucrative job that often seemed inhumane in its response to people, and oftentimes, to the very real challenges they faced.

As a bank foreclosure and collection supervisor, she began to experience tremendous stress, and during the last year on the job, she lost her hair in five spots. In an attempt to alleviate the job-related symptoms, she tried meditation, stress-management classes, and relaxation techniques, but none of them were able to relieve either the symptoms or the growing discontent within. Often she was forced to foreclose on people who were desperately trying to hold their homes and lives together but who had fallen behind in payments. While some foreclosures were of course necessary and dealt with people who weren't trying, a great number involved older folks or single mothers who were working hard to keep up. There wasn't much room for compassion in her job, and it was one she had come to dread.

Then came the moment of truth, an epiphany of sorts. Bobie's father became very ill, and she was spending a great deal of time at the hospital. While she was visiting him, she began to notice all the elderly people who were sick and uncomfortable, and she also saw that they were, for the most part, ignored. "Here," she thought to herself, "is where I could make a difference," and she challenged herself to explore just how this might happen. "I knew I could give these people more than just good care; I was capable of giving them the love no one else seemed to extend to them." At this point, a plan began to unfold. She made inquiries and investigated the possibilities. When she finally found a program that would allow her to work and learn at the same time, she gave notice at the bank and walked away from her higher-paying position.

Beginning at $5.10 an hour, she became an aide in a local nursing home. Here she was allowed to work under supervision while she became first a Certified Nurse's Aide (CNA), and then a Certified Supervisor of Medications (CSM). She also began taking classes through the local community college in Lincoln, Nebraska, in order to obtain a licensed practical nurse license with the ultimate goal of becoming a registered nurse. She is working hard, studying hard, and has little time for herself—but she enjoys it all. She states, "I feel that God has directed me into an area where I can really be of service." She feels that she is finally on her heart's true path. But it's been a long time in coming.

Born in January of 1954 to an unwed mother, Bobie was adopted when she was 22 months old by Art and Virginia Taylor, a couple who provided her with a loving home and gave her support in many forms. When she thinks of the women in her early life who empowered her, she gives credit to her mother, who always told her that she was as good as anyone and that she could do or be anything she set her mind to. "I also had an aunt who had the courage to live life the way she felt she needed to live it, regardless of anyone's opinion, and I admired her. It gave me an opportunity to see how strong a woman can be. However, for a few years I lost hold of all that."

Bobie married at age 19 and became pregnant almost immediately. While carrying her only child, a daughter, she began to get the first clues that this marriage was not working as she had hoped. However, not wanting to be termed "a failure" because she married against her parent's advice, Bobie concluded that it was easier to stick it out than admit her error.

Sometimes things in her marriage would seem better, and then they would fall apart again. She remembers, "I really lost self-esteem during this period of my life because of all the verbal abuse, but it's such an internal process and not necessarily conscious. It just happens and insidiously creeps up until it has taken you over." The moment of truth came when Bobie traveled to Nebraska to attend her brother's wedding. The extended family had gathered for several days of festivities, and suddenly she realized that this was how family should be, and she had never had this in her marriage. She didn't want to go back. "I had been set free," she says.

Bobie returned home to Portland, Oregon, and informed her husband that their marriage was over. When he responded, "You can't do this to me," but never even asked, "What is the problem?" or "Can we work on it?" she knew she had made the right decision. They tried for a time, for practical reasons, to live in separate parts of the house until things could be settled, but it soon became apparent that that wasn't going to work. Finally, her 12-year-old daughter pleaded with her to get out. She said, "Mom, Daddy has loaded guns." Bobie became fearful when she saw him lying on the bed with his shotgun.

Already gainfully employed, she went out and found an apartment to rent. In the middle of the night, while her husband was working the night shift at the hospital, Bobie moved out with the help of friends. Bobie filed for divorce, but she stayed in Portland, on the opposite side of town, for a year. However, even that became too close when she discovered one night that her husband had a .357 magnum pointed at the kitchen window of her apartment. As soon as the divorce was final, she solicited the help of her parents and moved back to Nebraska.

She and her daughter, Stephanie, moved into their own apartment, Bobie found employment at a local bank, and they began rebuilding their lives. Three years later, in 1991, Bobie married Mike Cutshall, a loving and supportive man. However, in spite of a new life, the job at the bank was not fulfilling, and it was at this point that Bobie's minister, Abby Wilson, became a supportive counselor and mentor. "Abby is a free spiritual being and assured me over and over that I could do whatever I chose to do. She always told me, 'It doesn't matter what you do as long as you're happy. You don't have to remain in the status quo'—Abby really brought it all together for me."

Bobie's self-confidence rides high these days, and her face shines with joy when she talks about what she is doing and where she is determined to go. She has a vision now and is finally emerging as the woman she always wanted to be.

JOYCELYN ELDERS, M.D.
From Sharecropper's Daughter to Surgeon General

---

*"If we allow ourselves to always choose in the safest
way—a way that has been adopted for us by others,
we will never honor the real life in us."*
— Marsha Sinetar

There seems to be a tendency in our country to maintain a code of silence on certain issues. We bury our collective heads in the sand pretending that the hard issues don't exist and refuse to face them in a new, healthy, and more honest manner. The ability to critically assess how we've handled these issues in the past, admit when those solutions aren't working, and then try to creative different options, often seems foreign to public policy.

Dr. Joycelyn Elders, as Surgeon General of the United States, attempted to do just that in many instances, but specifically in the areas of sex education and drugs. Like John the Baptist, hers was often a voice crying in the wilderness, but nonetheless, she was the harbinger that planted a cosmic seed in our collective national awareness, which one day may take root. There always needs to be at least one voice loud enough, prominent enough, and brave enough to tackle both the tough issues and the status quo! New approaches to solving these hard-core problems tend to prod people to confront them, to discuss them, and even to wrestle with them, and whatever the public opinion, those concepts are forever publicly and politically acknowledged.

That Joycelyn was asked to resign her appointed post as Surgeon General, a job that she was doing as she felt she had been asked to do and in the manner she felt it needed doing, speaks loudly of a political system gone askew. However, a firm believer in God and ultimate Divine Order, Joycelyn Elders believes that it was Divine Purpose that led her to Washington D.C., and that Divine Purpose returned her to private life and the work she is currently doing with enthusiasm and joy.

Joycelyn grew up in Schaal, Arkansas, and was one of eight children born into her sharecropper family. At age four, she started school and walked five miles daily to catch the school bus. "I was always encouraged by a mother and father who told their children they could do or be anything that they wanted to do or be. My parents often went without necessities for themselves so that their children could have nice things," she told us. "They were my first teachers."

In Schaal, there was no access to mass media, and she would never have known about the possibility of going to college if she hadn't been encouraged and supported by the United Methodist Women's group that gave her a scholarship. She worked her way through Philander Smith College, a black institution in Arkansas, as a cleaning lady. Two women, Dr. Edith Irby Jones and Dr. Rosaland Abernathy, were her role models and mentors. These two women were instrumental in showing her the strength and potential that women could develop, and they encouraged Joycelyn to maximize her own potential. After college she enlisted in the Army, where she trained as a physical therapist, and later she entered the University of Arkansas Medical School. She was the only black woman in her class.

Being in the center of controversy is not a new phenomenon for Joycelyn Elders. A woman of deep convictions, she is committed to making a difference where she can. She shook up the establishment in Arkansas when she tried to alert citizens to some of the major issues concerning teenage pregnancy and AIDS. She actively promoted sex education, birth control, and freedom of choice on abortion. When people in Arkansas asked if school-based clinics would dispense contraceptives, she replied, "I'm not going to put condoms on their lunch trays, but yes." Forthright and honest, she believes the consequences of irresponsible sex often produce children who will more than likely grow up uncared for, and she advocates alternative measures in order to prevent, or at least to reduce, that risk.

As an emerging woman, she has learned to be a risk taker and to confront challenges openly; in the process there is always the risk of controversy. However, she credits her ability to handle the vicissitudes of life to her husband, Oliver Elders, whom she married on Valentine's Day in 1960. He has been one of those rare men who has been a full partner with his wife in every facet of their life together. Oliver, who was basketball coach of a Little Rock high school team for 33 years, accompanied her to Washington, D.C., and was her strength during her tenure as Surgeon General. She says, "No matter what was coming at me, if I could just go home and talk it over with my husband, it didn't matter what the rest of the world was saying." Her husband is such a calm and centered person that his perspective alone is sufficient for her, but Joycelyn does recall other supporters as well:

> However, I did have lots of support while I was in Washington, and people like Ted Kennedy, Pat Schroeder, and Mark Hatfield were wonderfully helpful to me. Others like Carol Mosley-Brown, Barbara A. Mikulski, Paul Simon, Howard Metzenbaum, Luis Stokes, Cynthia A. McKinney, and the Black Political Caucus were always very kind and supportive and gave me encouragement. Mark Hatfield, even though he was a Republican, gave the nomination speech. The senators from Arkansas were out of town, and when Senator Hatfield was approached and asked to make the nominating speech, he graciously consented to do it.

Fired as Surgeon General when she spoke forthrightly about masturbation as a normal part of human sexuality, she still feels strongly that with a million teens getting pregnant each year, we need to confront the idea that children are sexual beings. "The more they know, the better prepared they are to make more appropriate decisions." Contrary to some interpretations, Joycelyn was not advocating teaching kids how to masturbate; she was asking us to discuss the topic openly and to eliminate some of the erroneous beliefs surrounding it.

However much some of us may lament the fact that she was not even allowed to complete the first term of the Clinton administration, her influence was felt, and the courage to voice her convictions despite opposition remains admirable. Thankfully, the voice has not been silenced; she currently teaches at the University of Arkansas for Medical Sciences in the School of Pediatric Endocrinology and has written her autobiography, *Joycelyn Elders, M.D.* She travels quite extensively—accepting invitations to speak to college students across our country. A receptive and appreciative audience, the students are prime targets to hear her timely message, and she has become a role model and motivator to literally thousands of young people. "It is so important for them to know and understand their power and potential—how can anyone do anything if they don't know they can?"

Joycelyn Elders certainly is the embodiment of all the characteristics that mark an emerging woman. She serves as a shining example for women of all races, showing that with enough effort, they can accomplish their dreams. As we bring our interview to a close, she says in a strong but gentle and thoughtful voice, "A favorite quote of mine comes from Dr. Martin Luther King. He said, 'The day you see the truth and cease to speak is the day you begin to die.'" Then with a lighthearted chuckle, she adds, "And I'm not going to be dead for a *long, long* time!"

STAR EUTHENE
Women's Advocate and Artist

"Give us the courage of the soul's high vision,
The heart to make and keep the brave decision."
— Marie LeNort

Star is a guide, a point of light, a capable and outstanding leader, a multitalented, multifaceted, loving personality. This women's advocate has been a model, motivator, and mentor to countless women who have passed through the Women's Center in Coeur d'Alene, Idaho, and for women of varied professions and circumstances who make up the Idaho Women's Network and the Idaho Coalition Against Sexual and Domestic Violence. She has also been a stellar spokesperson who educated countless people about the issue of a woman's right to safety in our society. She has spoken out in the media, in civic and growth groups, and in schools.

News reports of domestic violence or rape in the North Idaho and Eastern Washington area usually included a commentary from Star as Director of the North Idaho Women's Center. In statements characterized by their strong advocacy along with their calm clarity, Star focused upon what needed to happen for women to be safe.

Gloria Steinem was the model and motivator for Star's strong but nonstrident style of communication. When Star first became involved in women's issues, she observed that Gloria was making a tremendous difference and doing it with grace, strength, and dignity, without blaming or whining. Star explains:

> She [Gloria] spoke directly to the issues, never wavered, and spoke firmly and clearly, but did not demean others. I appreciated her style and recognized a desire in my own heart to be such a spokesperson and advocate for women. Blaming and crying do not build strength. We find strength by standing on our own and becoming clear. It's not about what "they" did to us, but about what we will do for ourselves.

Star and her friends Opal Brooten and Len Mattei were the first organizers when a National Organization for Women (NOW) chapter was being organized in Coeur d' Alene, Idaho. Opal was an older, experienced activist who had a history of committed action with respect to what she believed was right; she served as a model, motivator, and mentor for Star and Len and many others. Early on, Opal, Star, and Len went to Boise as representatives of NOW to talk to legislators about Idaho's archaic rape laws and to lobby for change. At that time, the concept of marital rape did not legally exist in the state. Even after six months of separation, a husband could legally force his spouse to have sex except in "cases of lunacy," and she could not file rape charges.

When Star first heard about this, she "saw red." She recalls, "Although I was not in a marriage myself at the time, I was outraged. I knew that I could not possibly live in a state with such primitive laws, and though I had no idea what it would take, I was determined to do something about it. That single issue became the catalyst for my development as an activist and leader in advocacy for women in the state of Idaho."

Star was shocked again when she arrived at the state capitol building with other women's advocates. They were advised to speak as individuals, not as members of a women's group because they might "appear too threatening." Unable to understand or accept that viewpoint, she spoke to the other women. "We don't have power as individuals, but I believe we can stand together and make a difference." And they did. However, when a proposal to change the rape law was introduced, the male chairman stood up, waved the proposal in the air, and said, "This will never pass in the state of Idaho!" The small group of women hearing that statement realized it would be necessary to elicit the support of more women from all over their state if they were to prove this legislator wrong.

In a very short time, Star and other determined women put together the Idaho Women's Network. In the beginning, they were mentored by The Women's Lobby Fund of Montana, whose members traveled to Idaho to support the Idaho women. By sharing organizing information, a mutually helpful network was formed.

The Idaho group was composed of teachers, social workers, nurses, members of Church Women United, and any and all women and men interested in helping to gain equal status and safety under the law for every woman. The women made a commitment to work as long as it might take to bring about positive changes in the law.

"Changing and influencing legislation is not about having degrees or being a lawyer," Star explains, "but it is about dedication and commitment, leadership and long hours. We learned that when we take a bill to the legislature and it doesn't get passed, the issue doesn't go away. We need to come back the next session and continue to work." In the beginning, the numbers were few, but they kept a focus upon their goal, and their ranks began to increase.

The second legislative session was another disappointing one, but Gail Bray, a senator on the subcommittee, managed to get the women's proposed change brought forward for the third session. This was a full two years after the original bill was introduced. However, awareness of the issue had spread because the Idaho Women's Network was gaining recognition among the legislators.

By the time the third session began, the group had gained so much respect and clout that they received a call from the legislators who were bringing the bill before the entire legislature. They wanted to know if the wording was acceptable to the Women's Network! It was acknowledged that they represented thousands of votes—and that's a substantial number in sparsely populated Idaho. Since then, the Network and Coalition have continued to gain power and respect. A woman who stands up for her beliefs and encourages others to do the same, Star often discusses the history of these groups when she speaks to groups of women and men about becoming involved in the political issues that affect their lives.

At the Women's Center, battered women are encouraged to stand up for themselves and to testify in court about their abuse. To do so often takes courage when the batterer is in court and usually in the hallway before and after court sessions hoping to intimidate the woman who will describe her experience.

Star herself has been threatened many times. Anytime an angry spouse came into the center, she emerged from her office and dealt with that person calmly but firmly and insisted that he leave. When she needed to testify in court about threatening behavior directed toward her, she experienced the same sense of intimidation battered women felt when the person they were testifying against glared at them from the hallway or courtroom. However, during her years at the center, Star never backed down, thus modeling a strength and courage the battered women needed to see.

Star is especially proud of one such young woman with three young sons, Linda M., who came battered and beaten to the Women's Center. After a stay in the shelter, she made the decision to divorce her husband and to take on the task of raising her boys alone. She began classes at the community college, volunteered at the Women's Center, and eventually became a part-time paid staff person. Star never ceases to be amazed at the courage and will of this young woman and her eagerness to learn and grow. Linda is now in her junior year, working toward a degree in social work, and she and Star have become what Star describes as close sister/friends.

Linda is a model for me. She is growing and learning so fast, doing all the right things we encouraged every woman who came into the center to do. The wonderful thing about motivating and mentoring women who are ready to move beyond their victim status is that I get to rejoice with them in their successes. It is incredibly rewarding to participate in such reciprocal relationships. Ultimately, it is a learning and growing experience for those who give help and encouragement, as well as for those who receive it and succeed.

After 12 years at the Women's Center and five years as its director, Star recently retired in order to freelance with her art and to embrace a more relaxed lifestyle. Currently developing her talent as a jewelry maker and sculptor, Star travels to juried art shows all over the country and is a regular exhibitor at "Art on the Green" in Coeur d' Alene, Idaho. She also is a model and motivator for public school students between 1st and 12th grades as a periodic "Artist in Residence." She encourages students' artistic expression in such areas as basketry, jewelry making, and papier mâche projects. "I'm very excited about my life right now." Star declares:

New doors keep opening for me, and I'm thankful I stepped out and trusted myself to succeed at something new. My spiritual life helped in that decision, and it just becomes more and more significant for me. I feel fortunate to be part of the extended Holo spiritual community [the authors' spiritual retreat] and appreciate the support of Ione Jenson, Julie Keene, and Masil Hulse. They help me believe that no dream is too big to come true.

LOUISE EVANS
Innovative Entrepreneur

---

*"You can aim for what you want and if you don't
get it, you don't get it, but if you don't aim,
you don't get anything."*

— Francine Prose

"When someone tells me I can't do something, that's when I determine to try that much harder," declares this entrepreneur who began creating her own successful businesses several years ago. "I found that you can't passively sit around and allow yourself to be defeated by obstacles," she explains. "Once I acknowledged myself as a free spirit and recognized I wanted to work for myself, the universe brought opportunities to me, and I found ways to make the most of those opportunities."

Louise acknowledges that it was sometimes difficult to reach her goals, especially when it was necessary to deal with well-entrenched systems, but she is a persistent woman. "I have been forced to work harder and think through issues down to the last detail in order to clearly explain them and gain support, but on the other hand, there's an advantage to that added pressure. I have my ducks in a row and am so well organized that I usually meet with success at whatever I try."

It's difficult to trace Louise's career chronologically because she thrives when she has several projects going at the same time. In 1990 she began her own health and safety consulting business and currently assists beverage distributors and lumber and utility companies in developing job descriptions, conducting work-site analyses of physical demands for each job, and setting up medical services with local hospitals and physicians.

At the same time, she created the health and safety consulting business, Louise was the owner of another enterprise she'd created 11 years earlier, a paramedic training school. When she and her husband decided to adopt a baby, they decided to educate themselves about emergency procedures. Louise took an eight-week cardiopulmonary resuscitation first-aid course and became friendly with the emergency medical technicians (EMTs) who taught it. She began to ride along on ambulance calls and eventually took the EMT training herself. Even after adopting a daughter and a son, Louise kept taking more paramedic courses and volunteering on the ambulance runs.

Eventually, the physician who directed the first paramedic training program asked Louise if she would coordinate a second course. She began working on a contract basis with a local hospital, and from there decided to start her own training school. "During the early years of this new training program, I visited many other EMT/paramedic training schools around the country and worked to constantly advance the level of training we offered," she says.

From the beginning, Louise worked diligently to get her school nationally accredited. This turned out to be a process that took skill, patience, and persistence as she worked with hospital and school officials and national organizations over a period of ten years. "The school is now affiliated with a private college so the students have the opportunity to take other college courses and receive a two-year or a four-year degree," she says proudly. "We became the first nationally accredited EMT/paramedic training school in Oregon. The two-year 1,500-hour program includes classroom, hospital, and ambulance work. We started with one class of 16 students, and 10 years later had 8 classes and 160 students." Even while Louise was zealously working toward the goals she had set for the paramedic training school, she continued to take on additional projects. One such project was to develop a model occupational medicine program for one of the Portland hospitals, which later became a regional program.

Eventually, after years of focused work, Louise felt that something was missing, that there had to be more to life than working 16-hour days. She became concerned after she realized she was being consumed with thoughts about money, tuition, school budgets, taxes, classroom equipment, and all the other elements she was juggling. "I knew I had to find a way to gain balance and harmony," she recalls. "I began to spend more time reading, journaling, and listening to my inner person." She found Stephen Covey's *Seven Habits of Highly Successful People,* which helped her sort out priorities and develop a personal mission statement.

At that time, Louise had been divorced awhile, and the children were grown. What would come next? In 1995 after 16 years of ownership, Louise sold the paramedic school. Although she is still active in her health and safety consulting business, life has become dramatically different. Wanting to create a more relaxed lifestyle, she recently decided to move to Montana.

I'm in the process of discovering a deeper spiritual part of myself. I'm proud that I've been able to accomplish so much in the business and professional world, and I loved the work I was doing, but I found that professional success by itself wasn't enough. I need balance and an opportunity for personal discovery. I feel fortunate to have figured this out while I'm still quite young, while I have so many years left to enjoy my children, my family, and my friends. I intend to stay involved in the business world doing a reasonable amount of work, but I also intend to remain on a path of inner spiritual discovery. I trust the universe to help me sustain my balance as I create a new and fulfilling life for myself.

LT. COL. MELISSA FRIES, M.D.
Balancing Head and Heart

*"Women have always been healers. Medicine is
part of our heritage as women, our history,
our birthright."*
— Barbara Ehrenreich and Deirdre English

"Continuing education is the underlying theme of my life," says Air Force Lt. Col. Melissa Fries. "Every few years I've made drastic changes, finally getting proficient in one area and then moving into another area and starting over and working my way up." At the present time, this top graduate in her medical school class is the Director of the Obstetrics and Gynecology Residency Program at Keesler Air Force Base in Biloxi, Mississippi. She is also a geneticist who works in prenatal diagnosis, identifying at-risk couples.

Although Melissa is a dedicated professional, she is also passionate in her desire to maintain a balance between her private and her professional life.

I'm proud of my expertise in my area of specialization, enjoy the scholarly aspect of research and publication, and care very much about the residents I supervise. At the same time, I'm devoted to my husband and my six- and eight-year-old daughters. I attempt to be a model of what a woman physician can be. She doesn't have to be a cold-hearted bitch who has nothing but her work, nor does she need to be an inferior doctor because she is closely involved with her family. I want my daughters to see how natural it is for a woman to be a good scientist as well as a warm human being involved in family life.

In her own early years, Melissa developed an avid interest in the natural world. "I read about Jane Goodall in *National Geographic*," she recalls, "and it was exciting to me that she lived in the jungle and studied chimpanzees. I knew I wanted to do something equally as exciting. When Jane married her photographer and had a child, she modeled for me that a woman can be a good scientist and a mother, too. I knew I didn't want to have to make an either-or choice between career and family."

Melissa witnessed her mother waiting until later in life to develop artistic talent and to find her profession of ministry. Melissa's military father had a scientific bent and encouraged his daughter's interest in science, but he once confessed that he was uncomfortable at the thought of his daughter being in a supervisory position over men.

It was her mother who went to the high school to protest the school's decision to place Melissa in a home economics class instead of a science class. Two other mothers protested, too, so there were 3 girls in the class of 30. "But they still made me take home economics," Melissa notes.

After high school, Melissa spent two years at the local community college. At 20, she married and moved to California with her military husband. With her mother's long-distance support and encouragement, she completed four years of college, majoring in biology. Then her husband was assigned to Okinawa, Japan. Unable to study for a master's in biology there and wanting to stay busy, Melissa volunteered 40 hour weeks in the eye clinic, veterinary clinic, and school libraries on the base. Later she worked as a teaching assistant to prepare high school dropouts to obtain their diplomas. "I discovered that I loved to teach." Melissa remembers:

> While in Okinawa, I went back to school at night, obtained a master's degree in education, and after returning to the United States, taught junior high science for three years. The pressure of 130 kids every day began to wear me down. There had to be something more I could do with my mind. I wanted to work with people in a scientific role, and although I'd seldom been around doctors, except for my own check-ups, I felt I wanted to become one.
>
> I applied to several schools and was accepted at a military medical school, which seemed to be a natural path for me because my father and husband were both in the military. However, by this time, my husband and I had grown apart and were divorced during my first year of residency.

One of 30 women in a class of 130, Melissa developed close friendships and a strong support system with her female classmates. "I knew early on that I wanted to be a woman's doctor," Melissa says. "I love women, and I enjoy being around them. Working in this area of medicine, I don't have to deal with male egos in my patients. Also, more women are going into this field, so there is more female colleague support."

The residency program in obstetrics and gynecology at Willford Hall Medical Center in Lackland Air Force Base Texas was one of the most challenging in the military. A male-oriented program that had been in place for over 20 years, it finally graduated a woman the year Melissa entered.

> I discovered that women and men go into this field for both positive and negative reasons. Some go into it because they truly like women as a group, and some go into it because they don't like women, and by being a woman's doctor, they are in a position of power over them. I feel the latter group is now diminishing, but it has been a powerful factor in the past. As I watched women doctors in staff positions not being given credibility, I became angry and said to

myself, "I'll be damned if they're going to treat me this way. I'll show them!"

Obviously, she has done a great job of doing just that—not only "showing them" but setting an example of success for other women who come along after her.

During this stressful time, Melissa met her husband, Ron. Listening to jazz music on a rare evening out, she found herself seated next to him and knew right away he would be important in her life. "He's a wonderful partner, and I couldn't function where I am now if it weren't for him," Melissa emphatically states. She goes on to talk about his specific help.

> He's a contractor and a helicopter pilot who sometimes works in real estate. Not in the military or the medical field, he provides a calm oasis for me. His parenting role is critically important. He's there when the girls get off the school bus, works at their school every Wednesday, and was recently selected as the parent of the year at their school. If I hadn't married a man like Ron, I probably would not have had children, and I wouldn't have discovered first hand exactly what my obstetrics patients go through!

Melissa feels fortunate to "have it all," and as she works with others, her goal is to demonstrate for her daughters and all women that they don't need to settle for less than a completely full and satisfying life.

JEANNE GIVENS
A Woman for All Seasons

"O Great Spirit, Whose voice I hear in the winds,
And whose breath gives life to all the world,
Hear me! I need your strength and wisdom."
— a Native American Prayer

A full-blooded Native American and member of the Coeur d'Alene tribe of Idaho, Jeanne Givens has both an infectious smile and the ability to articulate her views with power. Her intelligent approach to problem solving makes her an outstanding advocate for many causes, and over the years, she has been involved in a broad spectrum of activities that focus upon issues surrounding Native Americans, poverty, and women.

Jeanne has worked in the area of social services all of her professional life and also served a term in the Idaho State Legislature. She was not an experienced journalist when first approached to write a newspaper column in the *Idaho Statesman* about Native American issues. However, after listening to many opinions and formulating her own, she began to write about the tough issues and to produce a provocative column. She says with a grin, "The job is to create, stir, agitate, and provoke thinking."

Writing about the history of Idaho tribes and tribal relations at state and national levels, she uses her column to point out how tribes are often unfairly treated by state government and how some representatives are utterly disrespectful to the tribes. "It provokes, of course, and I get letters to the editor," she tells us, "but I feel fine about that, because this column expresses an opinion that hasn't ever been in the public press before."

"Journalist" is only one of the many hats that Jeanne Givens wears. She has been instrumental in creating a new organization called *Schee-chu-umsh,* meaning "the ones who were found here" in the Coeur d'Alene tribal language. This is a political action group concerned about budget cuts aimed directly at the Bureau of Indian Affairs as well as overall cuts that directly hurt the poor. The organization is involved in an intensive voter education and registration project. The group supports candidates locally and nationally who have these same budget concerns and who the group feels will be reasonable and intelligent spokespersons in Congress.

Jeanne was recently nominated by President Clinton to serve on the Board of Trustees to the Institute of American Indian and Alaska Native Culture and Arts Development. The group oversees the operation of the Institute of American Indian Arts at Santa Fe, New Mexico, and Jeanne is thrilled to be able to make a contribution to Native Americans at this level. The first and only minority to be elected to the Board of Trustees of North Idaho College, Jeanne Givens prefers to exert quiet leadership through empowerment projects.

She says, "This position satisfies my desire to serve institutions that are accessible, progressive, and willing to change to meet the demands of a changing population. We have an excellent program for women now, called The Center for New Directions, and I am working on a program aimed at attracting and keeping increasing numbers of Native American students."

When asked about the early influences that allowed her, one of six children growing up in a single-parent family, to become such an empowered woman, she was quick to reply, "As I was growing up, challenging circumstances helped frame my sense of possibilities.

My mother worked very hard as a secretary to raise six children on her own, and she was a powerful role model for me. Although some members of the family left home feeling 'short-changed,' I left feeling I had been given a unique viewpoint and an excellent impetus for gaining an education."

This ability to perceive positive aspects of the challenges she faced growing up poor and a minority is what makes Jeanne Givens such an excellent example of an emerging woman. Poverty, sacrifice, and watching her mother make difficult choices about what each child would receive helped Jeanne see how her mother established priorities. It was apparent that the world was not an easy place for poor people, and the affirmation Jeanne made for herself was, "I will work *with* and *for* people who are not socially, economically, or racially empowered."

On the tenth anniversary of her mother's death, Jeanne and her siblings planned a traditional Indian memorial to honor her life, along with an Indian naming ceremony for all her grandchildren. As Jeanne speaks, it is evident that her mother's legacy has been a powerful influence in fashioning the woman she has become. "Mother was a strong woman who had a good sense of humor and a good sense of who she was. Raised in the traditional Indian way, she didn't have illusions about what she wanted out of life. She knew she was Indian, that she would always be Indian, and she embraced the identity and culture."

Although married to a non-Indian, Jeanne has, nonetheless, found a full partner in her passions. She and Ray Givens met while she was on the Board of Directors, and he was the managing attorney, of the North Idaho Legal Aid Services. Ray was a strong and outspoken advocate lawyer with a keen sense of fairness who used the law as a tool for seeking justice. He had confronted the Health and Welfare department in court over 100 times on behalf of poor women, and today, Ray Givens is the Coeur d'Alene tribal attorney. What was at first a philosophical attraction evolved into love. Thirteen years after their marriage, at age 39, Jeanne gave birth to their first child, a daughter named Maria, and two years later, she had a son, Joe.

Jeanne's advice for young Native American women (and *all* young women), is to have a strong sense of self. She explains what that means to her.

Listen to the spirit within you that is uniquely given just to you. That spirit may be an unconscious driving force that causes you to paint or to be creative. In Indian people, the easiest way to identify that spirit working within is the sense of generosity. It's nothing you've framed, acquired, shaped, or even learned—it's something beyond you. If you young Indian women listen to that spirit and do not suppress or ignore it, but instead allow it to flow, you will have a much richer life. Do all your emotional and spiritual homework and get that out of the way so you can live your life the way it's meant to be lived. Music is another way of achieving that connection with your spirit, and Indian melodies which have survived hundreds of years are the songs of the earth and of the animals. They represent the lakes and mountains, and when we make music, that is Mother Earth using us as instruments.

Young Indian women, develop the ability to listen, and to be humble when it's appropriate. These are traits accessible to all humankind, but women are generally better able to express them through their personalities as they deal with the world. Develop intuition, foresight, and visioning. Prayer is a positive envisioning for yourself or for another. Spirituality can be a real working force in your development.

As we listen and breathe in this Native American's words of loving advice to her younger tribal sisters, it seems apparent that we can all learn from them. As emerging women, let us all willingly accept increased responsibility for modeling and motivating our young women of all races.

And finally, for all women everywhere comes a wonderful Native American concept. In the Indian culture, people are allowed to evolve into and through all the stages of life naturally. They honor the child, the teenager, the young adult, the mother, the worker, and all other phases clear through to the tribal elder. Older people are treated with love and respect, and they are a treasure to be shared with the community. They are listened to and are the advisors and dispensers of wisdom.

This tradition of honoring every person and acknowledging that everyone helps the wheel go around and around is one Native American custom all emerging women, perhaps without even consciously knowing its origin, are learning to embrace as we evolve toward becoming more *universal humans.*

HELICE GREENE
Gentle Leader

"There is no period between the soul and God.
Love is the tide, God the eternal sea."
— Bliss Carman

On a spacious tree-covered corner lot on a quiet street in Oak
Park, Illinois, a grand old Frank Lloyd Wright mansion houses a
charming and unique Unity church. An added sanctuary seats several
hundred people but blends with the original architecture. Halfway up
the magnificent staircase leading to the office of Rev. Helice Greene
is a large stained-glass window. The spacious second-story office
itself is graced on three sides by large windows that overlook the
serene setting below. We have known Helice for many years and have
seen her repeatedly express loving and peaceful thoughts and feelings, so it makes perfect metaphysical sense that we would find her
joyous and thriving in this tranquil and elegant atmosphere. We begin
by asking her to talk about her work. She tells us:

> One of the most important elements of my ministry is the inner
> work of prayer, journaling, and reading. As I consecrate time to the

journey of my own soul, I can more readily transcend the dark moments and see the gifts in the difficult times. After my time alone, the myriad interactions with others begins—everything from the celebration of a wedding or christening to the difficult moments of illness and other personal crises. There is also time spent with staff in planning, and time spent with classes and prayer groups. It's a busy and often demanding life, but I feel totally blessed to have the opportunity to immerse myself in what I love to do.

Because Helice meets people on every level of their experience, she discovers that she continually learns from them. "Sometimes even the mundane, everyday concerns lead us to deeper, more powerful answers within ourselves," she explains. She points out that it takes dedication and commitment to work in harmony with a large staff and congregation while working through differing perceptions about issues and tasks. Helice's goal is to come from a position of listening and loving. "As a group, we're committed to hearing all viewpoints," she says. "Then we take time for prayer and silence and ask, 'What is for the highest good for our ministry and the people we serve?' Sometimes we're surprised at the answers."

Helice's introspection began to emerge when she was 15. That was the year she was profoundly affected by her mother's illness and early death.

My mother was a foundation I could always depend upon. She brought laughter, joy, and music into our lives. My father loved and supported us, too, and participated when he could, but he worked long hours, so we didn't see him as much. Mother taught my sister and me the value and gift of family. No matter what ups and downs she faced, she always came from a loving space. Her illness was a tremendous challenge for all of us. She was only 39 when she died of cancer.

Although strength and support came from her older sister, Millie, and from her father and other relatives, losing her mother was a traumatic wilderness experience for this teenager. She questioned her own safety and how people could die so young. Her inner journey was tremendously deepened as she explored, often in solitude, what life was all about. "My mother's early death was instrumental in making me who I am today," Helice reflects. "The journey of the soul has threads of gold and darkness, all the things that make us who we are."

A later trying experience led Helice further along her path. Married and living in Santa Ana, California, she was having a difficult physical challenge and was facing surgery. A neighbor knew about the Unity church and its focus on spiritual healing, so Helice decided to go and listen. As Hertha Tautland spoke that evening, Helice was ready to hear her healing message. She spoke of how both the mind and emotions affect the body, and how we can't treat the body alone. She presented a metaphysical Bible lesson about the man at the pool of Bethesda. Although Helice didn't fully understand everything the minister was saying, she was touched at a very deep level and sat quietly weeping. She decided against the surgery, began to attend all the services and classes at Unity, and when she went back to the doctor, he said, "It must have been a misdiagnosis."

A year-and-a-half later, Helice and her family moved to Chicago and began attending Unity in Oak Park. She went on to take more classes and to become a licensed Unity teacher. Ultimately, after a divorce, she went on to Unity ministerial school. All through this process, Richard Billings, the long-time minister in Oak Park, was her supporter, friend, and mentor, and they continued to keep in close touch through the years.

Unity of Fairfax in Virginia was Helice's first ministry, and from the beginning it grew and thrived while Helice gained expertise and respect as a strong and loving leader. She also inspired and mentored several women in her congregation who went on to become ministers themselves. Two of them, E.J. Niles and Jane St. John, are currently co-ministers at their home church in Virginia. Linda Dominick is co-minister with her husband, Guy Lynch, at Unity of Today in Warren, Michigan. Dee Swinney went on to pioneer another church in Alexandria, Virginia, and Mary Anne Multer is a minister in

Charlottesville, Virginia. We ask Helice how she motivated so many women to go into the ministry, and she replies:

> It was a natural and informal part of the relationship I had with them. I'm interested in helping people move forward with their lives, so I often ask questions like, "What are your next steps?" or "Where do you see yourself going?" or "What is your vision for your life?" Sometimes I say, "I've seen this particular characteristic in you, and I can see you doing—whatever." I invite people to consider these things. This is a time when women especially seem to be willing to take more risks, to be flexible, and to set their sights on something higher.

After several years of ministry in Virginia, Helice was invited by her long-time friend and mentor, Richard Billings, to return to the Chicago area to co-minister with him at Unity in Oak Park. It seemed like just the right thing to do. Daughters Zandra and Heather and her grandchildren live in the area, and ministering with Richard in such a beautiful setting was appealing as well.

Helice has been back in Chicago for several years now, and she finds it incredibly rewarding to be working with her mentor.

> Richard is loving and authentic and exudes such joy, wit, and humor that everyone loves to be near him. He's one of the most loving, compassionate, and understanding people I've ever known. Always seeking to call people to a higher level of living, he sees the highest and best in them. Although he's been here for 30 years, we're working in a full partnership, which frees him to do more of the things that are in tune with his heart. It's great for both of us.

Helice is also enthusiastic about the church's renewed commitment to families and children.

> Here in Chicago, especially, we see children whose families don't have the basic skills to help them get an adequate start in life. We want to find more ways to support those families who come with-

in our sphere of influence. We sponsor special seminars for youth and families, and we're building a strong team ministry approach in our youth education system. More adults are getting involved with more children, and we're setting up prayer partners of one adult, one child.

Our vision is to make a positive difference in the lives of families and children, and we trust that the specific steps will unfold as we continue our commitment. The key to everything we do in life and in this ministry is the realization that we're all here to learn our lessons of love. The people and situations that help us learn those lessons are continually drawn to us.

We leave Helice with questions she often asks of others. We ask about her next step, her vision for her own future. She closes her eyes, and after a few moments, answers, "My goal is to continue to deepen my journey within, to honor the relationship with myself and with the presence and power of God. I want to be of maximum service to others, and I am open and receptive to the inspiration, guidance, and direction of the Spirit of Truth who continually shows me the next step."

CAROL HALE
Building Bridges of Understanding

---

*"May the teachings of those you admire become part
of you so that you may call upon them."*
— Sandra Strutz Hauss

"**M**ulticultural" has been a key concept in the life of Carol Hale, both personally and professionally. While working with the migrant education program in the state of Florida, she reviewed local programs for migrant children and designed training for teachers and administrators who work both with this population and with neglected and disadvantaged youngsters. She has served as a liaison for the Florida Department of Education to the Multicultural Education Task Force, which reviews the status of multicultural education statewide and facilitates its integration into Florida curriculum. She recently wrote a grant funded at $35 million, which will help ensure scholastic success in children from all cultural and economic backgrounds.

Carol spent 16 years teaching English to non-English-speaking adults and misses that direct contact, but she keeps in touch with many former students here in the United States and in several other countries. Whenever they see or hear from one another, it's always a joyous reunion. Carol explains the possible reasons for this rapport.

> When people first came into my classes, they often felt lost, and my heart went out to them. Perhaps I related to them so easily because my father emigrated from Iraq, and I grew up teaching him the subtleties of the English language and continued to send him materials and books for years. He died in 1994 at the age of 98, and I still miss him. People often seem amazed that I could teach a class of people who spoke several different languages, but it was never a problem for me. I've always felt comfortable with people from all over the world, and their enthusiasm for learning has motivated me to use all my resources to teach them well.

Carol began teaching English to non-English speakers when she accompanied her husband to Puerto Rico while he worked toward a degree in Marine Science. She found a position teaching English in a Catholic school and knew she'd discovered her calling.

After they returned to Miami, Carol began teaching foreign-born adults, mostly Cubans, in evening classes. Then came the Mariel boatlift of 1980, a period of heavy immigration, and her classes were packed. "The 'Marielitos' left Cuba with absolutely nothing," Carol reflects, "and they were willing to do whatever was necessary to make a new life in this country. I was very impressed with their fortitude. They often worked two jobs in addition to attending my English classes five days a week." As Carol's reputation as an effective and compassionate teacher grew, her classes continued to increase until they had to be split up into smaller groups.

With each move she and her husband made around the state of Florida, Carol found her niche teaching English to non-English speakers. At the University of Florida in Gainesville, she created and taught an English program for foreign graduate students and their families. The women in her class, mostly wives of students who already spoke English, came from 30 different countries.

They were far from home, far from families and support systems. I admired their resourcefulness as they made friends, shared ideas on childrearing and financial planning, and helped each other understand American culture at the same time they shared their own backgrounds. Women from nations that were currently at war supported one another without animosity as they struggled together to make their way in this new country. I took them on a community field trip each week where they could learn to interact in English on site and become familiar with situations and places they would likely deal with in the future.

She remembers one especially successful visit to a local hospital where the students were given a tour and taught what to do in a medical emergency. Several days later, the husband of one of the women was injured in a fall, and as a result of the field trip, she knew just what to do. The hospital later asked Carol's students to serve as interpreters in the emergency room if the need arose.

After four years in Gainesville, Carol's husband graduated, and it was time to move again. "I was very depressed about leaving my classes," she recalls. "The students planned a wonderful farewell party where each wore native dress, recited poems, danced, and sang their unique appreciation. I'll never forget the gift of themselves they gave that day."

The bonds Carol shares with her students have stayed strong, although several years often go by without contact. Recently, a former student from Brazil spent a year near Orlando as a school volunteer while her husband studied citrus cultivation. Although it had been 12 years since they'd seen each other, Carol spent the day with this woman, who is now an English teacher in her native country. She decided upon that career because of the kindness and inspiration she received from Carol, and she never forgot her motivator and mentor.

Currently mentoring a former student from the Philippines whose American husband recently decided to divorce her, Carol offers emotional support and helps this woman understand the legal aspects of the situation. "I'm willing to be an advocate for women whenever I'm needed, no matter how much time has gone by since they were my students," Carol declares. "Many of them have become my friends for life."

Recent changes in her personal life led Carol to take time off from her work. Now divorced, she shares custody of her two young children with her ex-husband. They also have a grown daughter. "Fortunately, we both care very much about our children and how they are affected by the choices we've made," Carol says. "We are keenly aware that we are their models."

Through all this personal change, spiritual development has become vital for Carol.

There would be a gap in my story if I didn't mention the influence of Julie (Keene), who was my first woman minister. She taught me a broader perspective, and I appreciate the sense of peace I've gained as a result of her counseling and wisdom. I was drawn to hear her every Sunday, and I consider her a crucial model and mentor in my life. Certain phrases stick with me, such as: "Nothing can disturb the calm peace of my soul," and her often-declared quote from Tennyson, "God is nearer than our breathing, closer than our hands and feet." She organized a Master Mind prayer group a few years ago, and the group I joined as a result still meets regularly. All our lives have been profoundly influenced by this supportive activity, which always brings us back to the belief that "everything is in Divine Order," as Julie would say.

Because of her focus upon healing and spiritual growth, Carol feels she has cleared out much of the mental and emotional debris she accumulated over the years. "I'm connecting with my mother in a new way and appreciating the gifts she gave me, and I'm building a closer relationship with my siblings," she says. "I am striving to become more sensitive and to extend love and understanding in such a way that I truly deserve the label of model, motivator, and mentor."

DONNA HANSON
Embracing the World with Compassion

---

*"The time when humanity will be able to think in
universal and global terms still lies ahead, but the
fact that we can speak of it, desire it, and plan for
it shows that it is possible."*

— Rama Vernon

Strong and persuasive words, spoken thoughtfully and gently,
transported Donna Hanson's listeners from the Unitarian Church
in Spokane, Washington, to Beijing, China, and from there around the
world. Donna's method was simple, yet brilliant. She simply allowed
women from a dozen different geographic areas of the world to eloquently speak through her. We were moved and appreciative of the
opportunity to expand our minds and hearts beyond local concerns
and soon realized we were in the presence of an emerging woman
who belonged in this book.

Donna's Beijing trip was only one of many she has made to sev-
eral countries of the world, sometimes in her official capacity as
Secretary for Social Ministries from the Catholic Diocese of
Spokane, sometimes as a volunteer, and sometimes as a concerned

citizen of the world. Donna expressed the sentiments of a member of parliament in Uganda, which aptly highlights the need for individual connections that transcend political systems: *What is the meaning of a free press when only 50 percent of the people can read? What is the meaning of a ballot to a starving woman and her children? Can they eat it? We must remember that we are a family of nations, and that a rising tide of global awareness and responsibility must lift every person out of poverty if there is ever to be peace in our world.*

For all her professional life, over 30 years now, Donna has dedicated herself to assisting people. She has been a school social worker, an instructor in sociology and human services, and project director for Early Childhood programs. Through it all, Donna has either worked or volunteered for the Catholic Diocese of Spokane. For seven years, she was the Executive Director of the Eastern Washington office of Catholic Charities.

"When I was asked by Bishop Topel to be the executive director," Donna recalls, "I was aware that only priests had previously held the position. I did not realize it at the time, but asking a woman to be director was revolutionary. In accepting the job, I did not set out to be a mover or a shaker. I had the academic credentials plus the experience as a part-time associate director, so it just seemed logical to say yes."

Centered and calm but always moving decisively forward, Donna's focus is upon connecting people to the services they need, regardless of their religious affiliations. "The majority of people served by Catholic Charities do not belong to our faith, but the world community needs to work together to create systems that improve the quality of life for everyone," she says.

As she works toward positive change, Donna often finds that her own life is profoundly impacted as well. At a Caritas conference in Rome during 1991, Donna met a young woman from Bucharest, Romania. The neglected children living in Romanian orphanages had been featured on ABC's "20/20" program shortly before their encounter, so Donna asked the young woman how quickly these abandoned children might be helped. The woman's haunting response, "That depends on you," spoke to Donna's heart, and upon returning to Spokane, she asked to be released from the diocese for a three-month working sabbatical.

> This young Romanian woman, Linda Pogorilovschi, and I became soulmates: she was my sponsor, my mentor, my housemate and my friend in Bucharest. I could not speak the language, and I have no sense of direction, so I kept getting lost. However, by living and working with the Romanian staff and volunteers at Caritas, I received a profound lesson in letting go of the nonessentials with which we fill our lives. I went to share with them what faith-based expertise I had, but in the midst of their reality, they had faith left over to share with me. I came away with my own faith renewed.

She observed the church, which many struggle to understand, delivering food, drugs, clothing, and supplies when virtually no other institution could get into the area. She saw appeals to the people in the United States turn into vital goods and services for people of all faiths and political parties. "I came home convinced that we gain a deeper understanding and love by simply walking in another's shoes, even if only for a brief time," Donna says. "I am deeply grateful for my Romanian mentor, who challenged me to walk in her shoes."

Models and mentors have abundantly blessed Donna's life, beginning with her family of origin. Supportive women teachers continued to mentor her in the Catholic Academy she attended through both high school and college. "Never," she says, "did any of these 'women religious' suggest that we couldn't do anything we might choose to do. I always felt supported, which included the encouragement to accept leadership responsibilities."

Supportive relationships have continued to bless Donna's life. Her husband, Bob, also a professional social worker, was a "man before his time," Donna says with a smile.

He was the oldest of seven children and helped rear his younger brothers. He was very comfortable with our two sons, even when they were babies, and household tasks have never been beneath him. His mother, my uniquely wonderful mother-in-law, was the kindest, most accepting person in the world. Whether I was working or volunteering, she offered her help, never once hinting that I was neglecting her son or our children. She was a profound role model to me; to this day I strive to be the same kind of mother-in-law. I have no doubt that such significant mentors make our lives not only endurable, but indeed a joy.

Donna's philosophy is illustrated by an experience she turned into "The Parable of the Batteries." While on a Caritas trip to Jerusalem, a woman in Donna's party arrived without camera batteries. Donna gave the woman her extra supply, but two days later her own batteries were almost depleted, so she suggested to the woman that they take turns with the fresher batteries. But the woman had another solution. "Give me one of your weak batteries," she said, "and I'll give you a strong one; that way we'll each have battery power for our cameras, and we can both continue to take all the photos we want. We do this all the time in my country of Tanzania."

Donna realized that putting together the weak with the strong so that each may benefit is the goal of her life and career. "No one loses anything when each works toward a beneficial outcome for all," she reminds us.

Ten years ago, Donna worked toward a beneficial outcome for all as she addressed Pope John Paul II in St. Mary's Cathedral in San Francisco. Her goal was to speak on behalf of the lay men and women who comprise 98 percent of the Catholic Church in the United States. She hoped to articulate the diverse needs and philosophy of Americans. While the tone of her comments was deeply respectful, it was also full of strength and integrity.

When I come to my church, I cannot discard my cultural experiences. Though I know the Church is not a democracy ruled by popular vote, I expect to be treated as a mature, educated, and responsible adult. Not to question, not to challenge, not to have authorities involve me in a process of understanding is to deny my dignity as a person.

She then invited the Pope to reach out and to be more inclusive of women, the inactive clergy, homosexuals, the divorced, and all people of color.

  Donna knows clearly from whence her strength and sustenance comes.

I have no doubt the only true strength is spiritual strength. Such an insight came to me in October of 1987 when I was in Rome. As I walked in the twilight across St. Peter's Square, the lights were just coming on, and water was cascading in the fountain and splashing onto the plaza. I thought: You are here at the heart of Christianity. Suddenly, with an astounding clarity, I thought to myself, No, Christianity is inside of me. It is not a place, even this place. Rome is beautiful; St. Peter's is special, and this is a unique moment for me. Yet, I carry Christ with me wherever I go.

As each one of us becomes aware of such a truth, life becomes even more challenging. . .and yet, infinitely easier.

CONNIE HARDAN
Fortitude Under Fire

"Pain is important: how we evade it, how we succumb to it, how we deal with it, how we transcend it."
— Audre Lorde

A smiling, soft-spoken woman, Connie Hardan's kind spirit and gentle nature are obvious. However, the heartbreak and pain she has experienced in the past is not at all evident. Abiding by her husband's wishes, she stayed at home on their farm for years, devoting her entire attention to her family. When her oldest child was a sophomore in college and the younger two were in high school, her husband informed her that he was leaving because he was in love with a twenty-year-old. The children decided to live with their father. "They were at an age where they appreciated the material things that he could continue to give them," Connie says with no trace of bitterness.

But in the end, she realized that perhaps she'd trusted too much. This quiet and unsophisticated housewife accepted her husband's aunt as a divorce attorney for them both. Although her husband was affluent, she ended up signing away everything except $500 a month for two years—this in spite of the fact that she'd recently been diagnosed with fibromyalgia (an inflammation of the body's fibrous connective tissues).

During that difficult time, Connie wrote:

> As I sit here looking down at my divorce papers, I find it strange that so many years of living can be summed up in five pages. The pages are stark white with black bold print, staring back at me, summarizing the best years of my life. No words on these pages describe giving birth, nurturing, supporting, encouraging my family. It is a document used by the court to say who gets what, and it states for all to see that this marriage is over.

Unable to accept her new status, Connie says, "I cried myself to sleep every night and prayed to God that I wouldn't wake up in the morning, and when I did wake up, I cried again in frustration and despair." She finally accepted the idea that perhaps God did have a purpose for her life and that she should find a way to begin anew.

Gradually, Connie found emotional and physical strength deep within herself. No friend or relative came along to support her, but she found an internal motivator and mentor. As she grappled with the need for employment and surveyed the job market, she recognized the necessity for further education and decided to enroll at Spokane Community College. However, school proved to be a struggle for her. Fibromyalgia caused short-term memory loss that forced her to review notes over and over and to read assignments six times in order to gain a basic comprehension. In addition, pain often kept her from sleeping at night. Only with sheer will and determination did she manage to get through each day.

Yet, other options and interests presented themselves. She soon discovered some of the other women students who had been divorced or had endured abusive situations. Connie began to let go of her victimhood when she co-founded a support group called Share Our Search. The group's first project was to collect and distribute Christmas toys. Many struggling students with children had no extra money for such luxuries. The Share Our Search group put up a tree in the student lounge and invited students, faculty, staff, and even the president of the school to get involved, and they all responded. The result was that every child in campus day care as well as many other children received toys. "It created a special Christmas joy that we all shared," Connie remembers.

An honor student in spite of her difficulties, Connie earned an associate degree in Liberal Arts/Communications. She managed to accomplish this with an income of only $500 per month and no financial aid. Right after her graduation, she found employment as a receptionist but still continued to plan for the future. During lunch hours, she attended and completed an accounting class. Later at a weight-loss clinic, she taught women about diet and nutrition, makeup, and self-esteem, and there she discovered her true calling—helping other women to gain strength and confidence.

At Spokane Community College, she offers women her services as Registered Counselor, Licensed Make-up Artist, and Small Support Group Facilitator. She has also recently earned certification as a Personal Trainer/Fitness Counselor with the Aerobics and Fitness Association of America and plans to create a video on muscle stretch for those with fibromyalgia. She's still taking college courses and plans to keep on doing so until she earns a bachelor's degree. Her biggest project at the moment is a new business, a Victorian gift shop called House of Hartline, where she sells books, cards, framed poems, antiques, stuffed animals, and other items. It seems that once Connie's creative energy took over, there was no stopping her!

"I've learned that the more I focus on the positive things I can accomplish, the more I empower myself," Connie says. "There *is* life after divorce!"

LOUISE L. HAY
Woman of Vision

*"The awakening of consciousness is not unlike
the crossing of a frontier—one step and you
are in another country."*
— Adrienne Rich

"The women I admire are powerful women who are strong,
independent, bright, empowered beings who have developed
great self-worth and self-esteem," declares Louise Hay, the bestselling author of *You Can Heal Your Life.* "They do not let anyone
suppress, repress, or minimize their worth in any way. They can
come from any walk of life. The women I admire understand the
principles of Universal Law—that what we give out comes back to
us, and the more we give to Life, the more Life gives back to us.
They are healers."

In her book *Empowering Women,* Louise says: "Women are now
the best they've ever been. So it is time for us to shape our own destiny. We have opportunities never available to women before. It is
time to join with other women to improve life for all of us." Yet, as
we questioned Louise about those women who might have helped her

along the way, she reminded us that we each must ultimately be responsible for ourselves.

> I can't single out any one woman who is responsible for making me the person I am today—except myself. Just as I accept responsibility for the negative experiences that I attracted as an adult, I also take responsibility for having turned my life around through self-help techniques, a dedication to wellness and fitness, and the adoption of healthy mental patterns that have created the wonderful life that I now enjoy.

As we examine the life patterns of women of accomplishment—some well known, some not—who have exhibited compassion and genuine caring for others, we often see their struggle with early painful experiences—those which ultimately made these women stronger. So full of love and compassion now, so self-assured, moving so easily in the world, the observer would never guess what events might have occurred earlier in their lives.

Certainly, such is the case of the beautiful, talented, self-assured Louise Hay. President and founder of Hay House, a growing book publisher; world-renowned lecturer and workshop leader; bestselling author of 18 books translated into 25 languages, and philanthropist (the Hay Foundation supports AIDS research and shelters for abused and battered women); she is model, motivator, mentor, friend, and just "Louise" to those who work with her.

But her life fits the pattern; she was put to some early and severe tests. While still a toddler, her parents divorced, and Louise was boarded out while her mother, Vera, worked. Hoping to make their lives better, Vera remarried, but the man turned out to be cruel and abusive. Then, when Louise was only five years old, a neighbor raped her. The doctor's exam and the court testimony were traumatic enough, but Louise was devastated when she was told the rape was her own fault. She continued to live in fear that the man would get out of jail and exact revenge upon her.

The central core of Louise's teaching now is the importance of forgiving the past, acknowledging and healing the inner child, and loving and honoring who we truly are. Her heart opened to the AIDS population early on when so many were treated as pariahs. An outcast child and teen herself, Louise stored up vast amounts of compassion for others in similar situations. She had no friends in school, dressed in shabby clothes, had a funny bowl haircut, wore ugly high-topped black shoes, and smelled of the raw garlic she was forced to eat every day to "keep the worms away."

Nowadays we hear about runaway kids seeking to escape from sexual abuse at home. Louise experienced that trauma, too. Once she became a teenager, her stepfather began forcing sex upon her. At 15, unable to tolerate the abuse and cruelty any longer, she quit high school, left home, and found mundane jobs in soda fountains and restaurants.

"Starved for love and affection and having the lowest of self-esteem," Louise recounts in *You Can Heal Your Life,* "I willingly gave my body to whoever was kind to me." Just after turning 16, she gave birth to a baby girl; she'd already found a good home for the baby and adopted her out when she was five days old. This all-too-common story continues in the same vein for many young women even today who stay caught up in a pattern of self-destruction. But that was not Louise's destiny. Hers was to break out of this negative mold and to teach others to do the same.

While working in a Chicago department store, she heard about a free introductory modeling class and subsequently enrolled in the Patricia Stevens Modeling School. At about the same time, she began working as a receptionist for an Arthur Murray Dance Studio. In the process, Louise discovered that she was capable, organized, and could deal with the public. Later, she moved to New York City and embarked on a successful modeling career.

Louise met a handsome international businessman in New York, and they were married for 14 years before he left her for someone else. Although Louise continued her modeling career after the breakup, it had lost its luster. "I look back now," she says, "and realize he freed me for what I really needed to do." The turning point came when she attended a Religious Science lecture taught by

Dr. Raymond Charles Barker. Afterwards, she began to attend Sunday services and classes, resonating to the thought system that would transform her life. "And it needed transforming," Louise remembers. "In spite of a successful modeling career, I had low self-esteem and felt my life was one disaster after another. I sometimes slapped my own face in disgust."

For the next three years, she studied to become a Religious Science practitioner and delved into a variety of New Thought teachings. During the interim between becoming a practitioner and studying for the ministry, Louise learned transcendental meditation and studied for six months at Maharishi International University in Fairfield, Iowa. With the completion of ministerial training, she had assimilated a vast array of tools and techniques and was ready to be of service to humankind. She taught classes, lectured, counseled, and wrote a metaphysical booklet entitled *Heal Your Body.* She seemed to have it all together.

But then her philosophy was put to the ultimate test—vaginal cancer. She met this challenge on every level. Asking her doctors for a three-month reprieve from surgery, Louise began working with a nutritionist and using healing herbs. She also worked with a therapist who helped her to uncover, heal, and release deep resentment and anger. After the three-month period, there was no sign of the cancer in her body.

Then came a move to California. Starting from scratch, she began to slowly build a counseling practice. Her mother, Vera, came to live with her, and they began their deep healing process. Louise continued to give of herself through counseling and workshops, and the universe supported her efforts. A substantial gift of money came from one woman who said that Louise "helped me change my life around." Another woman stayed with Louise for a year, helping with her work and assisting with Vera. Louise continued to attract people who wanted to support her as she developed a variety of workshops and a mail-order business to sell her books and tapes.

During this time, Louise and Vera deepened their love and communication. "A new understanding developed between us as we cried and laughed together," Louise says. Their business complete, Louise's mother left this planet in 1985. "I miss her and love her," Louise said shortly after, "but we completed all we could together, and now we are both free."

The effort that would catapult Louise into world renown had begun in 1984 when she wrote *You Can Heal Your Life*. Four years later, it was on the *New York Times* bestseller list. In the years since that first huge success, Louise has been a supportive employer and friend to those close to her, as well as a model and motivator for millions. She does not see herself as a mentor in a normal sense, although the women and men she has encouraged along the way might feel differently.

"I do my best to live the principles I teach," she says. "I don't want to be put on a pedestal or thought of as a guru in any sense. If the ideas I put out are helpful to others, then my work is worthwhile. I am a lady with a simple message—*love yourself and heal your life.*"

JEAN HOUSTON, Ph.D.
Audacious Social Artist

"My child, I live my life each day as if it were my last. And life in all its moments is so full of glory."
— Helen Keller to Jean Houston,
grade school student

With a dramatic voice full of passion, energy, and sizzling intelligence, Jean Houston challenges us to wake up to a new life. This global midwife, sacred psychologist, haranguer, and prophetess challenges leaders and ordinary citizens all around the globe to awaken their dormant potential and to push their growing edges as never before. Jean powerfully states:

> With the new millennium approaching, we are being called to reinvent the world while we reinvent ourselves. Thus, we can become designers and weavers of a new pattern to re-envision and re-enchant the world. We are living in the midst of the most comprehensive cultural transition the world has ever seen, and with the rise of women, we cannot even begin to determine where it all is going. As a woman, I myself am called into ventures that would have seemed impossible to my female forebears.

Traveling as much as a quarter of a million miles a year in her work with the United Nations, with individual governments, and with heads of state in a variety of cultures, Jean's mission is to implement teaching programs that enhance personal and societal capacities.

We simply have to use more of ourselves if we are going to survive and make a better world. Yet my work is not only about creating more optimal human beings. It's about taking people who are on a growth path and turning them into social artists. Otherwise, it just becomes galloping narcissism.

Jean urges strong-minded social artists in all cultures to meet regularly to share ideas, develop projects, and make things happen, which is definitely Jean's forte. Obviously, she came into the world with a mighty mission and was embodied with the intelligence, energy, and passion to fulfill it, but as we speak with Jean about her life, we can't help but wonder what obstacles she encountered along the way. She tells us about an early one she has only recently sorted out.

"I didn't take the path for which I was patterned and prepared," Jean says. "I grew up in a theater and show business family and was highly prepared to be an actor, director, and playwright. When I was 20, I felt virtually jerked from the safe and comfortable womb of that clear plan and pulled into a great unknown." The details of that stressful time remain clearly etched in her memory. Shortly after her college graduation, Jean was in Greece sitting in the temple of Athena mulling over three offers, including one from a Hollywood studio offering a seven-year contract. The most enticing offer came from Broadway producer Joe Papp, offering her the role of Viola in Shakespeare's *Twelfth Night*.

All of Jean's previous patterning shouted, "Yes!" But there was another still, small voice that said, "No." When she asked why, she heard: "If you do this, it will mean a life in theater and films; your kinds of skills are needed for something else." When Jean asked what that something else might be, all she received was silence. Reluctantly following her guidance, she went back to graduate school and experienced what she describes as a "hellish year" of confusion. However, she slowly began to create a whole new career based on human capacities research, "a career that virtually didn't exist then," she states emphatically.

Searching for words, Jean describes that struggle.

It's a very complex thing I've only recently become aware of. Whenever I've attempted to do things that deal with my original patterning—theater or television or anything like that, I'm always blocked, whereas if I attempt to do things that have to do with greater research or ways of social artistry or forms of deep teaching, I can't say it's a smooth path, but it is a clear path. When I said no to what was authentically part of my essential being, I had to rewrite, reloom, and repattern myself in very radical and dramatic ways. It's almost like I had to reinvent my being. The lure to theater is still enormous, and when I see a great performance, I see something in me that is not envy—it's way beyond envy—it's an enormous yearning.

I believe many women are struggling now because they're making their own unique choices instead of following old models and programs, and there is often a certain sense of loss. They're searching for ways to integrate the mothering of a company or project with the older more basic form of mothering. Yet, women's roles must expand beyond a preoccupation with childbearing to encompass all fields of human endeavor if women are to be available for the complex requirements of the emerging planetary civilization.

Although she chose to become a pioneer in a new field of endeavor, Jean's training and expertise in drama are apparent in all she does. "We live a fraction of the life we are given because we do not live out of a big enough story," she declares in her autobiography, *A Mythic Life*. Maybe that is Jean's answer to herself. Perhaps a life on stage and screen, even a hugely successful one, would not have been the biggest story Jean Houston was capable of living. As it is, the entire world is a stage for her, her consciousness not confined within personas created by others, even William Shakespeare. Instead, she is called upon to write and direct scenarios for the United Nations, for heads of state, and for people all over the world. And in addition to all that, she still manages to captivate audiences wherever she goes as she utilizes mythology, music, movement, and drama to motivate others to raise their sights and to use more than a tiny fraction of their potential brain power. "It's true that my workshops are very dramatic," she says. "In fact, my main working associate is a very fine actor who was for many years head of the Oregon Shakespearean Festival."

Those fortunate enough to attend her workshops or hear her speak are moved and inspired by her no-holds-barred zestful presentations that so dramatically illustrate her expanded consciousness and that push, prod, tease, and entice us into taking steps to expand our own. She reaches out and involves her audiences in multisensory exercises designed to engage neglected parts of our brain. For example, she has chanted encouragement to several hundred people crawling on their bellies, feeling their evolutionary journey from their life in the sea to life on the land. Merely sitting and listening passively to a left-brain lecture is not what Jean's audiences are allowed to experience. Rather, they leave feeling deeply stimulated and enlightened by their participation in the drama of life.

Artistry and a sense of drama spill over into everything Jean does. Her mind reaches out and draws in, constantly accommodating to a rich and varied input. This is reflected in the architecture and decor of her home, which she so vividly describes.

It was built in a whimsical manner by actor Burgess Meredith with 50-foot rooms, stages, and a three-story hexagonal tower. My avocation as an archaeologist and collector of antiquities means that it now houses an even more whimsical collection of ancient gods and artifacts, including an Egyptian mummy case, an intertribal calling drum from Kenya, a Ming Dynasty ivory statue, and an intricately carved Balinese bird-god. My mentor Margaret Mead once observed, "Such a strange place. Nothing goes with anything, and yet somehow it all works. Just like the inside of your mind, eh Jean?"

When the mind of anthropologist Margaret Mead met the mind of Jean Houston, the ground shook under each of them. Jean thought

Margaret had the most interesting intellect she'd ever encountered and asked to study it. Margaret agreed. "I discovered," Jean recalls, "that her many modes of thinking, learning, problem solving, imagery, memory retention, dream orchestration, and creative processing provided a living confirmation of the latent human capacities I had seen over years of laboratory research." Jean felt that she was observing the living emergence of a dynamic style of feminine mind and behavior. She recalls:

> For more than 50 years, whenever major or minor issues were called into question, more often than not, Margaret was there, speaking at conferences, networking the thinkers, innovating, challenging, scolding, and above all, making things happen. Whenever she tackled a piece of work, she immediately alerted her senses, set an agenda, and began racing. Each minute had thrust upon it the contents of an hour, each hour was laden with a day, and from her birth in 1901 to the time she entered my life in the early 1970s, she had probably accrued the experience of four or five lifetimes. She exhilarated everyone in her vicinity, and low-energy people tended to do their best work around her. She raised the nature of the possible in me, and there is no question that I owe the prodigality of my present output to Margaret's training.

During the extensive process of working with each other, Jean and Margaret became closely bonded, mirroring each other's unique personalities as their minds, hearts, and wills engaged in a mutually exhilarating wrestling match. Margaret acknowledged the depth of their connection. "You are like me," she told Jean. "You think in patterns, are as eclectic as I am, seem to be afraid of nothing, have invented a new profession, and are dedicated to making the world work. Furthermore, I need another daughter, so it's probably you." That is how Jean found the principal mentor of her life.

Jean also appreciates that she had loving and supportive parents who encouraged their only child's precocious nature. She inherited a flair for the dramatic from her Sicilian actress mother and was shown all manner of possibilities by her father, a successful comedy writer.

An array of offbeat characters, intellectuals, and celebrities passed through their home, and Jean often accompanied her father inside the Hollywood studios of the '40s and '50s where she witnessed characters from a variety of times and places casually mingling with each other. Her mind was continually challenged to accommodate new combinations and possibilities.

When she was eight years old, Jean accompanied her father as he delivered a script to ventriloquist Edgar Bergen. When they walked into the room, Edgar didn't notice the visitors at first. He was questioning Charlie McCarthy about the ultimate nature of life, and Charlie was responding with amazingly wise answers. "I don't know where it's coming from or what he's going to say next, but he's the wisest person I know," Edgar explained to the newcomers. This early demonstration of expanded brain capacities made a deep and lasting impression upon young Jean.

Our discussion turns to the plight of so many young women in our society today—the problems of addiction, low self-worth, and depression so graphically described in Mary Pipher's book *Reviving Ophelia*. Jean believes that we live in a time when there are not enough operative archetypes of strength and uniqueness for young women.

> Too many fall back on biological forms mandated and patterned by social pressures. This is why we see the rise of eating disorders, addictions, depressions, and teen pregnancies. We need powerful, spiritual, psychological, energetic, dynamic, creative archetypes. We have too many mindless bimbos and sexual predators as models. I appreciate such exceptions as Meryl Streep, and certainly Jodie Foster, who is trying for different kinds of images.

Jean and Margaret Mead once discussed the obstacles to women's empowerment, the sexism, the violence against women, the backlash. "You can't turn around the social order of thousands of years in a few decades without expecting a backlash," Margaret declared. Jean believes many women are caught in that now.

For example, I believe Hillary Rodham Clinton is caught in a backlash because she is a powerful emerging woman who is reversing the expected mode by her strong partnership with her husband. She becomes a target for those who fear change. Unfortunately, many young women would rather be anorexic than be a woman like Hillary Clinton.

Patterning is very deep. Families, societies and tribes expect a woman to act in a certain way no matter how much genius she may have for writing, artistry, engineering, theology, or whatever. She is always climbing uphill, remounting the slope of thought and social patterning. Although new opportunities have opened up, the old forms and expectations are still there and strong as ever.

Yet, in spite of the confusion and struggles, a significant number of women all over the world are awakening to their power and responsibility and are refusing to be held back. Jean assures us:

Herstory, rich and fecund, is coming into the light. The emergence of women is one of the most critical movements in human history, the biggest in 5,000 years. Women are joining with men in full partnership across the whole domain of human affairs. It's one of the biggest shifts in human history because everything will change with it.

Virtually everywhere I travel around the world, except in certain fundamentalist Arabic societies (and rumblings are beginning even there), women are taking on the fullness, not just of their power, but of their process. Their emphasis is upon making things work, cohere, happen, grow, rather than a focus upon ends, the ultimate product. The rich mindstyle of women that has been gestating in the womb of preparatory time lo these many millennia is now emerging in a time when it is essential that it emerge if we're going to survive and green our time.

If for a hundred thousand years or so you've been stirring the soup with one hand and holding the baby with the other, kicking off the woolly mastodon with one foot and rocking a cradle with the other, watching out for the return of the hunters with one eye and determining with the other on which cave wall you will paint a magical bison, then you are going to develop a very complex consciousness. This is a consciousness that is extraordinarily well adapted to orchestrating the multiple variables and the multicultural realities of the modern world.

A few years ago in a village in Kenya, a frail tribal wisdom woman whose name was Grandmother Herself spoke to Jean and several other women gathered around her bed:

> You all have new duties on this earth, you women. You have the responsibility to make the world work. The men are growing weak, and you are growing strong. Soon there will be balance. Soon the men will look to you as equals, and together you will grow a new nest, and a nest of nests. The spirits will help you, especially the grandmother spirits. They have become very tough and powerful. But now you must support each other, work and pray and dance together. You must remember what the men have forgotten. You must remember how to have a society without war and palm wine. You must stop "cutting the rosebud" [submitting to genital mutilation]. That belongs to the old ways that are dying, old ways that hurt women. And you white women, you must stop cutting yourself off from your souls. I see your souls standing off in the corner, like children who have lost their mamas. Take your souls back!

That admonishment is not unlike the message that Jean Houston delivers. As global midwife and sacred psychologist, she continues to chide, urge, teach, and support us as we emerge from our dormancy. She proclaims that it's time to plunge into the new millennium—strong, empowered, and responsible. She declares that it's time for all of us to embrace our emerging strength and to *"take back our souls."*

BARBARA MARX HUBBARD
Futurist, Philosopher, and Mystic

"I am a questioner grown used to solving puzzles,
expecting explanations, then held spellbound
by the unexplained, the grand mysteries of time,
of space, of life itself."

— Karen Ravn

Author and dynamic speaker, visionary and social innovator, Barbara Marx Hubbard beckons us to join with her in a commitment to actualize our spiritual, social, and scientific capacities. Her friend and mentor, R. Buckminster Fuller, inventor of the Geodesic Dome and himself a visionary futurist, said, "Barbara Marx Hubbard is the best-informed human now alive regarding futurism and the foresight it has produced."

In the process of expressing her spiritually evolving nature, this modern-day prophet opened herself to direction from the Christ spirit as she wrote a message of hope for the new millennium, *Revelation*. In it she shares her personal story, then offers a modern interpretation of the biblical Book of Revelation and maps a gentler path into the next phase of evolution.

There has been an evolution of religion itself into an understanding that we are all co-creative with the Divine. This knowledge is breaking down religious boundaries, and we are no longer limited by religious labels. We respect the traditions we come from, but when we become conscious co-creators, we are more than Christian, Jew, or Muslim; we are part of the Oneness of Spirit.

When Barbara was only 12 years old, her mother died of cancer, and that traumatic event precipitated her search for answers to the meaning of life. After the first atom bomb was dropped when Barbara was 15, her search intensified. She wanted to know the purpose of our awesome power. The years before she met and married Earl Hubbard were years of continued passionate searching, and she was attracted to her artist husband because he was also consumed with the larger questions. However, once they married, he wanted a family and expected Barbara to play the traditional role, which she did for many years as she became involved in the process of giving birth to and mothering five children.

In the '60s, she experienced what Betty Friedan described as the "problem with no name." Barbara explains, "*The Feminine Mystique* awakened in me the realization that what was *wrong* with me was not that I was neurotic, but that I had no vocation, no identity outside wife and mother. In my own eyes, my personal self didn't exist."

Gradually beginning to renew her quest for meaning and purpose, she studied Abraham Maslow's *Toward a Psychology of Being*, as well as the philosophy of Teilhard de Chardin. She came to believe that just as everyone has a genetic code inside, we have a genius code sealed inside as well. "The way to access that code," Barbara believes, "is to identify our vocation and to surrender to it. If we don't find our vocation, the sealed orders are never opened, and we die unborn." As a result of this awakening, she began a vision quest that has magnetized her for over 30 years.

In the spring of 1966, Barbara was blessed with a cosmic vision of planet Earth and the entire sweep of its history. She felt and saw the interconnectedness of everyone and everything on the planet. She was given the experience of the birth of a new consciousness of love, peace, and cooperation within herself and a preview of what our planet could evolve into. Then she was given her vocation: Go tell the story of humanity's collective potential! Go tell the story of our birth! She saw that planet Earth is one living body; all its systems are connecting. We are the first generation to be aware of ourselves as One and the first to be aware of our responsibility for the future.

As a result of her transformative vision, Barbara experienced "vocational arousal," the drive to evolve her potential and to pursue her mission without limits. "Vocations are not destinations," Barbara explains. "They are ever-unfolding destinies, pathways to full self-actualization and self-transcendence."

Barbara's dedication to her vocation eventually brought about the end of her marriage.

> When a woman is deeply aroused with a life purpose, it is often exceedingly difficult for the man who loves her to find his own identification in relationship to her. Yet, when a mother falls in love with her vocation and is called to it, she has a marvelous opportunity to gift her children with a model of fulfillment. I want to say to mothers: Be willing to evolve yourself. In choosing vocation, you give your child the gift of your evolving self, the gift of your meaningful life as a model, the gift of a sense of aspiration toward the fulfillment of their own unique potential.

When Barbara first talked with her children about the divorce, assuring them she loved them, her young son said, "Mother, we know you love us; you are doing what mothers are supposed to do. You are creating the future." Barbara is proud that her grown children are now deeply dedicated to their own vocations and that the bonds of love between each of them and their mother remain secure and strong.

Once fully dedicated to sharing her evolutionary vision with the world, Barbara began to successfully reach out to others she thought might share the same vision. Jonas Salk responded to a letter she'd written to one of his assistants, and he in turn introduced her to other influential people who shared a vision of a positive future. Years of productive and far-reaching work followed in the U.S. and all over the world.

Barbara has a gift for explaining very complex ideas so that they can be understood. She describes the co-creation she urges us all to embrace as "conscious cooperation with the process, direction, and purpose of evolution, the implicate order of the universe—God." This involves dedication to our own healing, to loving ourselves and each other unconditionally, to tuning in to our higher selves, and allowing the Universal Human, the co-creative person that each of us is potentially, to emerge.

Currently, Barbara is focused upon four projects, wherein she serves as catalyst, instigator, cheerleader, torchbearer, co-conspirator, encourager, model, motivator, mentor, and friend:

1. Women of Vision and Action: Barbara is co-chair with founder Rama Vernon of this network of transformationally oriented women from around the world who are planning to launch a creative revolution, a campaign for a new America and a for a new world. They plan to develop a Peace Room (rather than a War Room) that will track peaceful innovations and breakthroughs. Women of Vision and Action will hold mapping parties throughout various communities to find innovative, creative people who are building the new world, and then put these people "on the map" and invite them to meet for mutual support. Out of this activity, Women of Vision and Action will develop a design, a blueprint, for a positive future and form a design team who will present these ideas to the American public and to the world. Barbara believes that women's creative energies are launching a type of social uprising.

> This is motherhood at the next level. Besides experiencing the miracle of giving physical birth, we have the potentiality to experience the miracle of birthing a new society. The energy that has gone into procreation is now becoming available for co-creation. Nature is rising up in the feminine to lift us beyond the phase of maximum reproduction and early death. We are challenged to become co-creators through the actualization of our own potential. The same

energy and passion that produced our children can now be used to co-create a universal world community of peace and love.

The sexual drive to reproduce the species is now being transformed into the suprasexual drive to evolve the species. The feminine energy is refocusing itself to take the initiative in guiding science and democracy toward synergistic cooperation in the building of new worlds on earth and new worlds in space.

2. Master's Program in Consciousness Evolution: Barbara is now working with Professor A. Harris to develop a new field of education built around the question, "How can the human race consciously and ethically evolve?" In the past few decades, science has gained access to understanding matter. Through understanding of the atom, the gene, the brain, and the laws of energy and motion, technologically competent human life is gaining access to intervention in evolution. We are making new life forms, building new worlds in space, and changing our own genetic codes. We are at the point where we can destroy the earth through nuclear winter, or we can build at the atomic level through nanotechnology (the ability to construct at the atomic level) and radical breakthroughs in the science of matter. Barbara declares, "If we can't learn ethical evolution, we cannot survive. This is especially true now, for high technology societies are in danger of self-destructing. We're in a critical time frame because we have the power to co-create or to destroy, but we don't have the ethics, guidance, or vision to use this power wisely."

In the *social evolution* area of the curriculum, students will review the new cosmologies and the history of the idea that we might all be changed. Then learners will examine the present planetary situation as a whole system in transition from one phase of evolution to the next. Every functional system, such as education, health, government, and economics, is destructuring and restructuring. Barbara states, "We want to identify people who are major points of transformation in each of those areas and bring them into focus as an extended faculty that students could call upon to help them design ethical systems for the benefit of everyone. Teachers will study and work with those who are actually transforming the world."

In the *self-evolution* portion of the curriculum, learners review the evolution of consciousness and of our self-images; then they will develop a program of self-evolution. Students will develop "higher self-portraits" and seek to fulfill their potential through their vocation. Jacqueline Small will work with Barbara, along with Michael Grosso, author of *The Millennium Myth,* and Jerome C. Glenn, coordinator of the UN Millennium Project.

3. International New Thought Alliance (INTA): "I'm proud to be a part of this group that plans to extend and expand until we embody a universal spirituality," Barbara explains. "We'll bring people together from different fields who may not attend a church but who want to build a new world from a perspective of universal spirituality. We are creating a spiritual chalice for these creators where they can be honored in a spiritual context that comes from the universal aspect of all faiths." INTA has an annual transformational expo that is open to anyone who seeks to experience and express wholeness. The purpose is to be a vehicle for disseminating transformational ideas that empower and connect individuals globally. In 1995, INTA presented Barbara with that year's Humanitarian Award. "I hope many of the emerging women who read this book will be in attendance at the very special celebration for the year 2000, which will be held in Chicago and chaired by Dr. Johnnie Colemon," Barbara concludes.

4. Society for the Universal Human: This society was given birth at the Living Enrichment Center in Wilsonville, Oregon. Founder and leader Mary Morrissey invited Barbara, Jean Houston, Joan Borysenko, Father Leo Booth, Gary Zukav, and Gaye and Kathlyn Hendricks to serve as faculty for the society. The inaugural event occurred in February 1996 and drew together pioneering souls who experience within themselves the emergence of a more universal human. Barbara explains:

In the process of learning what it means to be a universal human, we are developing a curriculum to give birth, nurture, and empower ourselves to actually co-create a society that will manifest the kind of world we choose to live in. We've already had training sessions, workshops, and conferences putting forth these ideas, but not a supportive society for ourselves as a family, so this is an important breakthrough. No one fully knows what a society for, of, and by universal humans will be. Yet we feel that the genius to build a new civilization lies in our individual potential.

The four areas of Barbara's focus each provide an essential piece of the support people need as they commit to conscious evolution as co-creators. Women of Vision and Action promotes social action; The Master's in Consciousness Evolution provides intellectual understanding; INTA offers spiritual expansion; and The Society for the Universal Human encourages and supports the individual on the personal level. "I'm involved in a whole systems shift through these partnerships," Barbara reflects.

In addition, she has her own entity called The Foundation for Conscious Evolution and is working with partner Nancy Carroll to develop evolutionary circles for people to come together in small groups to experience spiritual growth, to learn the ideas of conscious evolution and co-creation, and to form a circle community over the Internet. The function of evolutionary circles is to grow the seed of the new person in the evolving world. Barbara invites us to pioneer with her into the next stage of evolution. (See the resource section at the back of this book.)

Barbara sees herself as a social architect, which she certainly is, but even that description seems too constricting for this dynamic spirit. In 1984, her name was placed in nomination for vice-president of the United States at the Democratic Convention, where she proposed a Peace Room in the White House to scan for, map, connect, and communicate what is working to create a more positive future. The Peace Room process is now being developed by the Foundation on their Website. Barbara's positive vision, coupled with her ideas for specific action, inspire those around her to realize they have the power to shape their own destiny. The emerging woman needs to play a significant part in creating our positive future. "The co-creative feminine energy must rise to leadership now, in partnership with co-creative men," she proclaims. "We must model the changes we'd like to see in the world."

MASIL HULSE
Newly Blooming in Autumn

"The art of life isn't controlling what happens,
which is impossible; it's using what happens."
— Gloria Steinem

She says she's slowing down. However, it isn't noticeable unless you happen to catch her napping a little more frequently than she used to, but even then, she still engages in enough activity to outdo most people half her age. In 1981, Masil and Ione Jenson co-founded The Holo Center of Idaho, where she, Julie Keene, and Ione still live and work. The Holo Community is located on five forested acres, so Masil, who has always had an affinity for nature, can still work with the land. She has created a lovely outdoor setting for our center and nurtures the natural growth that is so prolific in our Pacific Northwest location. A flowing fountain sits at the entrance to the house, giving us the sound of moving water, the only thing that we felt was absent.

Masil began oil painting when she was nearly 65 years of age and has produced many lovely pictures, including the one that graces the cover of this book, and another that took Grand Reserve Champion at the local fair. We call her our "Grandma Masil" after the famous primitive painter Grandma Moses, who began oil painting at about the same age. She is now actively involved with establishing and working at a local artist's cooperative gallery.

At The Holo Center where we write, do counseling, and sponsor one- or two-week-long Intensive programs with people who fly in from around the country, Masil's nurturing presence is keenly felt by all who pass through our doors. A nurse by profession, there is a natural, as well as a trained, healing quality about all she does, and her healing energy touches and blesses. She always knew she wanted to be a nurse, and even though she had no role model for that profession, she was determined to fulfill her dream.

Born in 1922 and raised in very small sawmill towns and rural areas, Masil always related deeply to the great outdoors and loved the natural environment. She is the only person we know who can spot the first buttercup of the season, 100 feet away, while driving down the road at 55 miles per hour. As a child, she spent countless hours wandering the meadows and hills and swimming and fishing in the creeks of the Oregon countryside. As the oldest of four children, it was often her only escape into solitude. "I always felt and thought differently than the other kids, so I was often alone by choice. It gave me time to think and to be."

Role models for Masil were 4-H leaders and teachers, and she fondly remembers the teacher she had in grades six through eight. In the sawmill town of Kinzua, the tiny school had no library, but a teacher bent on introducing her disadvantaged students to the joy of literature bought books for the classroom. It was here that Masil was encouraged to read and enjoy some of the children's classics.

There were several role models after she entered nurse's training who inspired Masil in her newly chosen profession. "And," she grins, "one of them made me a better nurse by demonstrating what I did *not* want to become." Due to her academic excellence, she was chosen to complete her last six months of training in the army at Madigan General Hospital in Fort Lewis, Washington. She fully intended to remain in the army after graduating, but World War II ended just as she finished her training.

Although she had never wanted nor intended to get married, she eventually did succumb to the societal pressures of the time. It was, for many years, a good marriage, and she and her husband, a wheat farmer, eventually adopted three children. Masil put her nursing skills to use in a new way as she took over and ran the pig nursery—an enterprise that gave them the necessary finances to continue ranching during hard times. Always versatile, it was not unusual to see her drive a wheat truck, ride a motorcycle, or pilot the family airplane.

In 1960, her two sons found dynamite caps and attempted to pry them open. Ten-year-old Danny died as a result of the explosion, and seven-year-old Davey was left blind. Masil shares what happened to her during that time of loss and crisis.

> I felt as though I had been lifted up and was being held in the arms of God so that I could function as a mother and a nurse. No one could understand what I was trying to tell them, nor did anyone have any answers for what I had experienced—not even my minister—so in time I chose to remain silent. After Dave went to the Oregon School for the Blind in Salem, I busied myself learning to read and write Braille so I could communicate with him. Many years later when Ione (Jenson) came into my life, we talked about my spiritual experience, and for the first time, someone understood. Ione and I did some deep inner healing work around the suppressed feelings surrounding the accident, and we also executed a physical healing of my nontropical sprue—an incurable allergy to all forms of gluten.

After Masil had completed her inner work and received her physical healing, she decided she'd like to be involved in spiritual healing work. When her last child, a daughter, graduated from high school in 1976, she began to work with Ione. A spiritual healing and retreat center soon became their collective dream, and they carefully and prayerfully kept lifting it up for Divine guidance. In 1981, they were led to Idaho and began to build The Holo Center—a project that they physically participated in constructing.

It was this deeper spiritual journey that finally spelled the end of her marriage. As Barbara Marx Hubbard points out, it is often very difficult for the man who loves her to embrace a woman's passion for giving birth to great personal and planetary transformation. Over the next few years after Masil's healing, it became increasingly difficult for her husband to accept the changes that were occurring. He had married a "wife," and he wanted to keep it that way. When it became an either/or proposition for him, she felt she had no choice but to continue her own soul's journey—a decision she's never regretted.

Masil, a sprite, often projects a childlike innocence and wonder at the world around her, but under that innocence is an active, creative woman who possesses courage, independence, and tenacity. Young at heart and broadminded, she is always willing to lend a helping hand to worthwhile endeavors. She greets each day with eagerness and anticipation and creates whatever it takes to keep us all from growing too complacent. On the spiritual pathway, Masil is, indeed, our co-conspirator and collaborator.

CAIT IRWIN
A Wise Soul in a Young Body

*"Without the period of lonely wandering, there
would be no artist, for she would long ago
have drowned in one ocean or another."*
— Jane Lazarre

One would not ordinarily think about including a 15-year-old girl in a book about emerging women. However, as Ione stood talking to this young woman in June of 1995, it became evident that this was no ordinary teenager; she was more like an "ancient sage" housed in a young body. Cait Irwin was, to say the very least, an extraordinary young lady.

Ione was presenting a workshop in Council Bluffs, Iowa, on our book *Women Alone: Creating a Joyous and Fulfilling Life*, and Cait attended that workshop with her mother. When we went around the circle and each participant explained what had attracted her to the workshop, Cait explained that in many ways she felt alone because her peer group often didn't understand the *different drummer* she heard.

She was an active and participating member of the group, and after the seminar had concluded and people stood talking for a few moments, Cait commented, "There was no age here today; we were all just souls sharing." Indeed, she was so right. Even though the chronological age, as measured in Earth time, ranged from 15 to 75 years, there was no sense of any age differences that afternoon as each person shared openly and honestly from their individual heart space. Thus, Cait Irwin entered Ione's world.

As they talked, Cait opened a book filled with her incredible art work. Ione was in utter awe of Cait's obvious depth of understanding. It was immediately apparent that this soul was born with a great capacity to understand her multidimensional existence and with an incredible talent to creatively express it in deeply original ways that are often steeped in metaphysical messages.

Maureen Irwin has wisely nurtured her child, and when asked to describe how she experiences her daughter, she said:

> She's wise and old, yet very childlike at the same time. I think she'll always be that way. She is sensitive, artistic, very loving, thoughtful, intense, anxious, driven, obsessed, a tomboy, athletic, romantic, intelligent, articulate, expressive, emotional, expansive, disorganized, original, curious, intuitive, persistent, productive, kind, a nature lover, and ambitious.
>
> I'm her mother, yet our relationship is an unusual one—very close—more like soulmates. I'm always in awe of what she is saying and thinking or doing. My challenge has always been not to control her, but to nurture, protect, and help her remain her unique self, and at the same time, to help her to function in the real world. People have always said, "Cait is so easy to have around; it must be easy to raise her." She is easy in many ways—not rebellious or demanding like some teenagers—but she requires a lot of energy. There have always been continuous questions and projects to keep up with; she's always inquiring, questioning, pondering, and reacting.
>
> She requires a substantial amount of emotional guidance and a lot of listening. She's very generous with her talent; she says it is a gift she wants to share. She has made money with her art, and she has a good head for business. She has been called a "walking ad agency" and a "cottage industry." I've always said that I know she is mine because I was there when she was born, but sometimes I think,

Where did this child come from and where is she going? She's always a surprise and a joy!

Cait's attunement to the world around her has always been astute; Maureen remembered that by the age of three, Cait became fearful of crime and environmental problems and asked, "Am I safe in this world?" If Cait saw a dead animal on the way to school, she would feel bad all day. Sometimes she would come home and say, "My heart was crushed today," when she had heard someone say something unkind to another person. She has never been able to understand how people can deliberately hurt each other.

Art became important early on as a way to express her feelings, and she would draw during class, under other papers, and explain it by saying, "How can I sit in this small space all day? I look out the window and wish I was a bird." She likes school and gets good grades, although she hasn't thought of herself as a smart person because she's somewhat disorganized, and her mind is not always "on task." Traditional testing never seemed to tap her abilities. Maureen remembers that Cait would need to come home and unwind as early as kindergarten saying, "School is so fast." By the sixth grade, she was thinking and speaking of metaphysical concepts and was always a challenge to teachers. Some handled the situation in positive ways, and others didn't.

Maureen, a rare and insightful mother, thoughtfully continues her comments about her unusual daughter.

Since the name of the game in junior high is conformity, this was a tough time for Cait. Luckily, she attended small schools most of the time, so she has been treated kindly. Nearly all of the students see her as an original—a unique kid—a character. Everybody likes her, but she feels somewhat isolated because she doesn't always enjoy the same things her peers are interested in doing. Cait laments, "Sometimes I feel starved for a good conversation," so she has always related better to older students and adults.

At age 14, the long shadow of depression cast itself over Cait's life, and for a time, she was suicidal and was hospitalized for nine days. It was a very difficult time for Cait and her family. Maureen took a leave of absence from her teaching job in order to support her daughter's healing process as they began their journey of medications, therapy, and so on. Since noise, stress, and concentration were so difficult for Cait, she only took those classes she could tolerate each day, and Maureen began home schooling in order to help Cait keep up with her assignments.

Her art became an integral part of recovery for Cait as she intuitively started to visualize her illness as a beast growing inside of her that she had to tame. Modern mystic that she is, she soon began to see her depression as a gift and feels that without experiencing it, she might not have come to her current depth of understanding about herself, others, and life in general. In her own words, she says:

> Going through depression, I realized and learned things about myself—who I was, what I was, and why I was. I found my connection with nature, and that's why I've become very interested in the way of the shaman. Native American beliefs have always seemed like common sense—living in harmony with the land. I'm also pursuing an underlying interest in herbology, reflexology, acupuncture, etc. I am interested in the ways the body can heal itself. Going through my illness forced me to mingle with my soul. Now I find it impossible to quit doing, dreaming, acting, and studying. I am trying to start a club at school that connects students with nature, and one that allows their spirits to encounter each other through writing, poetry, drawing, or other forms of self-expression.

> I see so much hate and violence in the world and think about how I can change all that. I guess you can't change people, but I've learned that you can inspire by example. Life is here to live—the ups and downs—all of it is part of the whole adventure, at least in this life. It would be nice if everyone could just enjoy the good and bad parts of each age, and not live in the past or the future, but the present. It doesn't matter how old you are, what gender or race; it's your spirit that matters.

Through Cait's experience with depression, she learned what makes her happy, balanced, and relaxed. She's become involved with meditation, relaxation techniques, and birdwatching; has found out who her real friends are; has learned how to pace herself; and has come to understand the importance of diet, rest, and exercise for a healthy body and a recognition of the mind/body connection. She showed such courage by facing her illness head-on and doing all the hard things to get better. She never stopped being the productive artist and also wrote a great deal of poetry throughout the whole ordeal. "Cait's my hero," Maureen says proudly.

She's doing very well now. She is the school artist and is called on to do all kinds of art work. Thanks to her, the biology classroom at St. Albert's High School is now a jungle, and huge lions, tigers, and gorillas surround the room. As Cait's imagination blossomed, so did the walls.

There is, however, one more amazing note to this story. When Cait begins a project, she never seems to know exactly what comes next until it emerges through her fingertips. And, somehow, one begins to suspect that in just this same unpredictable but divinely inspired manner, Cait herself is emerging.

IONE JENSON AND JULIE KEENE
Co-conspirators

*"Gratitude links us with God and with our
fellow human beings."*
— Angela Passidomo Trafford

Our separate stories will follow, but our current endeavors and passions are so intricately intertwined that it is appropriate to first share our common interests. Over the last several years, we have been involved in building community. The two of us, along with a third woman, Masil Hulse, share a home and healing center (The Holo Center—for a brochure, see the resource section) where we do psychospiritual counseling, inner healing work, and the teaching of spiritual concepts. Our goal is to help individuals, both male and female, to bring their personal lives into a place of healing and wholeness.

We are also writers and travelers. We have toured the country presenting workshops on various topics and have recently begun holding workshops on *Emerging Women*. Our current passion is to bring women together to confront their challenges, to look at their alternatives, and to commit to at least *one* specific step that will move their lives forward in a positive direction.

We also ask women to envision a perfect and peaceful society—locally, nationally, and globally—and to list the things that need to occur in order for a new reality to emerge. Together, the women begin to explore possibilities and look for some immediate steps that can be taken to move humankind in that direction. Finally, they decide what one thing, however small, they are committed to trying within the next seven days that will contribute to the manifestation of a more loving world.

Through these processes, we hope to help women connect both individually and collectively to the feminine spirit that is rising during this critical time in our evolutionary history. It is our belief that by healing our individual lives and then extending that healing into the world by the means available to us, we become part of the quantum leap necessary for creating a more humane planet. Therefore, the primary intent and focus of our writing projects is to extend our personal interactive ministry to a larger audience. These are the passions we share.

IONE JENSON
An Observant Learner

*"It is only through realizing the connection
between the inner and outer realities...that we are
able to walk in step with ourselves, each other,
and the universe."*

— Diane Mariechild

I think I was born to be free and independent. I vividly recall my first conscious assertion of independence when I was barely four years of age. My mother had just thwarted my plans. "Squaring off" with her, my feet slightly apart and firmly planted, my hands on my hips and my voice determined, I informed her: "Just wait until I grow up, and then I'll do as I please." Slightly amused, she responded that I'd never be old enough or big enough to do just as I pleased; it was a scenario that would be repeated often while I was growing up. However, shortly before her death in 1975, my mother confided to my older sister that she thought I'd come as close to "doing as I pleased" as any person she had ever known!

From the beginning, my thinking always seemed to be outside and beyond the cultural norms. I was always questioning the meaning of life, the force we call God, my purpose for being here, my relationships with other people, and what it means to truly love. I remember as a very young child growing up in the Midwest before air conditioning was widely accessible that on hot and humid summer nights I would lie on a quilt in our backyard and look up at the sky with awe and know that somewhere there were answers that I was seeking to questions I was not yet mature enough to formulate.

Early on, there was a constant flow of people streaming through my life, even for brief spans of time, that motivated me to recognize the vast potential that life offered. I was born to undereducated parents, but they always insisted on the importance of a good education, even though to them a high school diploma seemed like the pinnacle of scholastic success. Lena Jared, my first-grade teacher, awakened in me the knowledge that someday I, too, would be a teacher. She taught me the joys of reading. Pauline Benning, my second-grade teacher, taught me to unlock words with her persistent demands that they be "sounded out," and she opened the world of poetry for me by reading it aloud on a daily basis in her classroom. Evelyn Cross, my sixth-grade teacher, had me memorize and recite poetry at school assemblies, and empowered me to push my growing edge. She also helped me through a time when my father was very ill and close to death. She accomplished this just by being a warm, loving, and secure presence in my daily school world.

Vivian Ahlquist was the Sunday School teacher who encouraged me to sit on her porch steps or in her living room and ask the questions that often burned deepest in my heart. A spiritual questor herself, Vivian treated me like an adult and honored my "wonderings" by sharing her own—which were not much different from mine. This bond lasted between us until her death in the early 1960s.

There were high school teachers who modeled what it meant to be an educated woman. Both Ruth Moeller, my American history teacher, and Mary Beth Daley, my drama teacher, encouraged and convinced me that I was college material. Born and raised in a lower middle-class blue-collar home, college wasn't even a dream for me until these women helped me realize that I wanted more from my life than my circumstances deemed feasible. Each separately encouraged me to apply for an available $100 scholarship—which I was awarded at graduation.

I matriculated at the University of Nebraska at Omaha (UNO), worked in the Dean of Students' office, babysat, and did any other job possible to pay for my tuition and books. I completed two years of college before I married, and eventually returned and finished my teaching degree. My first year of teaching was at Franklin School in Council Bluffs, Iowa; it was the same school where Miss Jared, Miss Benning, and Mrs. Cross had been my teachers and role models.

At UNO, Hollie Bethel, the College of Education department head, exemplified the values that I would espouse and embrace as an educator. Alta Cunnan and Margaret Evans, my cooperating teachers, modeled excellent teaching techniques that stood me in good stead and helped me attain a professional reputation of excellence. Evelyn Piper, Director of Elementary Education for the Eugene, Oregon, public school system during the years I taught there, without a doubt modeled the highest standard of professional integrity I've ever encountered anywhere.

And then there was Sharon Beers, a young teacher ten years my junior, who taught in a school where I was developing and coordinating curriculum. Sharon's profound capacity to love and to be open to change and exploration flung open new doors and new avenues to search and embrace. She taught me about prejudice, about learning to be nonjudgmental, and she exposed me to a greater love for, and understanding of, all humanity.

As I consciously began my psychospiritual journey, the one I had been seeking for such a long time, Dorothy March and Daisy Lind, true soulmates and fellow explorers, enlivened my path as we learned and grew together. Also, Agnes Sanford, a wonderful spiritual pioneer and teacher, motivated me to expand my horizons and forever altered the way I would perceive my world. To all these wonderful women, as well as the many authors of literature, and spiritual and self-help books who constantly pushed my growing edge and modeled ever-expanding concepts about our multidimensional potential, I owe a profound debt of gratitude.

However, there are three women who were intimately involved in my life over a span of years; these are the women I call my *pivotal people*. These women have been outstanding role models, enthusiastic motivators, and unobtrusive mentors. To these three women go my love, my gratitude, and now my very public recognition of their special gifts and prolonged influence in my life, all of which have been indispensable to me as an emerging woman.

Lucille Pelzer

Lucille Pelzer entered my life in an in-depth manner during the summer of 1949 when she hired me to babysit her two young children. From the beginning, there seemed to be an important connection between Lucille and me, and I was fascinated by her life. She modeled a new type of woman for me; for unlike most of the women in my extended family, Lucille was not a stay-at-home wife and mother, nor was her forte having coffee and gossip sessions with the neighborhood women. I viewed her as an interesting enigma. On the one hand, she enjoyed creating a beautiful home with a loving and peaceful atmosphere, and she truly liked to cook and bake. She was a soft, loving, and demonstrative mother and wife. On the other hand, she nearly always held some kind of outside job to help financially secure her family's future. She also helped remodel her home, often taking the major responsibility for plastering walls, wall-papering, sanding, and so on. I was incredulous as I watched her gracefully move back and forth between these activities where there seemed to be no clear-cut or defined gender roles as there were in the homes of the people I knew. Never did she sacrifice either her femininity or her power. She merely took action on each challenge or task that presented itself and very effortlessly, or so it appeared to me, accomplished whatever she set out to do. Lucille gave me my first taste of a woman who was balancing her anima (female) and animus (male) in a remarkable and astonishing fashion. I doubt, even to this day, that she knows what an outstanding accomplishment that was back then, and still is, for that matter.

I watched her carefully, observed how efficiently she operated on many levels simultaneously, and I mentally catalogued every thing I saw her do. At the same time, I began to feel convinced that it would be easy for me to be equally competent, so I began to test my skill whenever an opportunity for me to do so presented itself. Lucille became a strong influence during those young and vulnerable years of my life.

When I married and our first house needed wallpapering, I successfully put wallpaper on room after room in our big old farmhouse after deciding to copy what I'd watched Lucille do so many times. Thus, I attempted and succeeded in doing many things that the other women in my family had never done. I took to the open road, as I'd observed Lucille do on numerous occasions, and drove highways, freeways, and eventually, often drove cross-country alone. She was such a strong and positive influence in my life that it still permeates my daily existence.

Whatever situation Lucille faced, she never complained; she just took constructive action and met the problem undaunted. Her greatest legacy was the knowledge and confidence that life always offered options, and if I wanted things to be different, it was up to me to find a positive way to create the difference. My life was greatly impacted by this woman of gentle power.

Glendora Burbank

It was in the fall of 1965 when I first glimpsed this vibrant redhead from across the room. We were attending a Head Start meeting, and with a degree in Early Childhood Education, I had just moved to Eugene, Oregon. Glendora Burbank was obviously a "mover and a shaker," and it was easy to see that this vivacious, well-spoken woman was one of the leading and influential forces in this new program. She was extremely well versed in the Early Childhood Education field, and she was well respected by those in attendance.

Often during those late-afternoon meetings, she would speak to the issues succinctly and with a depth of feeling that mirrored both genuine concern and fierce determination to give children the best educational advantages and opportunities possible. I was impressed with the professionalism of this woman, and I was drawn to her human, caring qualities. Over the next two years, we continued to work together on the school district's program for five-year-olds, and my admiration for her skills only continued to grow with increased contact.

When the Early Childhood program eventually had to be eliminated for budgetary reasons, I needed to find a new and meaningful assignment within the school district. Somehow, I felt that working at Awbrey Park School would offer me a challenge, a chance to continue educational pioneering, and an opportunity to learn under skilled leadership. I approached Glendora about openings in her teaching staff at the primary level. She invited me, instead, to be the resource person who would help implement and coordinate an integrated curriculum, and I eagerly accepted. She soon became my mentor and very good friend.

As we worked together on a daily basis, I observed Glendora in action and capitalized on the opportunity to learn from her. Aware of her effectiveness as a leader and touched by her concern for children, I begin to understand how power could be strong and gentle simultaneously. One could observe her being assertive and "tough as nails" when a principle was involved or when good education was at stake, and yet, one could also see the tenderness when she was touched by the needs of children. She could be poetry in action.

At staffing sessions, she was prompt, her superb organizational skills often kept her "ahead of the game," and problems were averted because of her foresight. When challenges did arise, we circumambulated the issue and looked at it from all sides. Then, taking the information, she led us into looking at solutions, and by the conclusion of the meeting, we were all clear about the issue, the various facets surrounding it, and the plan of action to be followed in resolving the problem. After four years of practice, it became an integral part of how I operate.

Glendora trusted me implicitly and constantly empowered me by giving me freedom, support, encouragement, and unequivocal confidence. However, her greatest gift to me was the gift of herself, her own "being"—a very real presence. Strong, assured, wise, and assertive, she was a woman before her time. I often stood in awe just watching her.

I respected and embraced her right-brain, softer side, but it was the other left-brain experience that I needed. Since I naturally tend toward being a right-brain person, I deeply needed to experience and learn those more practical qualities she so perfectly modeled. She helped me balance my heart and my head. As a result of this association, my life began to take on a richer blend of strength, tenacity, assertiveness, and logic. All these qualities enhanced my own natural inclinations toward positive thinking, spontaneity, and intuitiveness, and made for a rich legacy.

Recently, Julie and I went to lunch with Glendora. There, I sought permission to include the story about her influence in my life, which really, then, makes it "our story." When asked about the influences that allowed her to become such an extraordinary woman for her time, her answer sounded strangely familiar to me. She was born with an independent spirit, her parents weren't educated but always regarded education as a strong family value, and she felt she had good teachers along the way.

When asked about the women who might have motivated *her* to become such an empowered woman, it was astounding to hear her confide that the women who helped her most were the ones who had trusted her. She commented on how empowering it was to think that people had faith in her capabilities when she hadn't even yet recognized them in herself. Trust, faith, and affirming my talents were the very gifts she had, in turn, bestowed upon me.

Mary Krenk

The third pivotal person in my life is Mary Krenk. Mary entered my life when she invited me to do a radio interview during the years

I lived in Eugene and was publicly speaking out for the kindergarten program. We clicked from the first moment our eyes met.

Mary soon became a role model and mentor for me in my spiritual journey. After I'd moved from Eugene in 1972, I remember writing a letter and sharing with her my search for meaning through the psychospiritual. I concluded that letter with an assurance that I had not "jumped off the deep end." In the first return mail possible, Mary responded, "Perhaps it's the 'deeps' we're searching for, my dear. Go ahead and leap!" Then she went on to share with me her own years of exploration and some of the insights she had discovered in her search. From that moment on, our mutual love and sharing has continued unabated. (Mary's profile appears on page 159.)

JULIE KEENE
Spiritual Midwife

"To accept the responsibility of being a child of God
is to accept the best that life has to offer you."
— Stella Terrill Mann

Forgive and release the past—get on with your life! It's never too late to begin again! We are in the process of constant emergence! This has been the message I've whispered and shouted to myself over and over again and the one I've consistently shared with people as a teacher, counselor, and minister.

At first I was reluctant to reveal the specifics of my story because I was shamed and embarrassed by them. However, I came to realize that honest and authentic sharing was the key to my freedom and one of the most effective tools I have for helping others.

Healing beyond the effects of a traumatic past has taken up a great deal of my time and energy; if sharing my journey can help others be more skillful in their healing process, then I'll feel I've made a valuable contribution. It was not only a traumatic childhood I needed to heal and overcome; I needed to change the way I operated in the world as a result of my early experiences. I have dedicated myself to teaching others that we *can* get beyond our past. Our history is not our essential identity! There is hope and happiness for us if we are willing to do the psychological and spiritual work—and we don't need to wait years for positive results. They begin the day we embark upon that new path.

It's been said that angels rejoice when a soul transcends a negative pattern. Sometimes these patterns repeat themselves for generations. I rejoice along with the angels because with the help of God, Spirit, Principle, Higher Power, or whatever anyone wants to name it, I've managed to transcend many negative patterns. Neglected and molested as a young child, I was granted a reprieve from misery when I was adopted at age nine. It was like a dream come true for me when my new parents and three brothers accepted me as part of their loving family from the very first day.

Fortunately, even in the difficult earlier years before my new life began, a handful of positive influences kept a spark of my hope alive. When I was barely five years old, I remember being left alone for hours in an old house in the country. There was little furniture and I had no toys, but there was a radio, and I escaped by listening to soap operas. Today we see the soaps as a dubious influence, but in that earlier era they provided me with a relatively affirmative view of life. All the heroines in "Our Gal Sunday," "Life Can Be Beautiful," "Ma Perkins," and "Helen Trent" were loving, good, and courageous. They gave me hope that I could eventually find a better life. Other pockets of kindness and concern periodically surfaced in foster care, and with certain extended family members, and when they did, I absorbed the experiences and stored them away in my soul.

Those kind people who briefly inhabited my first nine years were varied, but after I was adopted, my mother, Mary, was a solid rock. She provided love, discipline, consistency, and I was blessed to be in a family that provided fun and new experiences. Soon after I arrived in my new home, my mother took me to the local library, which was only two blocks from our house. For years, I checked out books on all kinds of subjects, and Mother never questioned what I chose. Even at 10, 11, and 12 years of age, I had a deep curiosity about how people's minds worked and would try to decipher whatever psychology books I could find.

By the time I entered junior high school, my father, who worked as a lineman for the power company, had become an alcoholic. After several warnings, he was fired from his job. (This was in the days before companies had programs to help people with this problem.) As a result, the rest of our family learned to become survivors, but our mother led the way. With only a high school education, her options were limited, but she worked as a waitress; my brothers and I worked after school and weekends in restaurants and grocery stores, delivered papers, cleaned houses, and did babysitting—anything to make money for basic expenses. When we needed more, Mother decided to partition off part of our house to create a small rental apartment. We survived. Our father's alcoholism and subsequent illness and death was difficult and often humiliating, but in retrospect I see that we all learned valuable lessons in survival and, ultimately, forgiveness.

In spite of high school success and even a limited college scholarship, I simply didn't have money to begin college in the years before readily available student loans. A year after high school graduation, I fell in love with a tall, dark, handsome, and very sweet guy, and we married. He had only one "minor" problem: he liked alcohol. In my 18-year-old-naïveté, I believed my deep love would transform him and that he would "settle down." Too bad *Women Who Love Too Much* wasn't available then! I became a textbook example. The dramas and traumas of the next several years are documented in detail in my autobiography titled *From Soap Opera to Symphony* (ordering information for *From Soap Opera to Symphony* can be found in the resource section at the back of this book). Writing the book proved to be a healing catharsis for me. I revisited the sudden death of our nine-year-old son, the serious illness and handicap of our second son, the birth of our daughter, and then divorce and repeated patterns of frustration and unhappiness while looking for the Prince Charming who would fix my life once and for all.

When Ione and I wrote *Women Alone: Creating a Joyous and Fulfilling Life* (published by Hay House in 1995), I was often writing from the perspective of one who had lived through the challenges. Perhaps the most important element of my story, one that I hope provides courage and inspiration to others, is that I eventually sought and found a path to increased awareness, positive change, and spiritual growth. Deep healing began when I clearly realized that my life history is not so unique. Jungian Marion Woodman points out in the conclusion of her book *Leaving My Father's House:* "Individuation begins with the painful recognition that we are *all* orphans. And the liberating recognition that the whole world is our orphanage."

With the help of student loans and scholarships as well as encouragement from my brother, Will, who was already taking classes, I began college when I was 32. At that time, an instrumental mentor came into my life in the form of Mary Will, a Shakespeare professor and coordinator of the Honors Program of Independent Study at Central Michigan University. She encouraged me to apply for the program, and I was accepted. This allowed me to register early for all classes and to study independently. For one class each semester, I met with a professor to work out a plan of study and then reported in twice a month. I began to feel empowered to tackle projects on my own. As a result of this experience, I've not been fearful about venturing into unknown areas; I realized I could learn almost anything if I put my mind to it. All the professors treated me with respect, and Mary treated me as a total equal, encouraging me to go on for a higher degree and to become a college teacher, which I did.

It was natural for me to become a teacher of literature. Authors have been my models and motivators since I started reading voraciously at age nine, and I've continued to read avidly through the years for varied purposes. For example, starting in high school, and continuing to this day, whenever I feel discouraged, I find that it adjusts my attitude to read about the challenges others face and their courage in dealing with them. This focus never fails to help me put my own life in a broader perspective and is one of the major reasons I choose to share my own story. As Marion Woodman says, "Sharing our story can open our eyes to the ambushes we share with others and open paths to freedom."

Because feminist authors such as Betty Friedan and Gloria Steinem shared their stories, they helped open paths to freedom for me and for many women who began to reevaluate the '50s' ideas concerning women's roles in society. I had completely accepted the idea: "I'm nothing without a man in my life." My struggle to get beyond that perception to the understanding that I have worth and value, partnered or not, has been a long and difficult one.

Elisabeth Kübler-Ross has been another strong model and motivator. After the death of my son Richard, I went for years without going through the grief process, repressing my emotions and suffering because I didn't know how to resolve my feelings. Several years later, a good friend took me to hear Elisabeth speak. As I listened, my feelings about grieving and death were transformed, although it took months and years to totally complete the process that began that day. I heard Elisabeth speak several more times and read all her books and any material about her that I could find. She literally led me out of the "valley of the shadow of death." She helped me through the process of releasing Richard and helped me to know that I am forever connected to him in love.

Shortly after I embarked upon a deeper spiritual walk, I met Unity student Elaine Davis and instantly knew we were soul sisters. We shared an abiding interest in spiritual growth and began to facilitate a study group in Big Rapids, Michigan. Over the years, our deep loyalty and caring for each other have remained steady. I think of Elaine as my cheerleader. Just like my mother, Mary, no matter where I go or what I do, she is supportive. During a particularly trying period, Elaine offered tea and conversation along with her loving presence whenever I needed to laugh or cry. She has a great husband and two daughters who are also my friends, but no matter what else may be happening in her life, she always takes the time to nurture our friendship.

Just as so much support and inspiration has been given to me, I have a passionate desire to motivate women to claim their power by taking responsibility for themselves. Expecting a Prince Charming to magically heal our emotional wounds leads to disappointment and disillusionment. For years, I understood this intellectually, but couldn't feel it in my heart. However, I began to act "as if" I had myself emotionally together while I continued to look for psychological and spiritual answers.

After graduating with a master's degree from Central Michigan University in 1969, I began teaching composition and literature at Ferris State University in Michigan. Three years later, I created and taught a class in women's studies, and was proud to have my daughter, Colleen, as one of my first students. With me throughout much of my drama and trauma, she learned from my mistakes, and I rejoice that she has such a beautiful spirit and a loving and stable family of her own. (My future daughter-in-law, Lee, was also one of my first students. She and my son, Robert, have been together many years now, and they have handled the challenge of his handicap well. I am very proud of them, too.)

After 11 successful years of teaching, I had tenure and a comfortable niche, but I began to feel "divine discontent," the need for "something more." A deep desire to expand my teaching to include the spiritual dimension was becoming increasingly strong. I wrestled with the issue for two years before I applied to Unity ministerial school in Missouri and was accepted. The university gave me a two-year leave of absence "just in case" it didn't work out and I wanted to return to teaching. That action was incredibly affirming for me, and I'll always appreciate it.

Since ordination in 1982, I've led a flexible and fulfilling life as a "spiritual midwife," both in church ministry and as a workshop presenter, counselor, and part of The Holo Community. While Ione and I continue to travel with workshops, we are thrilled to be engaged in a new creative endeavor—writing. We have a deep desire to expand our horizons as we minister to people in our unique way through our workshops and through the counseling we do with people who come to us at our home at The Holo Center. (See the resource section for more information about the work we do there.) We see limitless possibilities and certainly no age barriers.

Fortunately, models of older women who disregard age barriers and who are vital, alive, and making valuable contributions abound.

When French actress Jeanne Moreau was interviewed on "60 Minutes," she was undeniably aging, but aging beautifully. Her philosophy is a model for me. "A true artist never stops working," she declared. She feels no need to hide away as she ages; she is not attached to her past physical beauty. At the time of her interview, she didn't have a partner, and she didn't view that circumstance as preventing her from enjoying life to the fullest. Mike Wallace asked if she missed the passions of her youth. She responded that of course she didn't miss them because she now knows the difference between love and passion: passion can be jealous, demanding, and agonizing, but love is calm, peaceful, and undemanding. No matter what Mike asked her, Jean's answers revealed depth and a serene acceptance of herself and her life. As I watched this authentic and wise older woman, I prayed that I might age so wisely and so well, and with at least a fraction of her grace and charm.

Yet, however much I appreciate the many models, motivators, and mentors of my life, ultimately I look to my own inner spirit, to my own fountain of love and wisdom. I finally know in my heart, not just in my head, that no other person can take responsibility for my life. Fortunately, I also know in my heart that I am never alone. The universal spirit of love and wisdom is available to us at all times. To the degree I identify with that Higher Power, I am at peace, and in that peace, I am able to joyously flow with life while encouraging others on the path of growth and transcendence.

SUSAN KREITZBERG, N.D.
Explorer and Pathfinder

---

*"We walk through so many myths of each other
and ourselves. We are so thankful when
someone sees us for who we are and accepts us."*
— Natalie Goldberg

"I am immersed in my experience," says naturopathic physician Susan Kreitzberg. "I eat, sleep, breathe, and drink in my work; it's all I ever wanted to do." Susan and her husband, Don Leathers, share a family practice in Bozeman, Montana. Susan, also a midwife who loves making it possible for babies to be born at home, came to her profession via a circuitous route.

Always strong-willed and passionate, a '60s rebel in the midst of a conservative Catholic family, she was determined to find her own truth in her own way.

> I've always felt driven by an inner sense of destiny. At crucial points in my life, I was given what I needed for the next step. When I first talked to my mother about wanting to be a doctor, she discouraged me. She felt such a long and expensive education would be

wasted because I would eventually want to stay with my children and not work outside the home. However, I didn't allow her to discourage me, because I knew I would not follow her path.

Susan began a pre-med program at the University of Oregon, but dropped out after two years. She became disillusioned with the traditional medical approach and felt she had to quit. She didn't know about alternatives such as naturopathic medicine, acupuncture, or any other unconventional therapies. Hurt and confused, she struggled to find a new focus for her life. Retreating to the mountains as part of the Outward Bound program, Susan became an instructor, and hiking, backpacking, and mountain climbing became her route to inner peace.

I would often go into a oneness with everything, but I didn't fully realize what was happening. I assumed that everyone who went backpacking had these kinds of experiences. Sometimes the young people I led into the wilderness complained about being wet, cold, and hungry, but I had a difficult time understanding their experience. I was in my own private heaven. Out of the mountains, my body felt heavy, but in the mountains I felt buoyant and uplifted and could have stayed forever, but that was not my destiny.

It was September of Susan's third year with Outward Bound. She was on the last trip of the season. She'd been in the mountains since May but didn't want the time to end. She sent her students down to a waterfall to take a shower and prepare themselves for their solo five-day trek. She looked forward to a delicious five days to herself before they met again. Then, partway down the mountain as Susan was playing in the snow, she slipped and fell 60 feet, landing in a rock pile. Her assistant instructor left Susan on the mountain and went out for help. She was alone for five hours before a helicopter arrived. Her back was broken in 12 places. "You'll be in pain the rest of your life," the doctors said. "You won't be able to do the things you've always done."

Although Susan was devastated, she was not defeated. She started a long road to healing. By wearing a back brace, she could stand

and walk for short periods of time. Without it, she had to lie flat. As she grew stronger, she began to substitute-teach, and she'd take her canoe out and run short stretches of river. That winter she did light cross-country ski trips. She was still in her brace, but she was moving. Almost nine months later, she was brace free and walking on her own. She went back to school at Portland State and finished a degree in literature and obtained her teaching credentials.

Susan had always loved literature, and teaching was something she felt she could do for fun, but she also felt it wouldn't be her life's work. Wanting to live in a small-town atmosphere, Susan took a teaching position in Dufur, Oregon, a year after her accident. There she met Ione (Jenson) and went to her for counseling. They became friends, although Susan was wary and skeptical because Ione was married to a minister. "Give me any God crap," Susan told Ione, "and I'm out of here."

The traditional religious philosophy of Susan's family never made sense to her, so she was determined not to be drawn into something like that. But Ione's approach was different. They talked about dreams, meditation, and inner healing, and Ione helped Susan understand that her experiences in the mountains were mystical ones and that through meditation, she could reach those places again without having to physically climb mountains. Susan says:

> Ione has been a model and mentor, the first person who could present spiritual things in such a way that they made sense to me. She was able to see who I was. She gave me my spiritual life. For several months, we met at her house one evening a week, and I felt I was making spiritual progress, but physically I was miserable. Back pain was cutting me in half; I woke up with it every morning and went to sleep with it every night. It was relentless. I began to think about going back up the mountain and doing a conscious suicide. Life wasn't worth this pain.
>
> I shared my thoughts one night with Ione and two of her friends and prayer partners. Ione told me to lie face down on the sofa and they'd see what they could do. They went to the encyclopedia and looked at an illustration of a perfect back and then laid hands on me.

My back started to ripple, my arms flopped around, my head was twisting, and my legs kicked. I remember thinking, "Oh shit, I hope they know what they're doing!" I couldn't imagine what was happening.

Afterwards, Susan stood up, looked at the others and said, "That's really weird!" and walked out of the house and into a healing crisis. She was pain free but went home and threw up and had diarrhea. The next few days she tested her new state of being by going cross-country skiing, chopping down some trees, limbing them, and then cutting and stacking the wood. She was still pain free. Then one night she had a dream.

My boat was sinking (my platform of reality at that time). I asked myself: Was I being forced to redesign my reality? Accept a benign entity that really did love humanity? How could I reconcile that with the religious upbringing I rejected? Where did Jesus fit into all this? Was there a real Jesus beyond the fundamentalist concepts I couldn't accept? I wished that it would be possible to sit down and have a chat with him, share tea and blueberry muffins.

About two months later, Susan baked her favorite blueberry muffins, left them on the counter, and went to sleep. Sometime in the night she was shaken awake.

It felt like someone had me by the toes and was shaking me like a rug! I heard, "Will you understand?" I opened my eyes, and the trailer was full of light, but my mind couldn't grasp what might be happening. I covered my head and went back to sleep. Again I was shaken awake; again the trailer was filled with light. This time I saw a white-robed figure standing in the kitchen area, next to the blueberry muffins. I got out of bed, although it was three o'clock in the morning. Totally freaked out, I fixed myself some tea and sat drinking it until dawn. I couldn't wait to phone Ione so she could help me sort out what had happened.

Susan was thankful she had Ione to help her try to comprehend her experience. As they explored together, and Susan tried to understand why the vision of Jesus came to her, she had a flashback to an early college experience. Her roommate was a "Jesus freak," always attempting to convert her. Tuning her out most of the time, Susan went about her business. But one evening, she finally snapped. Susan stomped out of the room and just before she slammed the door, she shouted, "I'll believe in your Jesus when I have tea with him in the middle of the night!"

From this point on, Susan had a totally open mind. Her back remained pain free and healed, and her mind began to turn again toward the healing arts, but in a new way. Her healing took place in January. She left teaching at the end of the school year and went to California, where a whole new world opened for her. She read a New Age magazine at a friend's house, loved every single page, and realized, "This is who I am!" Shortly after, she had her first polarity session, first body work, first sweat in a tepee, and dip in a hot springs.

Susan stayed in California and went to massage school, specializing in Touch for Health and eventually in Traeger. About this time, she met the man who would later become her first husband. They decided to move back to the country in Oregon and live simply, and when Susan became pregnant, they wanted to do everything as naturally as possible. They'd heard about a medical school in Portland where the women doctors did home births, so Susan and her husband arranged to have their baby at a friend's home near the school. In the course of the prenatal care, Susan fell in love with the doctors and naturopathic medicine.

> I knew I'd found my life's work. At the same time I thought, Oh my God, I'm pregnant! I'm excited about my baby and I want him, but how am I going to do this? I waited until our son, Forest, was two and then began to take pre-med chemistry and other science classes.

> My husband couldn't understand why I wanted to work so hard, why I couldn't be satisfied with the training I already had. It was the beginning of the end of our relationship. I couldn't be with someone who had so little vision for me. I'd never put limits on myself, and I couldn't allow anyone else to do that either.

Susan was accepted into medical school when Forest was 4 and she was 36. She was thrilled, but her parents ignored the fact and hoped she would give up the idea. Susan and her husband divorced during the first year. Fortunately, the school environment was supportive of family life, and students were allowed to bring their children to class if they didn't cause any disruption. The students, and particularly her study partners, Don (who later became her husband) and Mary, were helpful and supportive. They were in school 40 hours a week, which required a minimum of 33 additional hours a week to study outside of class. In the midst of this intense regimen, Susan started to do home births. Again, she received incredible support from classmates and had a list of several she could call upon.

Whenever I had to deliver a baby at night, all I needed to do was drop Forest off with his sleeping bag and lunch box. His substitute parent would fix his breakfast and lunch and take him to preschool.

Forest is a teenager now and proud that his mother is a doctor. He knows the work and sacrifice it took on both our parts. However, he's come through it all just fine. He's a self-reliant, well-adjusted, good-natured kid, and I'm so very proud of him, too.

After their graduation from naturopathic medical school, Don and Susan married, moved to Santa Fe, New Mexico, and practiced there for several years. They recently sold their New Mexico practice and now live and practice in Bozeman, Montana.

It's great to share my life with someone so dedicated to his own growth process and who is so supportive of mine as well. Naturopathic medicine is so right for us. We are trained to do Western diagnosis and such things as lab work, complete physicals, and Pap smears. Treatment modalities are proper nutrition, herbs, homeopathy, body work, massage, and hydrotherapy. Chronic conditions such as arthritis respond well, and we see incredible results. We see patients as whole beings and deal with their mental and emotional facets as well as their physical bodies. All three areas are reflections of each other. Thus, a person's story is important. I spend much of my day listening to stories, mostly women's.

As we speak with Susan, it is not difficult to understand how it might be easy to discuss things with her that perhaps haven't been shared before. In spite of a no-nonsense demeanor and her obvious competence, she exudes the kind of caring you'd expect from a beloved sister. She values her respected position, but does not use that role to distance herself from the patients she serves. She is model and mentor for women who see her flourishing in a professional life of her own, in addition to being married and being a mother.

I want to help every woman I see to know that she deserves a life of her own. So many feel selfish for wanting that, but as I listen, I hold space for these women to embrace their own dreams and visions because so much illness comes from lost will, broken dreams. I ask, "What keeps you from your dream?" And then we work on removing the obstacles—mental, emotional, and physical. I am committed to helping women understand that it's never too late to begin to take charge of every aspect of our lives in powerful new ways.

MARY KRENK
A Woman Before Her Time

*"There is no such thing as being
done with an artist's life."*
— Julia Cameron

"**M**ary is the brightest, most beautiful thing that ever entered my life. She has been a continual supporter and mentor in every area—in business, social life, education, and philosophy. She lives her ideals on a daily basis." This from Marv, Mary's husband of 55 years. But that is only a piece of the circle of well-deserved love and respect that surrounds this vivacious dark-eyed dynamo.

This unplanned seventh child of a remarkable mother was embraced and welcomed, which set a modeling pattern of loving kindness that Mary follows in her own life. She creates quality time for family, for friends, and for many others who are fortunate enough to be drawn into her sphere.

And what people have been drawn into that sphere! During her nearly 20 years of radio and television public service interview shows in Eugene, Oregon, she was the person who notables such as Eleanor Roosevelt and Charles Schultz called first when they came to town.

But Mary also sought out many lesser-known people who could offer valuable information and insights. Always open to new ideas, she focused on meaty, worthwhile topics without ever sinking to sensationalism.

Warmth, intelligence, genuine caring, and concern for all were traits that came across so clearly in her shows that people felt that Mary was their friend. Clearly model and motivator, she took the opportunities to mentor as well. Girl Scout leader for a group of teenagers before she was old enough to have teenagers herself, she taught and modeled personal integrity and community values that they could not always hear and accept from their own parents.

Because people instinctively felt her compassion, Mary received countless letters over the years. One came from a woman whose deaf daughter wrote poetry. The mother just wanted to share the poetry, but Mary visited the family, befriended them, and eventually produced a television program especially for the deaf—this in the days before closed captioning. Many people wrote to ask Mary to visit their invalid shut-ins, and she found time for them. A destitute young man once knocked on her door during a dinner party asking for a shirt to wear for a job interview the next morning. She excused herself and came back with a shirt and pants for him from her son's closet and blessed him on his way.

Incredibly, amidst her work and her automatic ministry to others, family was not forgotten or neglected, but always in the center of her expansive circle of love. When feasible, she took her sons with her on assignments. She once took ten-year-old Chris along on an interview with Eleanor Roosevelt, who thanked him for wanting to stay awake so late in the evening, and then shook his hand warmly when they left. "Chris put off washing that hand for as long as possible!" Mary reports.

Not surprisingly, Mary has never washed away her own memories of Mrs. Roosevelt.

I was surprised at how tall she was and surprised at how beautiful she seemed. There was so much more to her than photographs could capture, perhaps because her caring spirit transcended mere physical beauty. She was such an imposing and dynamic presence that it felt almost like I was in the presence of a queen. At the same time, I felt at ease because she was so gracious, so warm and approachable. She was a model for me because she was intelligent and committed to contributing to the world, yet at the same time, she was a mother who cared about her children and found ways to spend quality time with them. She too had sons, and I was impressed with how kind she was to mine. A great lady.

Mary's sons, Chris and Mike, have children of their own now, so the circle of Mary's caring has continually expanded. As soon as her grandchildren were only a few weeks old, Mary and Marv set aside every Friday evening and Saturday morning to be with them while their parents did other things, and they kept that schedule for years. A statement by Mary's granddaughter, Anna, when she was only three illustrates the rewards of that commitment and caring and characterizes the ongoing bond between the generations: "Grandma, we've been friends a lot longer than I've been alive."

It's been said that love knows no limits, that the more we give away, the more we have, and certainly Mary is a prime example of that theory. A special three-way ministry has been a key element of Mary's life. She met with her close friends Helen and Claire for decades for mutual support and to pray for one another, their families, and for others who came into their sphere. They were so dedicated that no matter where each was in the world, they coordinated the time so that they meditated at the same time each week. Currently, at 76, Mary is still expanding her circle of caring. Fun-loving, humorous, and unafraid to laugh at her own human foibles, she loves life, and that love pours forth spontaneously.

A major involvement and ministry for both Mary and Marv now is their teaching of international folk dancing to seniors. They never tire of taking the advanced dance group out to fairs, ethnic festivals, nursing homes, hospitals, elementary schools, and anywhere people can be uplifted by their energy and enthusiasm, their colorful costumes, and their willingness to talk and exchange ideas with the audiences. "It's gratifying to teach people to speak and to understand other languages and cultures without words needed," Mary explains. How symbolic of Mary's life that many of the dances begin with a circle. And that there's always room to welcome others into that expansive circle.

ELISABETH KÜBLER-ROSS, M.D.
She Changed Our World View

---

*"Our lives are mythic. We are direct participants in
the story of the soul of the world."*
— Jean Houston

This pioneering psychiatrist has helped people all over the world to cope with intense and stressful challenges, but she has not been exempt from them herself. "It's important to realize that strength and beauty often come from difficult journeys," she points out. "Should you shield the canyons from the windstorms, you would never see the beauty of their carvings," is one of Elisabeth's best-known quotes. "We must learn from every experience, no matter how negative it seems. Our purpose on earth is to heal, to love and help each other," she declares.

Elisabeth gained global recognition in the mid-'70s after the publication of her bestselling classic, *On Death and Dying*. Recently included in *Books of the Century*, a librarians' list of 159 books that have had "significant influence, consequence, or resonance" in the hundred years between 1895 and 1995, *On Death and Dying* describes the stages people move through while coming to terms with the death of their physical bodies. This book, along with her other research, writing, speeches, and workshops, revolutionized the care of dying patients. Hospice owes its beginnings in the United States to the work of this dynamic woman. She encouraged and supported Compassionate Friends (a grief support group for parents of children who have died), as well as another group for parents of murdered children. In addition, she has worked with Vietnam veterans and AIDS patients. Her interests have always been continually expansive, and she has never been afraid to be controversial. She was one of the first to research and describe near-death experiences and also one of the first to reach out to AIDS families in spite of threats from her neighbors in Virginia.

Is she a saint? There are many who would be willing to grant her sainthood. However, she would be the first to admit that she is very human. She has made mistakes—perhaps the most public one happened several years ago when psychics tricked her into believing they were manifesting her guardian spirits. It temporarily destroyed her credibility and nearly aborted the invaluable work she continued to produce. Because of her intense work in the twilight zone between life and death, Elisabeth may have been tempting prey for the unscrupulous. Nevertheless, she displayed courage and integrity as she admitted what happened and then moved forward with her work in spite of the negative publicity. She understood that her higher purpose in life was to love, to teach, and to heal. "I'd already dealt with adversity and conquered it many times," she remembers. "I knew that obstacles presented themselves in order to be overcome."

Born in Switzerland in 1926, her first challenge was to survive as a two-and-a-half-pound triplet. Her parents were conventional, but Elisabeth always had a strong mind of her own, a strong will to be an individual apart from her sisters and family. She became a lab technician at 16, and over her family's objections, traveled through Europe after World War II as part of the International Voluntary Service for Peace. Only 19 at that time, she cooked for workers cleaning up the rubble in bombed-out villages, and during off hours from cooking, she helped the work crews clear streets and buildings.

A preview of Elisabeth's strength and bravery came in France, where the men of the town were clearing mine fields that the Germans had planted. The Frenchmen were using German prisoners as human mine detectors, forcing them to walk ahead of them in the fields. Every day, two or three prisoners did not return. When Elisabeth discovered what was happening, she inspired her co-workers to join her in a protest. Standing in front of the prisoners, they declared that they would be the ones to walk the front line instead. The villagers soon gave in and stopped the practice.

The clear vision that allows Elisabeth to focus upon a situation and see beyond the usual human excuses developed early. Courage to tell the truth and to put herself on the line in defense of it has been an integral part of her character. Although she professes no specific dogma or creed, she teaches and lives within a cosmic spiritual framework. She has been incredibly giving and unselfish in her efforts to help others; perhaps that is why her energy remained high and steady for so many years.

In the spring of 1977, Julie (Keene) was invited to hear her speak at a gathering for doctors, nurses, and health-care professionals in Saginaw, Michigan. There were 2,000 people in the auditorium, most of them professionals. When Elisabeth emerged from behind a curtain and stood on the huge stage, she looked like a little grandmother in a house dress. A slightly built woman less than five feet tall, she began speaking in a thick accent that was at first difficult to understand. Wasting no time in an effort to establish rapport or talk about herself, she began to describe her experiences with dying children and their parents.

From the children's drawings, Elisabeth and her co-workers could discern the outcome of their illness and tell whether the parents were willing to see and acknowledge that outcome or not. She talked about how children believed that angels and those gone before were waiting to help them. She spoke about the love and beauty that surrounds the dying experience for those open to it. She related her absolute certainty of ongoing life, and shared a story of her first awakening to that knowledge.

I had been going through a crisis period and was on the verge of giving up my death-and-dying work. I was about to announce my decision to the minister I was working with as I was walking with him to the hospital elevator. However, before I could say the words, the elevator door opened, and a familiar woman stepped out. I realized that I knew her well but was blocked on how and where I knew her. The woman approached us and asked if she could talk to me in my office. It seemed important, so I put off announcing that I would give up my work.

As I walked back to my office with the woman, I began to realize she was a woman I'd worked with who had died of cancer. Unable to allow myself to believe what I was seeing, I began to fear I was hallucinating. As we approached the office, the woman opened the door for me, and then in a loving voice said, "I came back because I want to thank you for what you did to help me and to tell you that you must not give up your death-and-dying work yet." I touched solid objects in an effort to "get a grip on reality." The woman was persistent and made me promise that I would continue my work. At that point, I felt no one would ever believe this experience—maybe I would even talk myself out of it later! I handed the woman a sheet of paper and a pencil and asked her to write a note. With a loving smile, the woman wrote one, and I still have it in a frame. As you can see, I decided not to give up my work.

As Elisabeth spoke, she held the audience in thrall. There was no rustling of papers or noise of any kind. People were silent, hanging on her every word. Julie listened with an open heart and often with tear-filled eyes. Although her nine-year-old son, Richard, had died several years before, Julie still carried a weight of unresolved grief. At one point Elisabeth said, "You who have lost loved ones, know they are near you and watch over you and surround you with their love." Just after those words were spoken, Julie heard a clear, internal message that she strongly feels was a message from Richard: "See, Mom, I told you I'm okay. I love you." Although there would later be more healing and release work for Julie to do, a deeper understanding and acceptance was hers that day, and she will always be grateful to Elisabeth and look up to her as an inspired teacher and model.

There are those whose mission on earth is to facilitate a paradigm shift, to pave the way for others to follow, and Dr. Elisabeth Kübler-Ross is such a one. She paved the way for such people as Dr. Raymond Moody, author of *Life After Life;* and Dr. Brian Weiss, author of *Many Lives, Many Masters.* These professionals also risked rejection by a skeptical scientific community, but fortunately, they continued to do their breakthrough work. Their combined work then opened the door for the popular acceptance of books such as *Embraced by the Light* by Betty Eadie; *Saved by the Light* by Dannion Brinkley; and *The Other Side of Death* by Jan Price. As a result, many people have come forth to share their experiences and to validate and comfort each other.

And all this began with the pioneering work of an incredibly brave and brilliant woman whose ideas have always been ahead of her time. Elisabeth is now retired and living in Arizona. There, she struggles to deal with the aftermath of strokes, and grieves the loss of active life on her Virginia farm. This latest challenge is difficult for her, but she is determined to remain centered in love. She closed her final newsletter with the following words of wisdom:

> Be good to yourself, your Mother Earth, and to all the little ones you encounter. Always remember they have a long path ahead of them. Teach love, compassion, and understanding early, and always combat violence and abuse in any form, whether it is directed at people, Mother Earth, or at animals.

Millions the world over will continue to benefit from Elisabeth's work long after she leaves this planet. She is a towering example of the emerging woman: strong and focused upon her goals no matter what the obstacles, loving and compassionate, and a pioneer. As time passes, the windstorms of Elisabeth's life continue to carve more beauty into her heart and soul. We wish her well.

ELEANOR LeCAIN
Sister of Soft Power

"It's time for women to break the last strings of attachment to the old way and become the masters they are."
— Terry Cole-Whitaker

"The most gracious coming together of head and heart, dreams and reality that I ever experienced came at the first conference of The Women of Vision and Action Network," says the current president, Eleanor LeCain. One of the keynote speakers at the original conference attended by 500 women from all over the world and held at Georgetown University in 1994, Eleanor was dismayed to discover that there were no plans at that time to continue the networking. She stood up during the conference and spoke to founder Rama Vernon and the other women gathered: "The energy here is the energy we all need to sustain ourselves and transform the society. Anyone who would like to build on this energy and bring it forward in our lives and in the world, join me in this room later."

The 50 women who responded to Eleanor's appeal talked about

the possibilities, and they began mapping action steps. In the years since that beginning, women have come together in the network to liberate their creative capacities for healing and shaping the world. "We don't consider ourselves an organization in the traditional sense, but a loose network that links women already making positive changes in our society." The group made a conscious decision early on, Eleanor told us, not to advertise or publicly solicit members. They wanted growth to be a result of woman-to-woman contact. Their intent was to gather their resources and to become strong and clear in their mission before they subjected themselves to the harsh glare of the media. Eleanor feels the women are "sisters of the soft power," known to each other, but not necessarily recognized by the world.

The women have put together a wheel of transformation, with each sector representing a vital function of the whole social body. Some of the sectors are Peace and Security, Human Rights, Education, Media, Economics, Ecology, Religion and Spirituality, Health and Healing, Community Needs and Resources, and The Arts. The women explain the wheel.

> It is like a chalice holding our gifts. In gatherings, women choose interest groups corresponding to these sectors. Ideas and initiatives are placed into this evolving wheel of change to co-create a living blueprint for a new society. Visions and actions are sent to our national hub, recorded and fed back to members of the network. Through this social process, we discover the design of what is possible and the steps needed to realize this potential.

In the gatherings, women are moving away from podiums and speakers and working more in small groups where they help each other discover their life purpose and then find their unique work in improving the society. "The groups brainstorm resources, money, people, institutes—anything that could help women move ahead in their chosen arena," Eleanor explains. "The idea is to build links among women so we can identify each other and see where we can support, encourage, and nourish each other."

As we speak with Eleanor about her life and activities, there is no doubt that she is an empowered woman. She was one of the first female graduates of Yale University, where she obtained a degree in economics in 1977. Currently she is a writer, speaker, and consultant on issues that pertain to making companies more environmentally sound. Her principal client in the past few years has been Boston Edison, who hired her to lead a team to develop the next generation of energy-efficient programs. She has also been an acting CEO for a company that does environmental audits. "We actually go into a company and assess their resource flow, where they generate pollution and waste, and where they can cut back on resource consumption. We help turn trash into cash," she says.

This self-assured, confident woman has hitchhiked in Africa, climbed Mt. Kilimanjaro, managed three political campaigns (which all her candidates won), was Assistant Secretary of State for strategic planning, and started her own successful consulting business. "Where did I get the audacity to think I could do all that?" she laughs. And then she answers her own question: "I got that idea from two major influences. First, from my mother's belief in me and in the power of education, and secondly from a life-changing book I read while in high school."

Eleanor's mother gave up a four-year college scholarship in order to marry, and within a short period of time gave birth to four children. However, the marriage was not a happy one, so she left her husband and raised her children by herself. Eleanor reminds us that such a decision was remarkable for a Catholic woman in 1959.

> We were poor, and she raised her three daughters to recognize that we couldn't depend on a man to take care of us. She often reminded us that we needed to find our own way, get a good education, and know how to make our own living. "Then connect with a man if you choose," she said. I'm lucky to have escaped some of the conditioning that many girls received in that time period. I didn't think I had to run out and find a man to solve all my problems or meet all my needs.

In high school, Eleanor was very bright, but at the same time, very shy. She recalls:

> I was nearly catatonic. I didn't like talking to other kids or adults. I was miserable because I was very lonely. I felt like a social misfit, and I was. I had a big brain but an empty mouth. Then a book by James Allen showed me a way out of my dilemma. *As a Man Thinketh* reveals a truth that I immediately knew applied to "as a woman thinketh." I understood that I needed to change my thoughts and redirect them in a more positive way. I understood I was thinking myself into my own misery. As a result of reading this book, I began to focus upon the goals I wanted to achieve, and then I worked very diligently toward those goals.

Eleanor and her husband are now focusing upon a new goal, which is to bring love into the life of a six-year-old girl named Veronica. They want to adopt this child who suffered so much abuse and trauma with her birth family. They see how deep wounds can go, even at such a tender young age.

> She's in the hospital now, and some people there are saying she may never heal, that she's going to have behavior disorders forever and be in therapy for the rest of her life. However, we don't accept that prognosis. She doesn't need drugs; she needs love. We're trying to get her out of the hospital and home with us so we can give her the love and stability she needs to thrive. I see so much potential in her, and in every interaction I try to draw it forward and encourage it. One day while at the beach with Veronica, I was doing a barefoot dance of life in the sand, and as I finished, a thought flashed through my mind: I'm walking with Veronica on a journey in consciousness from wounded female to Divine Feminine. What a privilege!

Perhaps every emerging woman must take such a journey, and we will surely complete it sooner with the love and support of one another. As Eleanor draws out and encourages the potential in herself and others, she personifies the ideals and goals of the Women of Vision and Action Network. Early in life, she found a way to envision her own unfolding, and she has accomplished much as a result. She also reaches out to others, to Veronica on a very individual and personal level, to women in the network who positively impact our society and, finally, she makes a positive difference in such crucial areas as government and our environment. Eleanor LeCain, a woman who dances with life, is a woman of vision, an emerging woman, a sister of soft power, and certainly a model, motivator, and mentor. However, she refuses to rest upon her laurels. "I haven't done a tenth of what I want," she declares. "I feel like I'm just beginning."

SHARON LOWENSTEIN, Ph.D., J.D.
Passionate Advocate of Justice

---

*"Some exciting things begin to happen
when we dare to go beyond the stated boundaries
in order to discover more of ourselves."*
— Sheila Collins

A woman with a zest for life and a passionate dedication to her chosen work, Sharon is a fighter for justice. At the same time, she is a woman with an infectious laugh who loves to relax and play. A college professor of history before entering law school in mid-life, she's now an attorney who practices family law. She is also a court-appointed mediator in family disputes involving children, and a court-appointed guardian ad litem on behalf of children. "When I entered law school," Sharon explains, "I planned to be an advocate for women and children, and I only take clients whose causes I believe in. A number of my male clients have the HIV/AIDS virus, and I'm passionate about helping them, too."

The way Sharon practices law is influenced by her personal journey. As a young girl, she didn't question the traditional role assigned to her in the Jewish community: do well in school, obtain a higher education, marry well, have children, and put family above all else. As she grew older, Sharon became rebellious and chafed against familial and community expectations, but felt she had no choice but to accept them. This period was made even more difficult by her father's suicide when Sharon was 15. Married at 19, Sharon had three sons by the time she was 23, and she had a fourth son a few years later. All the while, she fought chronic depression without understanding the source. Then came the turning point. While working on her Ph.D. in history, she was in a serious automobile accident that almost cost her her life. After a lengthy hospital stay and a slow recovery, she decided to try therapy. She recalls:

> During this time, I began to realize I'd always resisted being a woman and was not comfortable with my female identity. Models and motivators had always been men. Even in social situations, I gravitated toward the men and joined in their conversations because I found their topics more stimulating. This was in the early '70s; the women's movement had not registered in my consciousness. I didn't study or incorporate women's history into my discipline. Therapy enabled me to deal with my father's suicide and then to discover and appreciate suppressed feminine aspects of myself. My female friends became more valuable to me after that.

Sharon remembers Sonia Krevitt Goldstein as an extraordinary woman who was always there for her. During the years that Sharon struggled to overcome chronic depression, Sonia was struggling to live with diabetes and its increasingly debilitating affects.

> She gradually lost most of her physical capacities but kept struggling to live all those years when I was suicidal. She was the one friend with whom I could share honest feelings. Although she was fighting to live at the same time I wanted to die, she bore no resentment about that. She understood.
>
> Eventually, she was helpless and in a wheelchair, facing further amputations. At that point, she decided to go off dialysis and to die in her own home. She shared her dying with her friends, just as she

had shared her living—with love and dignity. She taught me what it means to truly share.

The growth and change within Sharon resulted in a more open response to her history students. Kirsten, a German exchange student, enrolled in Sharon's course on the Holocaust. Kirsten felt terrible about the events that had occurred in her country during the war and wanted to learn more. She also enrolled in Sharon's class in American Jewish History. About two years later, Kirsten wrote to inform Sharon that she was at another university working toward an advanced degree in order to return to Germany and teach Judaic Studies. "My interest and ultimately my decision was sparked by your classes," Kirsten wrote. "Your personal interest and support meant a lot to me."

When the daughter of one of Sharon's acquaintances committed suicide, Sharon decided to reach out. She knew people often tend to stay away because of their own discomfort with suicide, which makes the family feel even more isolated and rejected. Sharon remembers touching the woman's arm and saying: "I'm the daughter of a suicide, and I know something of what occurs." That's all she needed to say. The two of them began meeting for an early-morning breakfast once a week, and the woman poured out her heart. Sharon shared the wisdom she'd learned from her own experience: "We are all walking wounded. The difference between you and me is that your wounds are now publicly exposed, and mine are not visible, but we all have wounds. Others are not focused upon you because they are too concerned with their own wounds." Subsequently, this woman went back to school and became an outstanding counselor.

After Sharon's children were grown and after her marriage had disintegrated, she experienced another major turning point. A university colleague asked, "If the first chapter of our lives consists of life in our family of origin, and the second chapter focuses primarily on raising children and establishing ourselves in the world, what are we going to create in the third chapter?" This casual question triggered Sharon's dormant interest in studying law. Shortly thereafter, she applied to law school and was accepted.

The first year was often brutal and demanding, but Sharon found herself in a study group of mature students who were a great support to her.

> The single most cruel and the single most loving and helpful of my instructors were women. They modeled how to be and how not to be. My female Family Law professor was the positive model and motivator. Unafraid to deal with feelings, she understood human relationships and had confidence in herself. I'm proud that she now sends clients to me.

As she describes her Family Law professor, Sharon is also describing herself. Always supportive of clients who turn to her for help, she also educates, motivates, and supports other professionals who deal with abused woman and children.

> A newly established female obstetrician-gynecologist was shocked by the abuse I regularly deal with and wanted to learn more about the issues, and we became friends. She now specializes in treating teenage girls. She has learned to become sensitive to cases of abuse and is more likely to consider the emotional and psychological ramifications.
>
> For example, this doctor had a five-year-old patient who needed vaginal repair surgery as a result of sexual abuse. The little girl was terrified of undressing in front of people. Sensitive to her needs, my friend arranged for only women to be in the operating room during the surgery. She also arranged for the little girl to stay fully clothed when she was wheeled in, and she wasn't undressed until she was under anesthesia. By the time she woke up, she was dressed again. This sensitive doctor could have been criticized for not having the most sterile environment, but she felt the child's overall well-being was more important.

Sharon, too, is sensitive to the overall well-being of those who need her help. One of her clients, a victim of sexual abuse, was hospitalized because she was suicidal and self-mutilating. The hospital was considering institutionalizing the woman against her will. While visiting the woman in order to discuss her legal rights, Sharon encouraged her to take control and to work with the hospital so as to avoid being committed. Sharon didn't share the details of her own history, but said: "I know some of what you are experiencing. I know some of what you're feeling. And I can say for sure that there is light at the end of the tunnel."

Months later, the young woman told her, "You can't know how much your words and your caring meant to me. I don't know your story, but I do know you were authentic. I realized that if you could be where you are, then I didn't have to stay where I was."

A few years ago, Sharon vacationed on the Greek island of Crete as part of an international woman's hiking trip. She knew no one at first, and most of the women were in excellent physical shape, while Sharon was not.

> I was touched when a fit and knowledgeable woman from England volunteered to help me. She rearranged my backpack and put the heaviest water bottle in her own pack. She reached out and helped me over the narrow and rough places. As a result, I learned much about hiking and made friends I'll keep for the rest of my life.

In her own work, Sharon reaches out to help people over rough and narrow places. Wise ones have said that in the very places we've been wounded and subsequently healed, we become the most effective helpers and healers. Unafraid to share her experiences where appropriate, Sharon demonstrates the truth of that philosophy. She is a woman who has moved beyond her own pain to a place of peace and empowerment that benefits and inspires others.

ALTHA MANNING
Leader and Teacher

"Adolescent girls need a more public place
in our culture, not as sex objects,
but as interesting and complicated human beings."
— Mary Pipher

A n educator and former Deputy Commissioner of Education for the state of Florida, Altha likes to be on the move and thrives on a change of scenery. She can't tolerate mental ruts in herself or others and has been a mover and a shaker in her various positions. Altha is presently Director of the Division of Safety and Health in the Department of Labor, which is responsible for workplace safety. The division's focus upon education and training for employers has resulted in increased voluntary compliance and hundreds of complimentary letters.

One of Altha's passionate interests is working on a more personal level with young pregnant high school girls and their families, urging them to move forward with their lives. "It doesn't have to be the end of the world," Altha declares. "I try to help them see that they can begin anew and work through their challenges. I help them to focus

 181

upon problem solving instead of giving up on their future."

Altha learned the value of these ideals as she watched her own parents raise six children on a tight budget. Her parents' priority was to see that their children had a good life and a sound education.

> My father was a college graduate, but he delivered mail because it paid more than teaching. My mother stayed home until my youngest brother was two. Money was always scarce, but my parents darned their socks, mended their clothing, and went without new clothes so that their children could have new school clothes. Even then I appreciated what my parents did for us and felt sorry for the children who didn't have such a stable home. I knew that someday I would try to help children like them.

As a result of her own early experiences, bringing young women into her office as clerks is only one aspect of Altha's mentoring. She understands the need for caring intervention in all aspects of a young woman's life. As a teacher, Altha made home visits to every student in her classes and understood early on that it was impossible to bring a student along without some involvement with the entire family. She believes that if the family needs help with basic needs such as food, shelter, clothing, medicine, and medical care, a student cannot move forward unless those family issues are addressed in some way. Her late friend and mentor, educator Ida Baker, set an example of caring and involvement that Altha tries to follow. Ida was the principal of one of the largest schools in the state of Florida but was never too busy to care about individual students, never too busy to intervene in a helpful way whenever she felt it was necessary.

The success story of a young woman named Monica (not her real name) illustrates Altha's style of caring and mentoring.

> I received a call from Monica's high school counselor because this 10th grader was ready to drop out. She couldn't think beyond today, but her counselor and I convinced her to stay in school for the immediate future and to come into my office to work part time. During many informal counseling sessions, I convinced her to

remain in school no matter what her current difficulties, and there were always many. After a visit to her home, I worked to alleviate some of the crises there and finally helped to get Monica's mom a job. In spite of her many difficulties, Monica managed to stay in school.

One day shortly after graduation, she stuck her head around the corner of my door as she so often did and offered a crudely wrapped package. "It's for you," she said. Inside was her high school diploma (the original, not a copy), her high school transcript, and an honor roll certificate for her last six weeks. "I've made copies for myself," Monica told me, "but I want you to have these because I never could have received them without your help and encouragement." She still works in the department and is taking some college courses. I believe in her and see that her life will not be wasted, and that is the most gratifying feeling on earth. Eventually Monica's sister became my protégé and is also doing well.

Making education at all levels exciting, dynamic, and alive has always been important to Altha, who was one of the pioneers of the integrated curriculum movement. "It's so important for students to understand how what they're learning fits into their lives and adds meaning to it," she explains. Altha had so much success in her own classrooms that she was asked to teach other teachers to implement her successful methods.

Although she has moved several times as a result of her husband's relocations, she has no regrets about any of the moves. "Moves have always been good for me," she laughs.

I've taught in areas where there were too many constraints— segmented periods with a requirement that subjects be taught unrelated to each other. I found it stifling, frustrating, and uncomfortable. I have never understood how anyone can teach the same thing for years and never change the textbook or the method. Fortunately, I've always been able to move on to...more interesting challenges.

Altha's husband has been a rock and support for her. He understands her need for variety and stimulation, and they've always had somewhat of a nontraditional marriage. He never expected her to be waiting at home for him with dinner on the table. "We're friends as well as lovers," she says, "and we respect each other professionally. I'm a fortunate woman in all areas of my life."

SUSAN MICHAELS
Following Her Quest

---

*"Our relationship to God becomes the chief thing
about us, exceeding and also conditioning our
relationship with each other."*
— Evelyn Underhill

The mission of this independent minister with a universal approach is to help everyone on earth understand that we all ultimately worship the same God. She recently returned from India, where she spent time with her spiritual mentor, Sathya Sai Baba. Susan explains that his name means "mother and father of truth." He urges the world's peoples to honor their divergent faiths and to stop fighting with one another. Susan shares his vision and looks forward to the day when all faiths recognize each other as valid.

In Susan's ideal future world, people would study spiritual truth according to their individual temperaments, customs, and mores in a language familiar and comfortable, but at the same time they would acknowledge the truth of all paths and remain consciously in unison with everyone.

In India at the gathering with Sai Baba, all religions were represented—there were Buddhists, Jews, Christians, Hindus, Muslims—and there was no proselytizing or criticizing. Fifty thousand people from over 130 countries came together singing praises to God, each person in their heart approaching God as they understood God to be.

"As they understood God to be," is a phrase Susan knows well. A member of a 12-step group for 26 years, she is still active. She conducts women's retreats for members, teaches meditation, shares her own experiences, and encourages women to remain steadfast on the path of sobriety.

Susan's own path was a difficult one. During an early marriage, she suffered several miscarriages, and she and her husband were turned down as adoptive parents. She resorted to alcohol as a way to dull her pain. A turning point came when her alcoholic husband insisted they watch the movie *The Days of Wine and Roses.* "That's our story," he told her, "and if we don't get help we're going to die." In order to help him, Susan began attending meetings for recovering alcoholics with her husband, but after three months she realized that she too needed the meetings and began to get honest with herself and to acknowledge her own problems.

At about this time, as a type of therapy, Susan started a small antique business. It was through this business that she met a motivator and mentor she grew to love. She became the loving and nurturing mother Susan never had, and her voice warms as she talks about this woman.

I first met Marilyn Pickering—everyone always called her Madam—when I received her mail by mistake. We were both in the antique business, but she was a seasoned expert who carried only the finest antiques. I'd heard rumors about how caustic and disagreeable she was, so several days later, with fear and trepidation, I stopped by to leave her mail.

A short white-haired stooped-over woman holding a cigarette in her hand emerged from a side door. I introduced myself as I handed her the mail. She took it and said, "Yes, I know who you are. I have business right now, but come back and see me sometime." I left feeling lucky to get away so easily.

A few days later, I received more of her mail, and when I took it around, she was outside on her hands and knees digging in her flower bed, a cigarette hanging out the side of her mouth. I began to reintroduce myself and she snapped, "Yeah, I know who you are, and what the hell took you so long to get back over here?" My West Virginia mountain background came through and I snapped something right back at her. With a twinkle in her eye, she said, "I knew we were gonna hit it off. Let's go have a cup of coffee on it."

From that day, Susan and Madam were bonded. Madam taught Susan the fine points of recognizing and buying antiques and insisted upon loaning her the money to purchase a Queen Anne tilt-top birdcage table that Susan eventually sold to the Baltimore Museum. Madam modeled for Susan how a woman, no matter what her age, could be in business for herself without having to rely on anyone. She was extremely intelligent, with a feisty and independent spirit and a wonderful sense of humor. A customer once pressed her about what year a chest of drawers was made. Madam said she didn't know, but the customer kept pressing her. Finally she said, "Do you want a chest or a calendar?" She later said to Susan, "I've had to lose a little of my femininity in order to toughen up enough to make it in a man's world."

Madam and Susan talked about all aspects of their lives. They embraced the same philosophy about the true oneness of all religions, and Madam understood Susan's intuitive hunches and encouraged her to honor them. "Madam often presented a rough exterior," Susan says with a smile, "but she was a beautiful lady underneath it all."

During this time, Susan's marriage ended, and Madam was there to support her. Three years later when Susan remarried, Madam, then in her eighties, was her matron of honor. She kept going strong until she was 87. About this time, Susan's doctor advised her to move to a warmer climate, but she didn't want to be so far away from her beloved friend even though Madam insisted that she go. Susan recalls:

She [Madam] said she was getting bored with life and that she would be ready to move on soon. She made me promise I wouldn't grieve because that would only hold her back. So we moved, but we kept in close touch. About a week before her death, she went into the hospital with pneumonia, and I went to visit her. After we talked, she smoked her last cigarette, then laid back on her pillow and never woke up. She taught me not to be afraid of death. She wanted me to rejoice in her freedom, and I do.

She also demonstrated for me that the aging process is not to be feared. I'm a single woman in my sixties now, and my life only gets more active. I revel in my work as I conduct retreats, teach meditation, and connect together the spiritual traditions of the East and West. As I share my gifts, sometimes wearing my minister's hat and sometimes not, the universe financially supports whatever work I'm led to do.

Susan just returned from a third trip to India, and this time she stayed a full month and came back with an assignment from Sai Baba. Her task, in addition to her other work, is to collect devotional English chants from all over the world to be incorporated into a book for international distribution. Susan explains that people around the world use chants from a variety of languages. "Let the glory of God be sung in all the languages in a variety of tunes," Sathya Sai Baba reminded her. In the course of her research, Susan has discovered a chant that acknowledges the feminine aspect of God, and it is one of her favorites:

> *Goddess of Love, Goddess of Mercy*
> *I pray to You, come to me.*
> *Goddess of Love, Goddess of Mercy*
> *I pray to You, set me free.*
>
> *Free from the ups and downs of life*
> *Free from sorrow and pain*
> *Free from the bondage of my soul*
> *That causes birth and pain.*

Make my heart an ocean of Love
Make me one with all
Let mercy be the flower of love
That grows in one and all.

Susan is excited about her project and feels privileged to be asked to do it. "The more we share our worship and our hearts with one another," she says, "the easier it is to acknowledge we seek the same Mother-Father God, the God to whom all worship ascends. May the flame of unity burn ever more brightly as we approach the next millennium."

REBECCA NAPPI
Journalist with Clarity and Vision

"We need to raise our voices a little more even as
they say to us, 'This is so uncharacteristic of you.'
Invisibility is not a natural state for anyone."
— Mitsuye Yamada

The *Spokesman-Review* in Spokane, Washington, is one of the newspapers we peruse every morning, and whenever we read one of Rebecca Nappi's editorials, we're enlightened in some way. No matter what the subject, Rebecca delivers a clear and thoughtful piece, and as avid fans, we never skip over anything she writes. We're delighted to present her thoughts about what it means to be an emerging woman. Rebecca relates:

One day when I was 12, I realized that men had more interesting lives than women. It was 1967, and not one of the women I knew worked outside the home, except for the mothers in the poor families in our church parish. They worked as store clerks and hospital aides, and there was always something a little shameful about the fact that they had to work. The women I knew best, including my mother, did things I found boring. They shopped, they cooked, they cleaned, they took care of kids. And mostly, it seemed, they waited for the men to come home from work so their real lives could begin.

I knew then that I wanted a different life. But I thought to have it I would have to emulate a man. And that's pretty much what I did for the next 20 years of my life until one day I realized I had so rejected the women of my childhood that I had rejected the good parts of their lives, too. It was a loss. But I wouldn't understand that until later.

I was often bored as a child, but luckily I loved school. I attended Catholic schools, including Marycliff, an all-girls high school in Spokane, Washington. The nuns were my first role models. Most veterans of Catholic schools tell nun horror stories, but the nuns of my childhood are directly responsible for the involved life I am leading now.

They ran our school. They balanced the books. They handled parents, teachers, students. They hired and fired people. They were tough, demanding, spirited. They assumed that we could run things, too. And if we girls didn't do it, who would? I served on the student council, and I was on the debate team all four years. The sisters insisted we use our brains. So we did. I graduated from Marycliff with a first-rate education and the belief I could do anything I set my mind to.

I entered Gonzaga University with fear and determination. I was afraid to ever end up dependent on a man for money. My mother and three older sisters were living a traditional life. They married young, had children young, and though my sisters worked part time, they still depended on their men to support them. They all had nice, dependable husbands, and my father was an attorney and good provider, but I felt that financial dependency made them vulnerable. I was determined to walk a different path. I desperately wanted a career.

I intended to be a lawyer, but my first semester in college, I wrote a story for the school newspaper, and I was hooked. Dorothy Powers, a *Spokesman-Review* editorial writer and columnist, taught journalism classes; she provided much support and encouragement and helped me get a scholarship for journalism graduate school at the University of Missouri.

I questioned my female teachers in college and graduate school to distraction. During my junior year abroad in Florence, Italy, my English teacher was a woman named Dr. Aranzula. I never knew her first name. She was British, married to an Italian man, and I felt she held all the answers to life. I was 20 and quite existential. I spent hours drinking coffee with my existential friend Meighan. One night, we walked several miles to Dr. Aranzula's house and rang her door-bell. She graciously let us in and answered our questions: "How do you balance career and family? How do you nurture your own creativity with two little boys?" I don't remember her answers; I just remember that she graciously took the time to answer them.

When I first started in newspaper journalism in 1979, there weren't many older women reporters nor many women editors at all. But I always took an interest in women's issues and made their stories part of my beat, no matter what beat I had. I did lots of "first women" stories—first women cops, fire fighters, district attorneys, and I asked them all how they balanced their lives.

In my twenties, I was extremely ambitious. I changed newspapers three times, always to a bigger paper, a bigger beat, a bigger salary. I had a journalism internship in Congress and at the end of it, I went to work for *USA Today* covering politics. In 1984, I reported primarily on the Mondale-Ferraro campaign. My career was going great. I was independent and leading an exciting life, but my relationships with men were terrible. I chose men who were unavailable emotionally or as busy as I was with their career. Deep inside, I think I associated marriage and children with the trapped lives of those women of my childhood. And I wanted none of it.

One March evening, though, I was walking along a beach in Texas. I had been sent there to cover spring break as a reward for all the hard work I'd done on political coverage. I was alone, of course. I thought: This is interesting and exciting at age 28, but if I'm still doing this at 38, it will be pathetic.

I knew then that I needed to change. I needed to resurrect the female emotional side of me that I'd quashed in my early teens, so afraid I would end up bored and dependent on a man. I didn't need to work on this too long. A few months later, I traveled home for vacation and "remet" one of my college professors who had gone through a painful divorce following the death of his oldest child. We fell in love. We married and I returned to Spokane, to a husband, stepchildren, and my big Italian family.

That was 11 years ago. I went to work for the *Spokesman-Review,* and my career continues to be a very important part of who I am. However, I see my older sisters and my mother in a different way than when I was younger and so judgmental about their lives. My husband and I tried to have a child, but unfortunately, I had fibroid tumors in my uterus and underwent an emergency hysterectomy at age 33. We decided against adopting, and my having to grieve this "no" from the universe helped me grow up more than anything else. I am 40 now and try to be a mentor to as many young women as I can.

I have always told my nieces, "Men are wonderful. We need them, but have something of your own so that if something happens to the wonderful man of yours, if he dies or leaves you, you can support yourself and your children." I think my message, and society's changes, have sunk in. I have seven nieces, and they all have careers or are pursuing them. Two of my older nieces had children before they turned 30. They worried that if they waited too long (like me) they would be unable to have children (like me). So they are doing much better at integrating their lives.

I also try to mentor women at work. After mentoring a Native American journalist for a year, and learning as much from her as she did from me, I began a newsroom-wide mentor program. Now, all young reporters are matched with an experienced reporter the day they begin. I also give dozens of speeches each year to women's groups, and I do a journaling class for women in transition—women trying to get off welfare and women going through divorces. I have kept journals since I was 12, and I tell them how the journals have provided me with snapshots of my emotional life.

I also tell them that we women apologize too much for ourselves. We say "I'm sorry" for almost everything. Unless we have truly hurt another, put the apologies away. They diminish us all. I also tell them that when I feel nervous or awkward in a meeting or a social situation, I take a deep breath and say to myself: "I have a right to be here." This line floated into my head about three years ago. I was standing at the milk machine at work, and several people were waiting behind me. Usually, I get nervous in those situations. Am I taking too long? Is someone getting angry behind me? Should I let someone go ahead of me? This time, though, I took my time and the words came: "I have a right to be here." Simple words. But it was the message the nuns passed on to me at a young age, the words my mothers and sisters told me, the lessons of my teachers. I have a right to be here. We women all do.

CHRISTIANE NORTHRUP, M.D.
Health Wisdom for Women

---

*"Who knows what women can be when
they are finally free to become themselves?"*
— Betty Friedan

In her unique newsletter, "Health Wisdom for Women"; in her best-selling book, *Women's Bodies, Women's Wisdom;* and in her Women to Women gynecology practice in Yarmouth, Maine, Dr. Christiane Northrup encourages women to listen to themselves and to take responsibility for their lives. She believes that every woman can create the health she wants by listening to her body's inner wisdom, and she has helped thousands of them cooperate with the physical, emotional, and psychological forces that shape good health.

The Women to Women practice, begun in 1985 with another female obstetrician-gynecologist (OB-GYN) and two nurse practitioners, was the culmination of her intention to create a holistic practice for women's health care. It would include all the useful elements, assurances, and balances of Western medicine and, at the same time, attention would be paid to the importance of emotions and circumstances in an individual woman's life. "However," Christiane remembers, "it was not all rosy by any means. Women resisted inquiries about their personal lives if they saw their problem as 'just medical.'"

Nonetheless, as Christiane got to know the same women over long periods of time, she clearly saw that what was happening with these women was not the same thing she'd been taught in medical school.

> Although there are many helpful things modern medicine and gynecology have to offer, in and of itself it's not enough. Depression is not a Prozac deficiency, and seven cases of vaginitis in two months is not a Monistat deficiency. Why send a woman to a therapist for pelvic pain when all we need do is explore her relationship with her husband, and ask her to consider where she might be leaking energy? We must take into account the whole person.

> I believe that our consciousness creates what is going on in our bodies, and we need to look at that. If we are in a constant war mode with the parts of us that are female, then we create that war mode in our bodies. I was shocked when very conscious feminist patients just wanted their uterus out. The feminist movement of the '60s and '70s was surely essential but, unfortunately, many threw over the female parts of themselves as bad or not good enough. Women need to understand that we have vital contributions to make as females.

Christiane encourages women to see their bodies as sacred and to treat them with softness and compassion. Women can be teachers for men in this area, she believes.

> As yet, men are not as in touch with their bodies as women are, but as I study gender differences in the brain, I see a rise in the feminine consciousness of men as well as women. That's encouraging because we are moving toward a place where both sides of the brain will be honored. Medicine itself is changing and becoming more feminized.

As a result of observing the doctors within her own extended family during her growing-up years, Christiane was sure that being a physician was the last thing in the world she'd ever choose to be. Her aunt and uncle were both doctors, "and I didn't like their lifestyle," she recalls. Her father, who was a dentist, spent time with his family and went on trips with them, while the others were tied to their beepers and practices. Christiane's interests while she was growing up were in biology, nutrition, the natural world, music, and ephemeral things such as angels and fairies.

A key person in Christiane's life was Gretchen Carroll. Now in her eighties, she still teaches exercise classes in nursing homes. A dancer, yoga teacher, and a metaphysician who studied with the Christian mystic Flower Newhouse, she was a friend of the family. One evening as Christiane was sitting with Gretchen's grandchildren, she saw an unopened book box that said "Natives of Eternity." Although she'd never done anything like that before, she couldn't resist opening it. It was a book about angels, and she was fascinated. After that, Gretchen invited Christiane to brunch so they could talk about angels and metaphysics. This went on from the time Christiane was 13 until she graduated from college.

From the time she was three, Christiane wanted to play a harp. She began lessons as a young girl with Dorothy Goodell, and then spent summers in Maine at a harp school run by Alice Chalifoux.

> I ended up going to college at Case Western Reserve in Cleveland because Miss Chalifoux was teaching there. They also had a strong science department, so I had music and science together. However, those were the years of the Glenville riots, and Kent State was just down the road. Those were difficult years for me, and after graduation I felt burnt out and exhausted.

On a long-planned European trip with her sister Cindy, Christiane concluded that it might be a better career move to have an M.D. rather than a Ph.D., "although I had no intention of ever actually practicing," she says. She loved the campus of Dartmouth in New Hampshire, so when they got back to the states, Christiane applied there and was accepted. At that time, they were just beginning to admit women. She recalls her experience:

For the very first time in my life, I loved school! I remember crying when I first saw a baby delivered. That was it. I knew I had to go into obstetrics and gynecology. So I went from "I don't even want to be a doctor" to "I'll get an M.D. but never practice" to the most labor-intensive, stay-up-all-night practice I could ever have imagined. And besides that, I married an orthopedic surgeon!

For ten years, until my own daughters were two and four, I delivered babies and loved every minute. It was as easy as breathing. I loved supporting women in labor, helping them to cooperate with the body's natural processes. However, the flaws in the system were a constant irritant. Pediatricians were too prone to rush babies to the nursery when there was no emergency instead of leaving the baby with its mother to bond in those precious first moments. The whole system was run by too much fear of "what if."

In 1985 Christiane left the old medical model and began her Women to Women practice. At that time, she stopped delivering babies because she wanted to spend more time with her own daughters during their growing-up years. However, she was free at that point to focus upon a more holistic approach and to learn more about herself in the process.

By 1987 I was still as burnt out and fried as I was in the old system, and there was no one to blame! I owned the business, and I couldn't blame the guys anymore—I'd had it within myself all along. That's when I went into a co-dependency recovery program. I realized my pattern began even as a child. I would get migraine headaches because I put so much pressure upon myself in school. I don't blame my parents or teachers. I don't blame the medical system. I did it to myself.

Women often believe that if we give voice to what we need and set about getting it, we will be disliked or even abandoned. Consequently, many women have relied on men to perform for them. But the women's movement won't get any further, nor will women's health get any better until we start to take responsibility for getting what we want and responsibility for taking care of ourselves. We must refuse to become victims.

It becomes clearer to me each year that the Source energy which keeps us breathing, keeps our blood PH what it should be, and keeps our heart beating is our true source of power. Unfortunately, we've been taught as women that our power and our source comes from our ability to get other people to love us. Then our lives fall under what Carolyn Myss, author of *The Anatomy of Spirit,* calls the "prostitute archetype." We try to fit ourselves into models that are not who we are. We lose our authenticity, and we leak away our life energy into relationships, people, places, or things that don't reflect our true essence.

Christiane feels that the success of the book *Reviving Ophelia* indicates that more people are ready to look at the issue of how girls in our present society are negatively socialized and too frequently drawn into a self-destructive path. Among her current passions and projects is a book about mothers and daughters. Her girls are teens now, and she's happy to say, doing beautifully. She visits their schools to teach about the body and mind and to encourage the students to support each other in speaking out, in being strong. She wants them to know that it's okay to be different, to be smart.

Christiane's book will deal with how to start girls on a more positive path, beginning in utero. "If we can do that," she points out, "there will be fewer Ophelias who need to be revived." Yet, in spite of current setbacks and backlash, in spite of fears of the massive changes we're now undergoing, in spite of the fact that many women are scared and are running back to what they think will save them, Christiane believes that a critical mass of women are pushing against inner and outer limitations. "Women will continue to emerge," she affirms.

Her parting words of encouragement: "Starting with small steps, find the courage to begin withdrawing energy from what clearly no longer serves you but which you may be terrified of letting go for fear of being abandoned. Allow Spirit to guide your life and supply you with your needs; I've never seen it fail."

RENA PERFECT, R.N.
Serving with Integrity

---

*"Your vitality evolves every time you give yourself
permission to pay attention to the deep-rooted
things you care about."*
— Carol Osborn

❝I feel a stronger peace now than ever before, but also an excitement; I can't imagine what the unlimited and boundless next 20 or 30 years will bring. I have learned from both the positive and negative events of my past," says Rena Perfect, "and I am content and comfortable with my chosen path."

Rena's chosen path led to her current position with Columbia Home Health Services in the tri-city area of Washington State. Having recently developed a home infusion program for Columbia Home Health, she now supervises nurses who deliver those services while visiting her own patients as well. Infusion, or intravenous delivery of medications, includes chemotherapy, pain medications, antibiotics, and nutrition for people unable to eat.

A registered nurse for over 20 years, Rena has spent time in hospital neonatal intensive care, adult intensive care, and pediatrics; she has been a hospice nurse, and has gained extensive experience in home infusion therapy. She is currently learning about management, marketing, and sales, and is developing a new charting and documentation computer system for the company. "I love my work," Rena says, "because there is so much opportunity to reach out to others. In my work with patients and nurses, my goal is to be a model of a peaceful person doing what I'm meant to do. We encounter people who are very sick, many of them dying. This is intense for the patient, for the family, and for the nurses."

Rena oversees a weekly case-management meeting where the staff discusses not only work challenges, but personal ones as well. It is a time of open communication and total support in every area. "I understand," Rena says, "that we cannot separate ourselves into pieces that have no relationship to each other. We are more efficient and compassionate nurses as we understand this. Because I've had more extensive experience working with dying patients, I share my own experience, thoughts, and feeling about death and dying. It's my privilege to help people through this passage."

She remembers one man in his eighties, a farmer who was dying of cancer. "He was a simple man with only an eighth-grade education. But he'd been a successful farmer, married young, and raised a family. He was not affiliated with a religious organization, but there was a sweet spirituality about him. Yet, I could see that he was experiencing a fear of the unknown journey he was about to take."

One morning near the end of his illness, he shared a dream of the previous night where he died and went to heaven. He was met by St. Peter, who welcomed him into a peaceful and beautiful place—so beautiful, he said, that mere words could never describe it. He noticed a group of people sitting in a circle, and walking over to them, he discovered friends and relatives who had passed on before him. They welcomed him into the circle, and he could see they were happy. He wanted to stay with them but realized he needed to get back to his family so he could tell them about this beautiful place. As he recounted the dream, it was clear that he no longer feared his death and that he hoped his family would not fear for him either. He became totally peaceful after that and died a few days later. "When I discussed the dream with the family," Rena recalls, "they could see the dream would be an important factor in helping them move through their grief. It is such a privilege to be of assistance to people during the most significant events in their lives."

However, before Rena was able to embark upon the more expansive life she now enjoys, she needed to break free of old patterns. A product of the '50s, she grew up steeped in the traditional role. She followed the same path as her mother before her, married young and stayed home as she began to raise her three sons. However, she felt trapped and yearned for a more stimulating life. "My husband was a good person, and my discomfort was not because of him; I just knew there had to be something more."

Two major events became the catalyst for change. The first revolved around watching the unfolding Vietnam war on television. "It seemed so senseless," she says, "and then I realized that it represented what I felt my life was." When the women's movement came along, she could recognize herself in Betty Friedan's description of those women who had "the problem with no name." Rena embraced the women's movement, seeing it as a way to freedom. Her role models were Gloria Steinem and other prominent women in the movement at the time. After her sons started school, she continued her own education and obtained a degree in nursing. Remaining in the marriage, she cooperated with her husband in raising their sons, but after they were grown, she knew it was time to move on and create a more complete life.

As she moved into her career, she learned from both the positive and negative models that presented themselves. The director of Rena's nursing school program modeled a quiet peace and strength. Admiring her qualities, Rena was motivated to emulate her. Once in the work force, however, she began to realize that there were aggressive and angry people who exemplified what she vowed never to be.

Rena's strongest model and motivator, Patricia Dee-Kelly, was the national nursing director of Home Nutritional Services. One of the original founders of the company, she conducted meetings for supervisors who traveled to New Jersey from all over the United States. As manager of two offices and two satellites in the Northwest, Rena attended the New Jersey meetings two or three times a year for five years, thus observing her model over an extended period and under varied circumstances.

Patricia was a tall, attractive blonde with a warm and approachable presence. Always dressed in a suit, she exhibited a professional attitude but was not afraid to display her emotions, and she gave hugs before and after meetings. In those years, that relaxed behavior was not the norm, and I related to Patricia's refreshing style. As she stood in front of our group, she asked us to help set up company goals and prioritize them. We worked cooperatively, developing them as we went along, so we felt invested and ready to work hard to accomplish them. She made us feel part of a team, and I loved it. I felt she was giving me permission to be who I was already; I didn't have to hide behind the "professional" mask anymore.

When the national company became so successful that it went on the stock market, it became a different company. The bottom line became profit. I watched Patricia's growing frustration under these circumstances and then watched her graceful exit. Unwilling to compromise her principles, she determined to follow another path. The company was eventually bought by another corporation, and its name was obliterated along with its earlier more humane mode of operation.

Patricia Dee-Kelly's decision inspired Rena to leave the company because her discomfort was also extreme at that time—and for the same reasons. Rena saw that Patricia was not devastated by the circumstances but learned from them and used them as a step in growth. Patricia later became director of the New York City Visiting Nurses Association, an influential position she still holds today.

Over the years, Rena has left positions because she was unwilling to compromise her personal integrity, resistant to staying in a constricting position just for the sake of security. "I sometimes question my decisions," she says, "but the next step always leads to something more positive and powerful."

Contentedly looking back over her choices and decisions, she says: "Now that I'm over 50 and not as concerned about pleasing others as I used to be, I trust my own instincts and make decisions based on my personal integrity. I'm my own person, and if others are empowered by observing that model, that's great."

MARIA POUNCEY
Making Limitations Disappear

"We are the electric light bulbs through whom
the light of God reaches the world."
— Agnes Sanford

"If we don't give back, we haven't really made it, no matter what our so-called important positions might be," declares this ardent advocate of minorities and women. We haven't advanced further because we haven't given enough to one another." Giving is what Maria's life is all about. Born into a migrant family of 17 children, her passion is to help migrant families find light at the end of what is often some very dark tunnels. She essentially does social work, but her official title is Migrant Education Program Coordinator for Gadsen County, Florida.

Maria's goal is to put children in school and keep them there, but this is not easy. Many have no birth certificate, no doctor, haven't had inoculations, and often they have no food, clothing, or even shelter. Sometimes Maria takes them home with her until she can connect them with the services they need.

Late one Friday afternoon, Maria found a family of five living out of a truck parked at a Laundromat. They had a nine-month-old baby, knew no one, and had nowhere to go. Catholic Social Services was closed for the weekend, so Maria took them home with her. "My husband has patience," she laughs. "He never knows when I might bring someone home. We've taken in abused women with their children, some for one or two months at a time."

Maria doesn't go around encouraging women to leave their husbands, she assures us. She does urge them to refuse to be abused, though. She wants them to see that drunkenness is no excuse for abuse. Unfortunately, many of these women often accept that excuse. This accepting attitude about abuse is passed along to the children. "The sooner the cycle of violence is broken, the better," Maria says. "My own son and daughter often go with me to the camps because I want them to see and understand how these people live and what needs to change."

Maria finds that many women want to attend school so they can find jobs other than back-breaking field work. A woman Maria helped to enroll in classes so she could obtain her GED is a current success story. She's studying to become a mechanic and working for an auto parts store. At first the auto store owner, who needed a bilingual employee, offered her $5.50 an hour, which she refused, explaining that she needed more so she could support herself and her children without Welfare. The owner then offered $7.50 per hour, and she accepted. As Maria tells this story, her voice reflects the pride she feels in this woman who called an end to an abusive situation, learned to fend for herself, and is now making it on her own.

Maria is also proud of the six-week summer school she organizes for children from three years old through fifth grade.

We often need to feed and clothe them and take them to doctors and the dentist. They will come to school running a fever because there's nothing for them at home while their parents are working in the fields. Every summer my daughter, who graduated as high school valedictorian last year, has helped with the summer school. She plans to be a nurse practitioner and work with children. She loves them and doesn't care if they're dirty; she simply wants to help them. I'm proud that my children have learned compassion.

Maria also appreciates her husband, Rich, who adopted her daughter. They also adopted their son when he was only seven hours old; his birth mother was a young, unwed migrant. Rich is a forester who attends meetings with Maria and occasionally takes off work to help get a woman or a family settled. "Although our budget sometimes gets tight, he never complains about the people I bring home. He's a very special person," Maria says.

As we spoke with this beautiful, articulate, and caring woman, we marveled at the distance she has traveled. The 16th of 17 children, she was born with blisters all over her body. Shortly after her birth, her migrant family dropped her off at an uncle's farm in Texas and made their way north to another survival job. No one thought she would live, but she did, and by the time her family returned, the aunt and uncle were attached, and her parents didn't have the heart to take Maria away. Her adoptive parents were poor, and they had five older children, but they shared what they had with love.

> These people were wonderful models. Mom was diabetic and a double amputee. She spent two years in a tuberculosis sanitarium. But no matter how sick she was, she got up, combed her hair, and put on makeup. "It's important to like yourself," she would say. She'd have my dad put her on the floor so she could mop, and other times he would carry her to the garden so she could weed. She did her own cooking and always had a big pot going so there would be enough for our family and anyone else who dropped in. She gave good advice and encouraged me to stay in school. She died when I was 12.

Maria's father and older siblings were also instrumental models and motivators. The sibling next in age to Maria was 15 years older, so in many ways she felt like an only child, even though her birth family visited, and she kept in touch with them. After her mother died, Maria's older unmarried sister, Luz, became her mentor. Luz worked hard so Maria could attend a private Catholic school, and Maria's father encouraged her to drop a high school romance and apply to a college in San Antonio. Although the deadline for applications was past, she was accepted and granted financial aid. "I promised my dad that if this happened, I'd go for at least a year, so I kept my word and went to the city," Maria says. "That was a big step for this country girl."

When she was a junior, Maria married and became pregnant. Her dad sent her a graduation class ring with the year 1979 on it, so Maria made it her goal to graduate that year. She managed to finish her senior year in December of 1979 while holding down a job and caring for her baby. "There was no way I was going to let my father down," she says.

With a major in business administration and a minor in operations research, she obtained a position with the government in personnel management where she worked while her husband finished graduate school. However, the marriage was not a happy one. "He couldn't adjust to fatherhood," Maria says, "so we divorced." Maria remembers that period of struggle.

> My ex-husband left me with our unpaid bills, so I moved into several different government positions looking for the highest-paying one I could find. Eventually, I became a prison guard at the Federal Men's Prison in Tallahassee. I was in my twenties and one of the first females in that position. They hired me because I was bilingual and a minority. The other guards didn't like me, and my supervisor gave me the midnight shifts. Although I wasn't trained in weaponry, I was loaded down with guns and sent out to patrol the perimeter. However, I was determined not to let these men defeat me. When I left, I wanted to leave on my own terms and in my own time. Their treatment just motivated me to work harder.

Finally, Maria was sent to a ten-week law enforcement training program, and she came out at the top of her class in self-defense and weapons handling. She was put on a normal shift after that and stayed in the job until her bills were paid. She had met Rich previously in Washington, D.C., and knew that someday they would be married, They were, just three months before she quit the prison job.

Seven years of working for the U.S. Attorney's office as a paralegal followed. Just before the seven years expired, she was put in charge of debt collections and became disillusioned.

> I knew this wasn't for me. I couldn't take things away from little old ladies who were more than willing to pay, while at the same time crooks were getting away with everything. I became anxious and depressed. I knew I had to leave in spite of the fact that I had 12 years of service with the government.
>
> I knew it was impulsive at the time, but I also knew I had to follow my heart. I wanted to help people, not be part of a system that was hurting them. I always had a nagging feeling that I needed to be doing something for my own people. My birth sisters would call from California to tell me their kids were in trouble and that my 13-year-old nieces were getting pregnant. I wanted to help them, but they were too far away. If they would have sent them to me, I'd have taken them in.

Maria was already volunteering with local-area migrants. She'd started the first Girl Scout troop for them and had become so well accepted that the natural step after she left her government position was to find full-time employment as a migrant advocate. "I finally found my true calling," she says.

Maria leaves us with "just one more" success story. A young high school dropout was driving a tractor for her dad, and he wouldn't allow Maria to even talk to her at first. Finally, Maria convinced him to allow his daughter to attend a ten-week high school equivalency course, and she graduated at the top of her class. A job at legal services came open about that time, so Maria convinced them to hire her, promising to teach her to type if they would only give her a chance. She's been there four years now and keeps getting promotions.

She asked what she could do to repay me, and I replied, "Give back to other minority students." She now tutors in the schools and shares her own success story. She is giving back, becoming part of the solution. I'm proud of her. When we make it, we can't forget about the others.

JAN PRICE
Voyager into the Light

"Thou dost not dream what forces lie in thee,
vast and unfathomed as the grandest sea."
— Ella Wheeler Wilcox

"Play, love, laugh, live for the joy of it. Have fun. Happiness is holy." These are words Jan heard in 1993 during a near-death experience after a heart attack, and she shares the details of her life in her book, *The Other Side of Death.* After previewing the afterlife, she has an enhanced appreciation for this one; yet at the same time she wants to assure us that, ultimately, death does not exist. The eternal essence we truly are simply exits the earth suit and goes into a different dimension.

The spiritual wisdom and sensitivity Jan Price now displays was an integral part of her being long before her out-of-the-body sojourn in 1993. A happy and serene childhood in a small town provided Jan with a calm foundation. Teachers fostered a love for books and writing, and the community in general delivered the message, "It's safe to get involved with life." Jan met her husband, John Randolph Price, "across a crowded room" at a party as he was getting out of the Air

Force in 1952; each felt they would be together from that moment on and were married in 1953.

> John is still my greatest mentor and inspiration. He sees only the best in me and urges me to express talents I don't always recognize in myself. We work and play together and delight in discovering and sharing new ideas. He often jokes that I'm his American Express Card—he won't leave home without me!

Their spiritual journey was launched in the mid-'60s as they began to study the Ancient Wisdom teachings. John was a successful advertising executive at the time, and Jan ran a car-leasing business. Their spiritual study took them on a search for the deeper meanings of life, which culminated in the establishment of the Quartus Foundation in 1981, a research and communications organization that probes the mysteries of ageless wisdom and seeks to integrate it with new discoveries of quantum physics. That same year, John published a highly acclaimed book, *The Superbeings*. In the years that followed, Jan and John became internationally known writers and speakers who teach that when the dynamics of mind are combined with the unlimited potential of cosmic forces, a door opens into a powerful new life that is both practical and rewarding.

Not ones to merely investigate possibilities, they jumped wholeheartedly into the laboratory of life. They planned and organized the first World Healing Day, which took place at noon Greenwich Mean Time on December 31, 1986. More than 500 million people all over the world joined in a simultaneous global mind link of peace and oneness—and the event has continued to take place each year on December 31st.

Also in 1986, seven years before she would have the heart attack, Jan and John were the co-recipients of The Light of God Expressing award from the Association of Unity Churches. The dynamic couple continued to work together in the writing of several inspirational books and are a powerful spiritual presence in the New Thought and New Age communities. Jan created and still facilitates personal growth intensives called "Freedom Flights." Limited to no more than 12 people, spiritual reality is revealed and energies are released that dramatically change individual lives. As a result of her experiences and teachings, Jan was able to write clearly about her near-death episode, which in many ways was a natural extension of her already highly spiritual sensitivity. She tells us:

> The sides of death are not that separate. Life resides in both places. The only real death is when we allow the light of joy to become extinguished.
>
> In the greater awareness of that dimension, I realized I'd carried a load of guilt all my life because my mother nearly died at my birth. I was shown that guilt precipitated my heart attack and that I needed to release it, and I was able to release it into the golden light. Although I had been a dearly loved only child, my soul had interpreted my mother's distress in the delivery room as anger at me. I'd assumed I had done something wrong and, so, felt guilty.

Another element of her experience provided great comfort. Her beloved dog, Maggi, who had died just three weeks before Jan's heart attack, immediately came to be with her in the next dimension. Maggi stayed with Jan as she moved through reunions with departed loved ones and was given instruction from higher beings. During this time, Jan was shown the importance of animals and the love they have to give the world. "And, yes, I saw that they have souls, too," she says with a smile.

Another highlight for Jan was meeting her higher spiritual self. "Awestruck, I was given a deeper understanding of the true magnificence of each one of us," she says. Jan's entire experience is beautifully told in *The Other Side of Death*, which we highly recommend. Yes, there have been similar books written in the past few years, but Jan's loving and wise spirit speaks so clearly and yet so eloquently in this one that the reader's heart is blessed in the reading.

The following is a portion of Jan's instruction from her celestial teacher:

Teach liberation. Fun and laughter are contagious, exposing all in their radius to the prosperous condition of happiness. Do what you really want to do. Follow the desires of your heart, and your blithe spirit will infect others. As you free yourself, your deeds and words will inspire others to break through the prison bars that have kept them from fulfillment. There is so much joy. So much good. Embrace it and express it, radiate and luxuriate in it.

It's obvious that Jan is following these instructions and becoming ever more aware of the Light of God expressing through her.

MARY LOU REED
Making a Difference

*"If I don't agree with a part of life, then my work
has to address it."*

— Maya Angelou

B ecause she is so friendly, approachable, and relaxed, most people feel comfortable talking with Mary Lou Reed, a woman who
listens and cares. She blends into a room of people and never seems
to be impressed with her own importance. She's like an old friend,
easy to be around. However, there is fire and steel underneath her
quiet exterior, and for most of her life, she has found a way to crusade
for what she believes is right. As an Idaho state senator from 1985
until she was defeated in a close election in November 1996,
Democrat Mary Lou Reed displayed a passion for making the lives of
women and children better and a passion for preserving our environment. She says:

> I wanted to do whatever I could to make sure kids weren't losers
> before they got started, and out of my affinity and respect for the nat-
> ural world, I worked to protect it from the kinds of human impact that
> can destroy it.

I've always been a political animal. Wherever the action was, I wanted to be there, so I was in student government from grade school through college. Mills College, a small private women's college in Oakland, California, gave me a nurturing, encouraging environment in which to develop a strong individuality. We were treated as individuals and expected to express our unique selves. I earned a degree in religion and philosophy and went on to Columbia University.

After she married her husband, Scott, Mary Lou dropped out of graduate school and later stayed home to raise their two children. "It wouldn't occur to young women these days not to finish their degree, and it wouldn't occur to me today, but back in the '50s, the mentality was totally different."

However, Mary Lou never stopped being interested in what was going on in the world around her. In every decade, she found herself active in some kind of political movement.

The '50s was the era of Joseph McCarthy, and I fought against his threats and repression. Scott and I were just moving to Idaho at that time, and it was even more conservative then than it is today. People feared a communist was under every bed. This was not an atmosphere I wanted my children to grow up in.

The '60s brought the women's movement, and I remember discussing Betty Friedan's *The Feminine Mystique* with friends. I enjoyed my children, but I was probably one of those women who should have had a job. I always felt the pull toward doing something meaningful and was always busy, sometimes in a productive way, sometimes not. I've found over the years that using time and energy productively within a political and organizational context is incredibly satisfying to me.

From the '70s on, Mary Lou and her attorney husband became deeply committed to conservation and environmental causes, and they helped found the Idaho Conservation League. "I spend much time amid the beauty of the outdoors; it feeds my soul, and I'm going to make sure I do all I can to ensure that future generations inherit a healthy environment," she affirms.

Once she became a legislator, Mary Lou received a personal political lesson. "I can't convey to you how male dominated the legislature was when I first arrived. In 1985, many men in the senate didn't believe women should be there as colleagues." One of 6 women out of a total of 42, she soon found an ally in Gail Bray, a senator 15 years her junior who took Mary Lou and another newcomer under her wing and taught them the ropes.

As always, I found that the best way for women to be effective politically is to group together to get something done. We're more likely to work in collaboration, while men tend to compete with each other. Yes, there were two or three women in every legislature who related to and identified with the men, and their tactics were the same. Perhaps these women were not as eager to work collaboratively with other women because they didn't respect themselves as females. Fortunately, the Idaho legislature became more women friendly over the years. I was minority leader for two years, and the Republicans have also had women in leadership.

While in the legistature, Mary Lou worked diligently for Head Start funding and for "Reading Recovery," a innovative program developed in New Zealand that has had phenomenal success in helping every child read by the end of first grade. Specially trained teachers take the children who are at risk of not learning to read and work intensively with them for about eight weeks. These children are helped before they can be labeled failures. Although Mary Lou helped get the Reading Recovery bill passed in the Senate, it lost in the House. "The problem was expense," Mary Lou explains, "but we need to be more foresighted. The state's budget is doubling for juvenile corrections. If children don't read early, they may never recover academically and thus be more apt to get into trouble later. I hope this progressive reading program will eventually make it into the Idaho schools."

Mary Lou's enthusiasm for good education and the political process was passed on to her son, Bruce, who is now the director of President Clinton's Domestic Policy Council. "Growing up in our house, he was naturally exposed to our passion for making a difference by working politically. When he was only 14, Bruce managed a political campaign. Of course his father and I are very proud of him."

Recovering from her own political campaign of 1996, she readily admits that "losing was not exactly a fun experience." However, Mary Lou's resilience and optimism are apparent as she continues to dedicate herself to helping bring about a better world. As a private citizen, she will be closely observing how Welfare reform affects the well-being of women and children, and she will involve herself as their advocate in the areas that affect them. Mary Lou also will be working with other citizens to reform the present system of campaign financing. "As you can see, a political defeat is not the end of my world." She smiles. "Life goes on, and happily at that."

Caring and involved from the time she was a young student, never allowing the repressions of any decade to intimidate her, Mary Lou continues to be a leader and an emerging woman making a positive difference in her world.

GEORGIE RICHARDSON
Agent of Transformation

"Mastery is an accumulated inner strength."
— Gail Sheehy

Nurturing, authentic, relaxed, and fun-loving, Unity minister Georgie Richardson revels in her role. "I love motivating people to stretch and to express the energy of their Higher Selves," she says enthusiastically. "I love mentoring those who want to heal emotional wounds and live in love."

As is the case with most teachers and healers, Georgie needed to move past her own emotional wounds as she sought to unearth her authentic self. Many of those issues arose through her association with powerful women in her early life who modeled what she didn't want to do or be.

One of Georgie's earliest female employers, Rose, owned the local credit bureau in Butte, Montana, where Georgie grew up. Georgie worked as an office clerk and errand person and later was trusted with credit reports. Rose, strong and powerful in her own family and in the community, ruled with an iron hand, and often humiliated her employees. Georgie remembers:

She'd strip you right in front of everyone. I felt powerless and didn't understand how to take charge of my own life. It saddens me to look back and see how intimidated I was around Rose's powerful negative energy. However, that experience taught me about being sensitive to the feelings of people with whom I work.

After Georgie married, her neighbor Marion was another type of model for her. Those closest to Georgie expected to be privy to her every thought and feeling, to have unlimited access to her inner life. "Marion encouraged me to guard my private thoughts," Georgie recalls, "and I followed her advice and began to gain a sense of myself as separate and unique."

A major turning point came when Georgie read a book about reincarnation, *Here and Hereafter*, by Ruth Montgomery. She recalls sitting in the chair devouring it, snapping her fingers, and thinking, But of course! This clears up so many questions!

The material excited, but also frustrated, her because she knew she could not indefinitely tolerate her life as it was. "This information wasn't cocktail party material," she says. "It was life-changing material I resonated to from the depths of my soul!"

However, there were other matters she needed to attend to before she could think about making drastic changes.

I wanted to complete my contract for this lifetime with my husband, Bill. I also needed to help my disabled son grow and mature in a safe and loving home. About ten years ago, my husband died. By then my son Scott was grown, employed in a sheltered workshop, and living in a group home. Bill's life insurance was more than adequate, so then I had the time and the financial resources to investigate the material I'd read about.

Georgie began to attend a Unity church. A major influence was the minister there (whom she refers to as Jane in order to protect her privacy). Jane was strong and powerful, yet gentle, and she encouraged Georgie to believe in herself. "She told me that she was just brushing my dust off," George remembers with a smile, "and that my soul knew these truth principles already. She said it was exciting to teach me because I was like a thirsty sponge."

Shy at first about participating in the fellowship and activities of the church, Georgie blossomed under Jane's tutelage. After a year of church attendance and weekly counseling, Georgie was hired as a church secretary. She soon became a platform assistant and was given responsibilities for the daily operation of the church. Eventually, Jane asked Georgie to give Sunday talks when she needed to be away. "I loved the speaking experience," Georgie recalls, "and a desire for my own ministry began to grow."

To Georgie's dismay, a tragic flaw began to appear in her model and mentor. Jane refused to take time for counseling and self-renewal. Consequently, her emotional health began to deteriorate, but she hung on even after it was obvious she desperately needed help. Georgie reflects, "I began to take over more work in the office because Jane was losing her grip. I was trying to keep everything going in the background so she could function. But I could no longer cover up for her after the Sunday she lost it from the pulpit in front of the congregation."

Several years later, Georgie is still deeply saddened by her mentor's departure from the ministry. "I feel such an ache in my heart for her. She was a vital instrument of change in my life, and I learned from her mistakes as well as from her successes. I'll always respect her pivotal role in my life. Her ministry remains alive as long as I minister, for I internalized much of her style and many of her stories and her beliefs."

Now in her own ministry in Salem, Oregon, Georgie is much loved by those in her own congregation, and her influence runs deep. She is grateful to God for her journey and where she currently finds herself. But she doesn't take it for granted. She is committed to taking adequate time for herself, to ongoing inner work, and to facing and healing her own shadows.

She is also deeply committed to living her life from the inside out—a process she calls Concentric Living. She declares:

I make my own choices about what to do, where to go, how to spend my money, and how to interact with others that are in alignment with the movement of light inside myself. My consummate goal is to not allow outside elements, family or societal, to dictate my decisions. It is vital that I give the greatest weight to my inner guidance. My most powerful controlling force, my ultimate mentor and motivator, is the Lord of my Being, the Spirit of Truth Within.

MARY BETH SEAY, M.D.
Medical Innovator

---

*"I have always had a burning desire to see how
the universe works, what life is all about..."*
— Shakti Gawain

Pediatrician Mary Beth Seay has a most unusual practice, and possibly the only private practice of its kind nationwide. Using a multidisciplinary approach, it serves the needs of children medically, emotionally, and educationally. Until recently, the staff consisted of Mary Beth and an assortment of counselors and therapists with a variety of skills, but she has now added another pediatrician to help with an ever-growing clientele. They have become the main referral system for all pediatricians in the city of Tallahassee, Florida, who have patients requiring this unique approach to treatment.

After 16 years of private practice, Mary Beth dared to pursue a new dream, and Consultative Pediatrics Family Center opened in 1988. It was originally established to help children and families cope with life-threatening medical issues. Very aware of the body/mind connection, Mary Beth realized that while she was dealing with the medical problems of her young patients and their families, there was also a strong emotional component that needed to be addressed. Therefore, she opened her new facility with an art therapist as part of her support staff. As the new practice grew, they began to pick up increasing numbers of children who had fallen through the cracks of both the medical and mental health communities and who needed crossover work between the two systems. With an ever-increasing caseload, she soon found herself needing to add to the number of therapists. In turn, more support staff created a shortage of office space; so after a relatively brief time, she moved into a new facility, a very large house that she converted into a warm, welcoming, home-like atmosphere.

The practice now deals with large numbers of children diagnosed with ADD (Attention Deficit Disorder) as well. Coordinating that kind of crossover effort and developing a community outreach into the schools and other areas of the child's life requires a tremendous amount of time and effort. The main challenge is to put together a complete program that works well and is adequate to carry the child over a long period of time, if necessary. Therefore, an essential element of the staff's work is to train parents and teachers how to work with these children more skillfully. Since there are no "pat" answers, the staff is required to create an entire workable system for each individual child.

A strong, but gently persevering woman, Dr. Mary Beth Seay has the ability to clarify issues and to pick up on subtleties that often go unnoticed by others. She then excels at presenting those perceptions in an easily understood context. A balanced blend of scientist and potentialist, she finds that through the years she has developed a sharp intuitive edge. Often these "hunches" or "flashes" lead her to a rapid and correct diagnosis supported by subsequent medical testing. She says:

> When I listen to what people tell me, my intuition kicks in and it's frequently right on or at least not far off the mark. This helps narrow down the wide range of possibilities into the ballpark where

things are. The kinds of youngsters we serve are ones with symptoms that could be at least a hundred different things, so this intuitive perception is extremely helpful in diagnosing.

Mary Beth discovered her life's mission while still in elementary school, but it came as a surprise to her as well as to her family. Born into a family of educators, it was always assumed that she would be a teacher, and while she knew that was not what she was going to do, she didn't quite know what she would finally choose. One day when she was in the sixth grade, her teacher asked the students what they wanted to be. When it was Mary Beth's turn to answer she said, "A doctor."

I don't know where those words came from, but it was clear from that point on. Somehow, in speaking those words, I knew it was right, and I never wavered. There had never been a medical role model in my life, and my parents were of two minds about my choice. On the one hand, they were proud, and on the other hand, they felt I had chosen an unfeminine profession. My grandmother voiced her concern and once told me, "You'll never get married or have children. You won't have a normal life." Sometimes those messages were overt, sometimes subtle, but they just impelled me to continue. Finally, everyone gave up their futile attempts to change my mind.

Although often wondering if she had been "dropped in from somewhere else" because she was so unlike the rest of her family, she did have a paternal grandfather who was her childhood delight. She was very close to him, and he related to her on a level no one else did. Mary Beth recalls, "He didn't have expectations, didn't get disappointed, and would go out of his way to do anything I wanted him to do. I loved spending time with him in his shop, tinkering, pounding, and getting messy—which was allowable in that situation. He always had animals around, and I loved animals, so that was another common bond we shared."

As she moved on to medical school after college, she was one of 3 women students in her class of 60. Her peers were quite accepting, but an instructor bluntly informed her that she was taking up space that could have been better filled by a man. He believed a male would practice longer, work full time, contribute more to the profession, and would pull more weight. During the last two years of medical school while on rotation, Mary Beth fell under the guidance of a female psychiatrist. This woman was her staff supervisor, and she became a mentor as well.

Today, there are many ways in which Mary Beth passes along her own gifts. The young art therapist who became her partner in starting this unusual pediatric practice is still working with her. At first, she was without professional credentials, and Mary Beth knew that in order for her to continue working in the medical arena, this very talented young woman would need to expand her education. With Mary Beth's support and encouragement, the young art therapist went back to school while continuing to work in the office. She followed Mary Beth around the hospital, mingling with health-care personnel in order to learn the medical aspects necessary to their practice; she now has her Ph.D. and is a fully credentialed psychologist.

By 1980, Mary Beth had been in private practice for eight years and had done very well, accomplished her goals, and had all the patients she could handle. But her service and outreach to other human beings on the planet didn't stop there. One day while talking to a woman who was going to Haiti as part of a church project, Mary Beth asked about medical needs in that country. Although the program the woman was involved in didn't include medical services, Mary Beth called the missionary in charge, who consented to let her come and provide some of those services. It was so successful that Mary Beth was invited to return, and she ended up traveling to Haiti for 10 to 14 days each year—taking with her a medical team, lay volunteers, and medicine.

In the fall of 1995, Mary Beth went to Hanoi to help evaluate the medical system available to support a brace shop. In Vietnam, braces are used as a treatment much more than in the United States because they don't have the resources to do many surgeries. They have often used heavy metal braces or bamboo braces, which aren't very effective. Since Mary Beth's trip, the brace shop now supplies lightweight plastic braces—a real improvement for the Vietnamese.

When asked if she would like to return to Vietnam, Mary Beth replied, "I would love to go back to see what could be done to improve the pediatric health care system. I see the big picture, and children are an important key in this picture. Children have the future capability to make the world better and to bring us all to another level of functioning."

There is no doubt that many hundreds of children's lives have already been made infinitely better because Mary Beth Seay has viewed the "big picture" and contributed her best efforts toward the evolving of a new humanity through her service to children.

DEE SHEPHERD
Master Teacher

"I see the mind as a volcano with two vents:
destructiveness and creativeness. And I see that to the
extent we widen the creative channel, we atrophy
the destructive one."
— Sylvia Ashton-Warner

Walking through classrooms at Shepherd Academy in Tallahassee, Florida, a casual visitor may wonder, "What makes this school different from any other private school?" At first glance, the difference is not obvious. Students are busy studying a variety of subjects at which they are expected to excel, and teachers are there to guide and encourage. However, once some time is spent observing how the program functions, the differences do become obvious.

Dee Shepherd, mother of two children and the grandmother of two, is founder and principal of the academy. When Dee left a salaried position and opened her own school in 1978, it became necessary for her and her children to live on food stamps while she built up her business. The children also received free lunches, and she recalls how humiliating the experience was for all of them. As she revisits that period in her life, Dee emphasizes that it gave her a clear understanding of how she didn't want her life to progress. However, the sacrifices were short and temporary and allowed her to follow her heart, which ultimately has made a profound difference in vast numbers of young lives. When asked to describe the academy, Dee explains:

> I have a program for children with alternate learning styles. We serve a population that spans ages 6 through 18. We work with kids who don't achieve in traditional school situations. Most private schools can't serve this population, and the public schools serve them on paper, but in reality, they aren't really serving them either. These are the kids who "fall between the cracks," and as they grow older, they become more depressed, act out more, and are more often involved with the law.

These are the students that Dee refers to as the "injured" children because of the experiences in their life, their family's life, or in previous school situations. Many of the children, particularly in grades one through five, are medically challenged youngsters. One child has multiple problems with hearing and underdeveloped arms, one has had an aorta transplant, another was premature and doesn't grow very much, others have a variety of learning disabilities or neurological problems. In grades 6 to 12, the problems tend to be more psychological than physical. While some students do have medical problems, many of the teenagers have actually been in psych units. Some have attempted suicide, suffer severe depression, and exhibit out-of-control behavior. Others have been diagnosed with Attention Deficit Disorder (ADD), and while they have high I.Q.'s, they've had so much practice failing through traditional methods of instruction that they continue to do so.

The staff at Shepherd Academy consists of Dee and her son Will, who is her administrative assistant. There are seven teachers and two aides who are employed full time, and one teacher and aide who work half time. The student population currently numbers 55, and Dee says: "A lot of focused energy is involved in educating these kids." Small class size and the student/teacher ratio helps account for some of the success students find here, but it is also much more than that. There is a total philosophy that permeates the air, and a visitor doesn't have to be around very long to spot what makes this school so effective in comparison to others.

The differences emerge under close observation, and it is soon evident that one of the major distinctions is the manner in which these children are perceived. They are looked upon as normal, evolving human beings who just happen to be in a body that might be different. It is also quite clear that some of the success is due to the fine balance the staff members have achieved in being both accepting and demanding at the same time. They accept the children's differences but, simultaneously, they demand that all students perform to their full potential.

The exceptional staff provides a therapeutic, nurturing environment conducive to academic success. The requirements for teaching at Shepherd Academy are stringent, and academic preparation is simply not enough. Dee requires her staff to be flexible, caring, creative, and centered, with strong, healthy self-images. "It can't be a threat if a child says, 'I hate you, you're the worst teacher I've ever had!' They must be able to accept the child's feelings without taking it personally." When asked how she finds these outstanding teachers, Dee confided that she looks at credentials but never hires on that basis alone. She does several interviews with every applicant and then finally hires on intuition. "That works," she affirms. "Twice when I tried hiring on the strength of credentials and experience alone, neither worked out. So I rely on a way that works well for me."

If Dee's staff is exceptional, it only reflects the rare genius of their leader. When we asked why she would want to work with this population of students, she laughed, and replied, "That's a *darn* good question." Then, getting serious, she confided, "First, in reality, it's because of my needs. I have a need to problem solve, to greet challenges, and to work at something stimulating—I don't want to be bored. These kids meet all those needs. Every day there are always four or five challenges to confront and a tremendous amount of problem solving to be done."

How did Dee Shepherd evolve into the empowered woman she has become? We sought the answer to that question and discovered some wonderful insights into this extraordinary lady. Dee was born the eldest child of four; her parents were both graduates of Duke University. Their household was a happy one, with lots of action and interaction. Dee fondly remembers her growing-up years.

> My father had a wonderful wit, and my mother had a good sense of humor. We spent a lot of time being silly and having fun. We were all readers, and many evenings were spent by the fire with the entire family reading. Even television didn't change that. We would watch a few programs, but we'd all still have a book in our hands reading it as well.
>
> My mother was a spontaneous woman who always made experiences available to her children. She might load us all in the car, take off, and drive three hours just to get to the beach or to some other place where we could see or do things that were of interest to us. It was a very enriched childhood—an easy one. I never remember adolescence being difficult. I would have to say my mother was the most important role model in my life. My mother loved and accepted me unconditionally, and yet she taught me about discipline, limits, and responsibility. It helped me gain a great sense of self-worth. I admire my mother because of the way she feels about people. She is non-judgmental, accepting of change, very open, loving, and caring and has always retained her wonderful sense of humor. If my life can be half as good as hers, I will be really proud.

When she was in the fourth grade, it was discovered that Dee had a severe vision problem. During a routine school screening, she was asked to read the first line of the chart, and she didn't know where the chart was. Her parents were told that if it wasn't correctable, she would be classified as legally blind. Dee hadn't realized that people were supposed to see leaves on trees and anything but shapes and shadows at a distance. This limitation, however, served to strengthen her. She recalls, "During those early years, I spent so much time in my own world, which was often limited to what was in my head, that without knowing it, I built an arsenal of inner resources. I developed both mental powers and an acute sense of intuition as a result, and I feel that I still retain most of that."

As a school administrator, Dee has the ability to meet people where they are. If parents come in upset or angry, she just meets them in that space where they are angry. They start from that point and try to problem-solve. They discuss the current situation or dilemma, what the school can do, what the parents can do, and what the child needs to do.

Further evidence of Dee's ability to meet people where they are can be seen in her interactions with students. A teenage boy enters her office and bursts out with, "Dee, I just need to talk to you, and I can never get time out of class to do it." He says he's worried about how much money his parents owe for his tuition, but as Dee pursues the issue, it's clear that he wants to talk about his parents' impending divorce. She talks with him a bit about how it's affecting him and helps him develop some strategies to cope with the transition. Then she walks to her desk, takes out a yellow card, and writes, "Mike is to see Dee anytime, anyplace" and signs it. Mike leaves in a noticeably different frame of mind from when he entered. This is the aspect of problem-solving Dee loves.

> I ask myself, "What is this kid really asking for?" He needs some support, some understanding, someone who will listen but not cry with him. He needs someone who can help him clarify the problem, clarify how he is feeling and experiencing it, and make that okay. But he also needs someone who can help him begin to cope.

It is this very down-to-earth approach that works like magic and that makes Dee and her staff so effective. Dee embraces a deeply held personal spirituality and repeatedly shows her students how lucky they are to be together. "It is no accident," she tells them. "You're the right kids, this is the right place, the right time, and the right teachers.

We're all very lucky to be together, because we're 'there' for each other." It's an accepting atmosphere, but it's also safe because the boundaries are firm and the students are not going to be allowed to be destructive to themselves or others. Dee explains:

> I guarantee it's safe. It's so safe that if someone gets out of control, someone will hold them in their arms until self-control is regained. I'll call the police if necessary—that's how safe it is.
>
> It's not all about tough love, or "I care about you"' soft love. It's a fine balance, and we're in business to help kids refine their behavior and redefine themselves. It is our job to help them be successful.

That is exactly what Shepherd Academy excels in doing. And just a final note: Dee Shepherd will never have time to be bored!

KATHY SILVER
Law Student and Philosopher

"This has been a most wonderful evening.
Gertrude has said things tonight it'll take
her ten years to understand."
— Alice B. Toklas

Kathy Silver is excited to be in her first year of law school at the University of Texas in Austin, this after seven-and-a-half years of working full time as a legal secretary while attending night school at the downtown campus of the University of Houston. Because she knew that a straight-A average would help her get into law school, she refused to settle for anything less. She says, "By virtue of working in prestigious law firms in Houston such as Vinson and Elkins; and Beck, Redden, and Secrest, I've seen the résumés of people with stellar qualifications. I saw the need to excel in undergraduate and in law school to even be considered for a position at most law firms."

This 32-year-old has been a legal secretary since she was a senior in high school, and when she began law school, it was the first time since she was 15 that she was able to focus solely upon her education. In addition, she enjoys sharing time with fellow students.

I love to learn, and I especially enjoy sharing ideas with intelligent and motivated people. I love to debate issues, to get beyond the trivial. Perhaps that's why I have such a deep desire to become a lawyer. I'll be required to think and reason my way through all kinds of issues, and the law is so broad there won't be a limit set on how much I can learn or how much I can challenge myself.

When we asked Kathy what area of the law she wants to specialize in, she wasn't sure, but she likes the idea of being a trial lawyer. She loves the matching of wits, the fast pace, and the high pressure. She's happiest when challenged with a lot to do in a short time. "However, I don't really want to work 90 hours a week for the rest of my life," she laughs. After she becomes a lawyer, Kathy plans to do pro bono work for the elderly and for single women with children:

Many poor people have minor legal problems and get cheated out of money they may need for survival. In some instances, all it might take is a letter from a lawyer to help. The legal system supports the rich, and that's one aspect of it I don't like. Not that I can single-handedly change the world, but if I help tip the scales for even a few people, I'll feel it's a worthwhile endeavor.

A model and motivator for Kathy is Linda McCloud, an attorney in her office who had to work very hard to get where she is now. Raised in the Welfare projects, Linda was told she could never go to college. Rough years followed; she went through marriages and divorces, had three children, and became an alcoholic. The turning point came when she joined a 12-step program 18 years ago and decided to reclaim her life and energies. She started law school when she was 40, worked full time throughout law school, and graduated with high honors. Outspoken and honest about her life experiences, Linda is very supportive of others. Kathy and Linda have talked about how surviving difficult experiences helps them function in diverse situations. "Those who've had everything perfect often have trouble when things go wrong," Kathy believes.

Kathy did not grow up in a perfect setting. When she was seven, her parents divorced, and her mother worked at a sales job that required long hours. Nonetheless, she still managed to do all the necessary things for Kathy and her brother.

> I wish I'd been more helpful and supportive as I was growing up. While taking great care of us, my mother excelled at her own job and eventually started her own successful company. She showed me, by example, that you have to work hard and depend on yourself, take pride in what you do, and have faith in your own ability. She taught me to stand on my own two feet, and I truly appreciate her. She is the single most positive influence in my life.

Awhile back, Kathy learned a lesson in balance. Naturally fun-loving and outgoing, full of energy and vitality, she seemed to have no problem with her long hours of work and school. Then it all caught up with her. Shortly after she'd taken the law school admission exam, she had a severe panic attack, so intense that she went to the hospital because she thought she was having a heart attack. A friend urged her to see a therapist, and she did.

After taking up yoga and meditation and learning how to more readily express the caring, sensitive part of herself, she realized she could be intellectual and analytical *and* nurturing and caring. She is beginning to understand the importance of setting boundaries and priorities.

> I used to believe I wouldn't make a good parent because I feared I couldn't be patient enough, but I now can see good things I might pass on. I'm capable of committing to a permanent relationship, and that's what I want. I have a passion for the law, but I'm learning not to allow my career to keep me from a rich and full personal life. I still work and study hard, but I've learned to take time out to laugh and play with my friends. I'm learning to laugh at myself. It's all a matter of balance.

SHAY ST. JOHN
Expanding Horizons

"Courage is the price that life exacts
for granting peace."
— Amelia Earhart

Reaching out to ministries around the world as Development Director for the Association of Unity Churches, and through the *Our Incredible Journey* workshop she facilitates with her husband, Shay St. John is model and motivator for many. Approachable, authentic, and willing to share her own deep challenges, she has come a long way from her uncle's farm in the deep South where she grow up in the '40s.

Shay's feisty Southern mother dared to break family patterns at a time when most women accepted society's more restrictive guidelines. This mother's mettle began to be tested when, at 13, she was confined to a tuberculosis sanitarium. One of her lungs was collapsed to prevent the further spread of the disease. After seven years, she was finally well enough to be released. In spite of fragile health, this Loretta Young lookalike was determined to become a model in New York City. She not only became a model, but a successful one.

Later, after Shay's birth and then a divorce, she returned with Shay to an uncle's home in Virginia. The small community did not welcome this divorced woman and her daughter. Shay explains the painful situation they encountered:

> I now know that the people believed divorce was contagious, almost like a cold germ that could be spread. Other children were not allowed to play with me because their parents feared I might bring my divorce germ into their homes. The local fundamentalist church even condemned my mother to hell.

However, in spite of the many rejections and restrictions, Shay watched as her mother disregarded them and bravely asserted her authentic self. She didn't waver from her decision to remain single, and she found employment as a secretary and bookkeeper at *the* place to work—the railroad. She constantly assured Shay, "You can do anything you want to." The seed was planted in the soil of Shay's receptive child's heart, and there the roots of a vision of higher possibilities for herself grew strong.

That vision was reinforced by school and teachers. Shay's responsive mind stood out in the midst of a community of children who saw school only as a place they were forced to attend and whose families resented the time school took away from chores at home. Mrs. Scott, Shay's fourth and fifth grade teacher, drawing out the broader potential in her pupil, made Shay a classroom assistant and then followed her progress closely throughout high school. The first in her family to graduate, Shay did it with honors and received college scholarships to boot.

William and Mary, Mrs. Scott's alma mater, was the college Shay held out for—a school where it was almost impossible for a female without powerful alumni connections to gain entrance. However, with Mrs. Scott's mentoring and glowing recommendation, Shay was accepted. In spite of resentment and ostracism from her extended family, who shunned anyone who dared to move beyond the confines of their limited existence, Shay remained focused upon her educational goals, never forgetting her mother's encouraging words: "You can do anything you want to do."

At a very early age, the life of the spirit became vital to Shay, despite the narrow fundamentalism doctrine (including a vengeful God) that would condemn her divorced mother to hell. Shay knew a God of her own—a loving creator who accompanied her as she climbed apple trees, dreamily watched white puffs of clouds in the blue sky, or roamed the forest near her home. "I always felt God's joy during those solitary times," she remembers.

Shay's mother, too, embraced a loving God. A prayer asking for help with Shay was found in her Bible after she died:

> *Dear God, Help me to live up to the faith I see in my child's eyes. Help me to be the person she thinks I am. I am so very human. Yet, to her I am wise as a sage. I am so very frail. Yet to her I am a tower of strength. I can bind her cuts and bruises, I can soothe her small hurts, both physical and mental, I can give her love, I can protect and cherish her. Yet I can never be half of all I must be without You to guide me. Watch over her, teach her things that are beyond my power.*

This mother's prayer was answered in a special way when Shay encountered Kathryn Rowbotham, a minister at the Unity church in Roanoke, Virginia.

Kathryn acknowledged the loving God that my mother and I knew, and taught the concept that "everyone is a minister." It took only two weeks to know I'd found the right path for me. Kathryn, along with her spouse and co-minister Alan Rowbotham, took me under their wing, and I became a student in every class they taught and an eager volunteer in every area of the ministry.

I began to study to become a licensed Unity teacher, and Kathryn and Alan offered classes that I could use, always looking for a way to encourage me. In a leadership training class, we were required to write our credo, a summary of our belief system. At the end of the training, students were given ten minutes to present their philosophy.

After I'd finished mine, Kathryn led the class in a standing ovation. That day I began to believe in myself in a new way.

Kathryn and Alan encouraged Shay to pioneer a new Unity study group in nearby Christiansburg, Virginia. The group began with just three people and quickly grew into 30. Then Shay stretched her wings even further and went on to Savannah, Georgia, to establish a new Unity church in the heart of the deep South. That ministry continued to grow and flourish after Shay moved on to a larger congregation.

As a result of hard work and dedication, Shay became ordained by exception as a Unity minister in 1982. Along the way, she married, gave birth to two daughters, divorced, grappled with serious health challenges, grew through other relationships, and then married Al Sears, her current partner and co-leader of the *Our Incredible Journey* workshops.

For several years, Shay helplessly watched the painful illness suffered by her daughter, Debbie, and then more recently had to accept her death at age 26. "Debbie modeled to me courage, conviction, and an assurance that God was with her," Shay reflects. "Unity was not her choice. Yet, we communicated through the windows of each of our belief systems to share a mutual love for God and for each other."

Currently, Shay continues her work at Unity headquarters, and leads workshops with her husband. Their purpose is to support and encourage forgiveness, healing, and growth. "As we give up the attitude that we're victims of the circumstances of our lives," Shay explains, "we begin to claim spiritual power; we become victors instead of victims." The following appears in the *Our Incredible Journey* workbook: From a victor perspective, we see clearly. Joyously, we share out insights with others.

> *To our enemies, we give the gift of forgiveness.*
> *To our opponents, we bring the gift of tolerance.*
> *To our brothers and sisters with whom*
> *   we experience this life's journey, we give love.*
> *To the children who watch us as we walk our*

walk, we stand as a good example.
To ourselves, we give the gift of respect.
Here, in victor awareness, we feel whole and complete.

Shay points out that even in victor awareness, we are all confronted with life's changes and transitions.

There is much for us to do, many challenges before the world. The healing of AIDS, feeding the homeless, caring for abused women and children, promotion of "green living," transforming fear into faith—there is so much that needs fixing. Our passion gifts us with the energy to do the work before us, and we do that work joyously. Our job title makes no difference. Whether we are a server in a restaurant, a social worker, a teacher, a minister, or a truck driver, we minister unto those with whom we come in contact, and others feel the contagion of our Light.

GLORIA STEINEM
Torchbearer

---

*"I cannot and will not cut my conscience
to fit this year's fashions."*
— Lillian Hellman

"The inner and the outer journeys must be linked, or neither works," declares Gloria Steinem, one of the original firebrands of the women's movement. After years of intense involvement, she realized she was feeling fragmented and "the world was fading from color to shades of gray." She found herself reacting rather then acting.

> I burned myself out with a total focus upon the outer, without understanding I needed to have inner sustenance as well. Unless we have inner uniqueness and authority, we aren't equipped to defy outer unjust authority. And it is important to defy that outer unjust authority, to be active in the outer. Passivity and navel gazing will not get us where we want to go.

Gloria is quick to admit that she sees things such as meditation as a tool of revolution and considers "inner space more important to explore than outer space." She feels she is now exploring the "other half of the circle," but points out that this is not a rejection of the past because she believes we build the future on the past, even though they may appear very different. By embracing both the inner world and outer reality, Gloria is, in essence, finding the balance she didn't previously possess, and she has discovered that both are equally valid. This knowledge has become a new source of strength in her life. She now exercises her power against societal rules and role expectations in a new way; she simply "no longer pays tribute to them by either conforming or confronting."

Gloria feels lucky, although we might question whether *luck* is the right word for it, to have spent her life doing the things she cared about most, things that were "close to the bone of my own and other women's hopes." No doubt Gloria Steinem is model, motivator, and mentor for vast numbers of women, and has been one for several years.

Her independent spirit was born early in life as she took care of her mentally ill mother who couldn't take care of herself. Her father, a traveling antique dealer and small resort owner, often took Gloria and her mother, Ruth, along on his travels.

> It was a blessing that I was rarely in school before I was 12 years old. I had time to read and to dream, and I didn't get programmed early on that girls couldn't do whatever they wanted. As I went through school, even college, I observed most women teachers choosing to go along with the patriarchal system.

From the age of 10 until she was 17, Gloria lived alone with her mother; her older sister had gone off to school, and her father left. Gloria writes a moving account of her family and her early life in a section of her 1983 book, *Outrageous Acts and Everyday Rebellions*. As we speak with her, we tell her we're impressed that she managed to survive what we would term today a severe dysfunctional situation. As counselors, we see many people who become immobilized for years with less trauma than Gloria experienced; these people often require extensive therapy to gain the strength and insight to move ahead. We wondered how she managed to survive so well. "As difficult as those years were," Gloria answers, "I always knew I was loved by my parents, and I also understood they couldn't really take care of themselves, so they couldn't take care of me either."

Consequently, Gloria learned independence and resourcefulness very early. Yet, it's obvious she didn't take on a role of self-pity or helplessness as a result of those early adverse circumstances; over the years she has used her energy in a dynamic and constructive way. A mobilizing force in the early women's movement, she continues her fight to enhance the quality of life for all women everywhere.

In her book *Revolution from Within,* Gloria reminds her readers that "It's Never Too Late to Have a Happy Childhood." Displaying a deep compassion for children who have been abused and neglected, she includes extensive expert advice on how to heal the traumas and move on to living a more productive life. Gloria is certainly no Pollyanna as she discusses these situations, and she clearly recognizes the pain and trauma that others have experienced. At the same time, she manages to see the gifts in her own early circumstances. She recognizes that her mother, handicapped as she was, was able to break the pattern of her own upbringing, a pattern of too much discipline and not enough love. Their mother often told Gloria and her sister that they were loved just as they were, that they didn't need to earn her love; they automatically had it. While Gloria admits that her childhood was difficult, she, like her mother before her, found the strength to approach life differently. Gloria's mother had tried an early career in journalism but became bogged down by life and mysterious inner circumstances. It has to be some satisfaction to Gloria that she picked up the same career and took it to lengths beyond what her mother might have ever imagined.

Gloria admits that her early childhood models came from films and books and tended to be performers, "models of escape and defiance." In college, she admired authors such as E.M. Forster, Dostoevsky, and Edna St. Vincent Millay. Female role models weren't too prevalent when Gloria was growing up, and while she could certainly admire a woman such as Eleanor Roosevelt, she felt that the only way her lifestyle was attainable was to marry the President.

However, as fate sometimes happens, a model presents itself ever-so-briefly, but makes a strong and lasting impression.

> I remember walking on the street in New York in the '60s, and I saw the French sculptor Nickki Staphael striding down the street in a man's coat, cowboy boots, and hat. She looked so free. I knew who she was and that she was doing her own work on her own terms. I was greatly impressed by how wonderfully free she seemed, and I wanted to be like her.

The list of Gloria's accomplishments is long. She is a journalist and the author of several books, *Ms.* magazine co-founder and editor, and so much a catalyst and integral part of the women's movement that her name seems to be synonymous with it. We found her to be a very approachable woman who also has the courage to let herself be vulnerable and to share on a more personal level. We admire her as she strides freely through life, making her own choices and standing by them. Although, for many of us, she is a symbol almost bigger than life, we see that she exudes the qualities of a warm and intro-spective human being moving through the inevitable and sometimes painful passages of her own life—not unlike the women she has championed for so many years. She inspires us to do what we can, right where we are; her example encourages us to make the lives of women and, ultimately, all people, better.

Having entered into her sixth decade of life, Gloria is still setting before us a new vision of what the emerging woman can look like. Her experience and wisdom, born from experience, shows us not only the necessity of discovering our inner life, but the powerful change that can occur with the translating of that life energy into outer reality.

Gloria Steinem—an outstanding woman who is always evolving and emerging and sharing so much of herself with women around the world—is certain to remain a positive role model for generations to come.

PATTI STEWART
Peace Corps Volunteer

---

*"We're either going to take the leap to have more
fun and be ourselves, or turn in our chips
and become old in spirit."*

— Laurel King

Life often seemed to conspire to keep emerging woman Patti Stewart submerged in pain and old patterns. A mentally ill mother. A mean-spirited and neglectful father. An alcoholic husband who left her for another woman. An irresponsible husband who expected her to work to pay his debts—and she did. When does the moment come when "enough is enough"? When does the time arrive when a woman is ready to rely on herself and her own strength and talents? There's a song that says that it's in every one of us to be wise. Well, when does that wisdom begin to kick in?

Perhaps it's been building all along. A kindly, elderly neighbor modeled kindness and compassion for Patti and her sisters in their early years as she "watched out for them." A wise and compassionate woman 30 years Patti's senior was a close friend, advisor, and mentor for many years until her death.

Married very young and believing she was nothing without a man in her life, Patti was bereft, helpless, and hopeless when her husband left her. Desperate, she sat crying in the back of a church in Dufur, Oregon, where Ione's (Jenson) husband was pastor. When she walked out, Ione followed her and offered counseling, inner healing, and friendship, which Patti gratefully accepted.

Yet, recovery and self-actualization are part of a process that happens over time, and often patterns are repeated until somewhere deep in the psyche, we "get it." Patti entered into another marriage with a charming but irresponsible man. He led them both through many enterprises in real estate and associated businesses. The debts would pile up, and Patti would work overtime selling real estate and managing a restaurant to pay the debts. This scenario occurred over and over again for several years until, finally, enough was enough.

After the divorce, Patti had no problem supporting herself; in fact, it was easier because she had only one set of bills to pay instead of two. After she purchased a home for herself, she relaxed and began to question the meaning of her life. She was ready for an adventure and had no one to please but herself.

Always an energetic person and a hard worker, she was not afraid to try new things, to stretch her physical, mental, and emotional limits. She applied for the Peace Corps, was accepted, and is now working in Guatemala. She is finding that it's never too late to break free, to emerge into a new consciousness, a new confidence. She says:

> I am the only American for miles around, and no one speaks English, but I am teaching classes in it. My Spanish has improved through necessity. The people here are a great help, and I hope to have some students with me soon who can speak English. It is lonely sometimes, but I have gotten to know and accept myself. I don't fear my loneliness anymore, and I'm proud of my ability to fend for myself. I guess I have always done that, but I thought I needed a man, so I never accepted my own strength and ability.
>
> I am so self-sufficient now. There is very little water, sporadic power, nothing handy, easy, or convenient—including cleanliness, but I'm managing just fine. I can saddle my own mule, cut down

trees, chop wood with a machete, change my own bicycle wheel. I cook everything from scratch (no mixes here!) and bake in a Dutch oven over a wood fire. I can grind corn and make my own tortillas, and even though I don't like them, I eat them! After walking 8 to 14 kilometers a day, I'm hungry—and tough as an old boot!

Yes, it is within every one of us to be wise! And self-reliant, adventurous, and giving. Pushed by life's circumstances, Patti made the decision to rise to the challenges; she chose not to become submerged in self-pity and victimhood. She stands as a shining example of the emerging woman, and a model, motivator, and mentor in her own right!

PATTY BALL THOMAS
Children's Champion

"I am me. I belong to no race or time.
I am the eternal feminine with its string of beads."
— Zora Neale Hurston

From the time she was six years old and began conducting classes for neighborhood kids in her backyard under the oak tree, Patty knew she loved being a teacher. Her father reinforced that desire by often referring to Patty as "little teacher." When her father died when she was only eight, Patty promised herself that she would become a real teacher. "Of all the titles and positions I've been privileged to have as an adult," she says, "the one that still means the most to me is 'teacher.'"

Fortunately, her mother continued to reinforce Patty's ambitions to excel in school and to teach. Patty and her sister were placed in a Catholic school, which Patty feels was a distinct advantage. She felt very safe and nourished growing up in that environment, went to church every day, and took her prayers and religion seriously.

In the seventh grade, Sister Mary Williams made such a big impression on Patty that for a while she wanted to become a teaching nun herself. "I was completely mesmerized by this incredibly charismatic woman and the habit she wore," Patty recalls. "She was quite young, poised, never raised her voice, and obviously loved the children she taught."

One day Sister Mary took the girls into the kitchen for a talk about the meaning of "becoming a young woman." The scene is indelibly etched in Patty's mind.

> Several of us were sitting on the floor, and Sister was sitting on a stool. She reached down and picked up the hem of her habit and folded it back over her knees. She had on black stockings, and we were awed as she crossed her legs and began talking to us about women and men and the facts of life: "When the other Sisters and I go to the beach, we don't wear our habits," she said. "We wear bathing suits, and often men will approach us looking for intimate relationships, which of course we refuse because we've given our lives to Christ."
>
> She went on to admonish us not to allow males to see us only for our bodies and instructed us about how to stand up for ourselves under pressure by boys. It was a great thing for me, because my mother never was able to talk to my sister and me about such intimate things as our body functions or possible relationships with boys.

Patty's experience with Sister Mary Williams and the other nuns reinforced her determination to become an educator, and she was such a good student that she graduated from high school when she was 15 and finished college by the age of 19. "I began teaching third grade in Jacksonville, Florida, before I was considered an adult," she recalls. In the following years, Patty went on to teach in several elementary grades, to supervise tutors, to specialize in reading, to become a research grant consultant, and eventually to become a director of Florida First Start in the Florida Department of Education. She currently has responsibility for two major programs: Florida First Start and Even Start Family Literacy.

The First Start program targets children from birth to three years of age and their parents. These children have been identified as "at risk" for future school failure, so a considerable part of the program is designed to support parents as they learn to be their child's first teacher. Skills are taught in their homes, and parents become involved in group meetings and parent-child play groups.

The Even Start literacy program helps break the cycle of poverty and illiteracy of low-income families by integrating adult literacy and adult basic education and parenting education into a unified family literacy program. Both programs empower parents to become advocates for their children. "I have a passion," Patty says, "to help families and children get that little extra boost that can make all the difference in their lives, which can help them to become productive citizens."

Throughout the years since her childhood, Patty has remained dedicated to a spiritual path. After leaving the structured church, Patty and her husband, Walter, kept up spiritual study in their home. Eventually, they began to attend a church with their son, Frederick, and there the Thomases dedicated themselves to working with teenage youth. Eventually, Patty was asked to become Youth Education Director and held that position for several years before moving on to help another congregation organize an adult education program. She is looking forward to soon becoming a licensed Unity teacher.

As we talk with this charming, energetic, and upbeat lady, we wonder what she feels is the biggest challenge she's had to overcome, and she replies:

> Sad to say it is trying to be a successful black woman in a white culture. Too often people prejudge because of color instead of waiting to get to know me. However, because of my commitment to spiritual truth, I also know that "what people think of me is none of my business." I've had some difficult challenges lately, but I remain steadfast in the knowledge that it's my job to love unconditionally, to do the best I can under all circumstances. I refuse to allow the judgments of others to influence me in a negative way. My strategy is to smile as I go forth to do my tasks in a professional manner. I strive to live according to the spiritual truths I've known since childhood.

SONJA C. THOMPSON
U.S. Army Chaplain

"There are many, many gates to the sacred,
and they are as wide as we need them to be."
— Anderson and Hopkins

"The passions in my life are God, the soldiers I serve, and my family," declares Chaplin Sonja Thompson. Foresight, persistence, and faith in God's plan helped Sonja accomplish her heart's desire to become not only a chaplain, but the first one to represent Unity School of Christianity in the military. She kept jumping over the obstacle of "it hasn't been done before," but because she never doubted that her desire came from God, she hung on to her vision.

However, it took five years and the overcoming of many obstacles for Sonja's vision to manifest. After a separation from her military husband, she moved her four young children and her ill mother to Lee's Summit, Missouri. There she worked in Silent Unity's prayer room for two years before applying for the ministerial program. All during this time, Sonja nourished her dream and began taking the necessary steps toward her goal.

By the time she was ordained in 1982, she had already completed the proper military paperwork for the Armed Forces Chaplain Board. Because of an age limit, Sonja needed to be accepted within just a few months. Coming down to the wire, she wrote and rewrote the board, each time providing more required information. Someone in the system suggested that she wait until the month of October to submit her material. "There will be a more accepting atmosphere with some new members coming on board then," she was told.

Several years later, Sonja was talking with a senior-level colonel over a cafeteria breakfast when he asked, "Do you want to hear how you were selected by the Armed Services Chaplain's Board?" He reached into his briefcase and took out Unity's *Daily Word*, explaining that he'd entered the military as a young Methodist chaplain, but his secretary read the *Daily Word* every day and insisted that he read it, too. "It soon became a habit for me, and I still read it," he said. "The October you applied, I was selected to be on the chaplains's board, and yours was the first application I saw. Because I knew so much about Unity, I was able to strongly recommended that Unity be represented."

As Sonja reflects upon how doors kept opening for her, she has no doubt that her life has been patterned by a higher power. Her life as a chaplain hasn't been an easy existence. In the last 15 years, she has spent considerable time in tents and foxholes, often wet and cold, but she has never stopped loving what she does, which is to provide spiritual and psychological support for soldiers.

For a time, Sonja was stationed at Walter Reed Hospital in Washington, D.C. She was senior floor chaplain and ministered in a ward of severely wounded soldiers from Somalia and Haiti. She says:

> I'm always in awe of the vitally alive spirit of these young people as they fight to survive, and it was a privilege to pray and to talk with these soldiers every day. One young amputee had been manning a check point in Haiti and nearly lost his life. I was honored to be with him when he was awarded the Purple Heart. I can't do enough for these troops who do so much for all of us.

The roots of Sonja's love for soldiers runs deep. Her father was career Air Force, and the family traveled all over the world. Sonja points out that about half of her life has been spent overseas. Her father was in a plane that was shot down over Italy during the second world war; he ended up in a prison camp but managed to escape. His bravery and determination was a model for Sonja. The services Sonja attended with her parents in military chapels all over the world also made a tremendous impression. "Chaplains don't make a point of their denomination, so I grew up in that eclectic mode," Sonja says. "I remember loving to sing the great old hymns, sometimes behind a pot-bellied stove, sometimes in a tent."

As a child, Sonja was a free spirit who loved nature, often climbing trees and hiking in the woods. "There's still something special about being outdoors in nature that brings me closer to God," she explains, "so working in the field with soldiers is especially gratifying for me." Another major spiritual influence for Sonja was her aunt, who sent Unity's *Wee Wisdom* magazine for children.

> I read these over and over and absorbed the philosophy that we are all part of God, and our prayers are always heard and answered. In a way, I've come full circle. As I focused attention upon other career goals through the years, my purpose of working for God sometimes took a back seat, but now that strong, simple faith of my childhood is very much with me.

Certainly Sonja needed that faith and was able to call it forth as she went through her ministerial training. The child support she was receiving from her ex-husband was minimal, and somehow it had to be stretched to take care of the household that included Sonja's mother and her four children, who were between the ages of 5 and 18. "When I was married to my husband, there was no worry about money," Sonja explains. "But that changed drastically after the divorce. Financial emergencies were a regular occurrence, but so were God's miracles."

As Sonja reflects upon this time, the awe and gratitude in her voice still shines through as the tells us about the day God graced her with a double miracle.

My oldest daughter, Chanel, was to start college, but we didn't have the $200 for her first tuition payment, which was due at five o'clock that afternoon. I was also concerned because a new ministerial term was coming up, and I didn't have the money for my own tuition, either. As I prayed, a picture came to me of the stack of old purses on my closet shelf, and I somehow knew that the answer to the prayer was to look through them.

I remembered that we had some savings bonds we'd never cashed, so I began to look for them, but they were not there. Puzzled, I went back into prayer. This time I intuitively heard, "I didn't tell you to look for bonds; go back again; you missed something." So next time with an open mind, I went through each purse and every item. And then I found it—an old, uncashed check from the prayer room for $199! We searched for odd change around the house until we had the $200 and raced to pay the tuition just before the five o'clock deadline.

Back home and feeling relieved, Sonja and the children were relaxing and giving thanks to God for miracles, when a knock came at the door. One of Sonja's classmates explained that she and her husband had just received an insurance check from their son's fatal accident. "We'd like to do some special things with the money," she said. "Would you be offended if we paid your tuition?" Sonja and her family were thankful that, once again, God had come through for them. Sonja reflects, "I'm grateful that my children continue to see those days in a positive light. We've remained very close over the years, and I'm thankful that they've all gone on to lead happy and productive lives."

As we speak with Sonja, she is just finishing training at the Command and General Staff College in Leavenworth, Kansas. She will soon be stationed at the European Army Headquarters and will be placed in a new position of increasing responsibility. She will influence the policy and training for all the chaplains throughout Europe. She says:

I welcome the opportunity to mentor young chaplains of all denominations, both male and female. As I travel to places like Bosnia and wherever troops and chaplains are deployed, I'll assess our policies and training. Are the chaplains doing the best job for the soldiers who are often in very hostile and dangerous places? We're always looking for ways to improve how chaplains can improve quality of life and provide a ministry of presence.

We need to be attuned to the feelings, fears, anxieties, and sometimes boredom, that soldiers go through. Our goal is to help our troops feel that God is right there with them in difficult times. Certainly, the chaplains themselves, who are with the soldiers 24 hours a day, also need support, affirmation, and validation.

Another aspect of Sonja's focus will be to design support programs for the families of the troops. "We're demanding more from our individual soldiers as our army downsizes," Sonja explains, "and they may be deployed up to six times a year. This can be very difficult for a family, so it's important to support the spouse and children who are left behind."

Although Sonja is engaged in serious work and relates with soldiers and their families at the very deepest levels, a core of joy within her shines through as she goes about her work. "This is what I was meant to do in this life," she says, her warm voice full of gratitude, "and I love it!" Perhaps that's why she smiles so often and why she allows her innate playfulness an appropriate expression. Certainly, those around Sonja are uplifted by her light touch as well as by her compassion, warmth, and sincerity. Those who know her readily agree that her nickname, which is "Sunny," fits her perfectly.

RAMA VERNON
Visionary Bridge Builder

"Integrity, honesty, commitment, compassion—
these qualities speak out, not because of words we
use, but because of the actions of our lives."
— Donna Hanson

"Whenever I get inspired to begin a project, I become a victim of my own creations," laughs this founder of six successful nonprofit organizations, including the California Yoga Teachers Association, which publishes the *Yoga Journal*. Undoubtedly, the planet is truly blessed by Rama's expansive inspirations, as well as her genius for bringing people together in cooperative efforts that bring those visions into concrete form.

She is the founding president of the Center for International Dialogue, formerly known as the Center for Soviet-American Dialogue. At the height of the cold war in 1984, the center created a framework for American and Russian citizens to overcome stereotypes by mutually exploring commonalities as well as differences. As a citizen diplomat, Rama made 47 trips to Russia in 7 years for the purpose of organizing over 200 citizen summits.

Since 1984, over 10,000 Soviets and Americans have participated in more than 700 joint projects that helped catalyze policy changes between the two countries. Rama's 48th trip to Russia took place during the summer of 1996. In conjunction with medical groups from the United States, she delivered medical supplies, love, and personal attention to Russian orphans. Not one to rest upon her laurels, Rama continually expands her vision and her outreach. "My mission is to integrate the spiritual aspect of life with social and political action," she declares.

The success in Russia led to an invitation for The Center for International Dialogue to expand its work into the Middle East, Ethiopia, Central America, and Africa, as well as into the inner cities of the United States. During the Gulf War, Rama initiated a series of round tables that brought together Kuwaitis, Saudi Arabians, Syrians, Lebanese, Jordanians, Israelis, Palestinians, Egyptians, Libyans, and Moroccans.

Another project was initiated in 1995 at the United Nations conference on women held in Beijing, China. Rama met before and during the conference with women from several African countries who asked for help in developing an African women's peace conference with a focus upon conflict resolution. "Africa is the most disparate continent on our planet," Rama explains. "Internal wars have destroyed the infrastructures, and families and children suffer. Fifty percent of Rawandan women are widows. These women cry out for sanity, peace, and protection for their children."

Although Rama's vision now encompasses the globe, it wasn't always that way. As a West Coast housewife and mother of five, she laughingly confesses that originally she couldn't think past the Rocky Mountains. However, she had studied yoga from childhood, had hosted many Indian teachers when they came to the United States, and made several trips to India herself as both teacher and student. As a result of her deep commitment to yoga, Rama embarked upon an expansive project in 1983 to bring teachers of yoga disciplines together for a West Coast conference—which was so successful that she was asked to organize many more all over the country. Later, she was asked to organize a yoga conference in Russia. She reflects upon her feelings and perceptions at that time.

I didn't even know where Russia was. I was shocked to discover that Russians were being jailed for teaching yoga or putting out spiritual material, and even interrogated and possibly jailed for having contact with foreigners. Consequently, an enormous amount of preliminary work was necessary. Finally, I proposed to the Soviets that we arrange one-on-one dialogues between our grass-roots citizens and their officials, using the professions as a convergent meeting point.

Something larger than myself took over. Here I was a yoga teacher, a housewife, and mother who couldn't speak Russian, and who had no background in international relations or political science. Yet, I ended up interacting with Russian leaders! However, this amazing result required work, up to 18 hours a day, 7 days a week. There were no fax lines, and phone calls had to be booked days in advance. That's why I had to travel to the Soviet Union nearly every month.

Returning home from her first trip, Rama realized that many more such trips would be required, but she had no money for additional journeys. She clearly remembers her prayer: *"Dear God, I don't know what to do now. If you want me to continue this work, then you have to find a way for it to be done because I have no money, no way to get back."* On a filled-to-capacity plane going out of Finland, she had moved three times trying to escape the cigarette smoke and felt lucky to find a seat with an empty one next to it. As the plane started to taxi down the runway, Rama was just finishing her prayer when the plane stopped and turned around, went back to the gate, and picked up a man who had no choice but to sit next to her. Rama describes how her prayer was answered.

After the plane was in the air, the distinguished gentleman and I began conversing, and he mentioned that he was the Northwest representative for Fin-Air. I shared with him what I'd been doing in

Russia, and by the end of the trip, I had all the free tickets I needed. Besides, Fin-Air gave us a computer and printed our first stationery! I realized then that Divine Will was behind this work, so I had no choice but to continue.

Nevertheless, Rama faced serious challenges. She was newly divorced, had a house and children to support, and had no income other than yoga teaching. Sometimes it felt to her like she was walking in darkness. She wasn't sure what she was doing but knew that she was following her inner guidance.

I was very frightened, and a part of me wanted to quit, but the work wouldn't quit me. Spirit was guiding me, but on the human level I felt paralyzed by fear. For many months, I had a vision of myself standing on the edge of a cliff in total darkness. The path behind had disappeared, and I couldn't see forward. I needed to take a tremendous jump to make it across the chasm.

For months, I stood there on the edge of the cliff too frightened to jump. Feeling like a spiritual warrior, I finally got the courage to take this prodigious quantum leap. I couldn't see the other side, but a hand held mine and I was carried over. The work began to accelerate after that inner breakthrough, and many of the Russians seemed to recognize and appreciate its spiritual aspects and even be attuned to them.

However, there were still obstacles to overcome. People in both countries criticized her work and tried to sabotage it. "I still didn't know what I was doing, so I kept relying on heavenly guidance," Rama says. At a low point, and seriously thinking about giving up her work, the Russians took Rama to visit Mother Teresa. They both happened to be in Washington, D.C., during the Reagan-Gorbachev Summit. Mother Teresa was working with AIDS patients and was talking to the Russians about the possibility of opening orphanages there. Rama describes their encounter, her voice still full of amazement:

When I was brought to her, she grabbed me, kissed me, hugged me, kissed my hands, cheek, forehead. She kept blessing me over and over for the work I was doing. She had no human way of knowing what was going on inside me, but she kept saying, "Don't stop what you're doing. You must continue because what you're doing is so important." This was a deep experience I still carry with me. And of course, I kept on with the work.

Eleanor Roosevelt has been another beacon of light for me. When she saw a need, she didn't care about the politics or her own image. She simply went forward in her efforts to fill needs, whether for starving children or for those in danger of losing their human rights. This caused her to be greatly criticized because she was threatening to men in powerful positions, but she kept on with her work in spite of the criticism. This statement of hers always comforts me: "If our desire is to serve humanity, we will be crushed and brokenhearted. But if our desire is to serve God, then no amount of ingratitude can keep us from serving our fellow human beings." Although I don't always announce it to people, for me, it's all about loving and serving God.

Spiritual and humanitarian ideals were instilled in Rama early by her progressive parents, who conducted a naturopathic school for holistic health and healing in their home. "They were 50 years ahead of their time," she says, "so I grew up with all the things that are now more easily available in our society." Her parents' home was a mecca for people who were expanding the narrow boundaries of traditional spirituality, and Rama remembers visitors such as Ernest Holmes, founder of Science of Mind; Gaylord Hauser; Adele Davis; Normal Vincent Peale; Dale Carnegie; Joseph Murphy; and Gina Cerminera.

Rama's mother studied with Paramahansa Yogananda; thus, Rama was exposed early to Eastern philosophy, but her experience went even beyond that. The family attended several different churches each week because her father spoke Aramaic, and the churches wanted him to translate the original Old Testament for them and speak to their congregations. He'd taught in Damascus in missionary schools earlier in his life before coming to the United States. "My

Lebanese father was nearly 30 years older than my Norwegian mother, so I learned to respect elders through family and old-world culture," Rama says. "I had an incredibly happy childhood, had full run of the house, and was always creating projects."

And Rama has never stopped creating projects. One of her current ones is the Women of Vision and Action Network. In 1992, Rama was asked to extend the work of The Center for International Dialogue to the Middle East, where dialogue was urgently needed between Israelis and Palestinians. She met Miriam Nour from Lebanon, director of "Sama House," a place for spiritual retreats in the United States. Miriam had escaped from Lebanon during the war with only the clothes on her back, and despairing of peace in the Middle East, she dedicated herself to finding *inner* peace.

As Rama sat talking with Miriam, trying to understand her pain and wanting to help in some way, Miriam suddenly shared a vision, which Rama immediately understood. "Perhaps there is a way!" Miriam declared. "Let's bring the women together. The women are the key, not only to peace in the Middle East, but to peace throughout the world!" Two weeks later, Miriam and Rama brought 20 Arab and Israeli women together from all over the United States, and they began to share their stories with one another. The women came in spite of being warned by husbands, fathers, or sons that they might be in danger of being attacked by "the enemy." But there were no attacks that day. As an Israeli woman spoke of the pain of serving in the army of Israel and the horrors of seeing her friends killed and maimed, she began to cry. An Arab woman across the room who had been through similar pain from the other side of the "enemy lines" began to cry in sympathy. Then they each stood up, rushed toward one another, and embraced, mingling their tears. That action symbolized the love and understanding that broke through entrenched patterns of enmity and distrust during the day's sharing.

The ripple effect began to spread throughout the country and expanded far beyond the original Middle Eastern focus. New groups formed, and the women's vision and prayers for peace reached out to highlight the need for peace in other areas of the world. Indeed, the popularity and momentum of these groups was so powerful that the women Rama had met with in living rooms throughout the United States requested a national conference.

As Rama visited individual groups and collected their ideas about how to create a blueprint for a more peaceful world, her notions about working with women's groups began to change. "I was in touch for the first time with the pulse of womanhood, and it was a nurturing experience for me," she recalls. "I had always shunned women's groups, believing them to be merely support systems for one another with little potential for impacting the national or international community."

However, as Rama became deeply engaged with the Women of Vision groups and began to gather others into the planning circle, she recognized a powerful potential for good. After two years of working with small groups, the first national conference was held with 500 women in attendance. It was called "Women of Vision—Leadership for a New World." Held in Washington, D.C., with Barbara Marx Hubbard as a keynote speaker, the challenge was laid out. Could women be called upon to hold the vision of peace and justice and then act upon it in the midst of a turbulent world? Rama believes this goal is possible.

> We have vision keepers and activists in our organization. Eventually both capacities need to come together in each person. Sometimes people with a global perspective become too busy for inner work, so they crash and burn. Others become so involved with inner processes they become selfish and implosive; their energy becomes static. We must do our inner work, then take appropriate outer action if we are to become balanced.

As Rama continues her work in the Women of Vision and Action Network and the Center for International Dialogue, as well as with other projects and organizations, she challenges every emerging woman to reach out in new ways.

> Our planet is in crisis. It is time to step forth, not out of anger for the injustice that prevails in the world, but out of love for all

humankind. It is time for the Divine Feminine to express in the voices and actions of women. We can no longer remain apart from the suffering of others, "hoping" for improvement or change. We must involve ourselves in the peaceful transformation of our planet. We must bring our visions and dreams out into the world of manifestation and become catalysts for moving humankind into the outstretched arms of a peaceful new millennium.

DOREEN VIRTUE, PH.D.
Writer and Metaphysician

"If we treat miraculous prinicples like toys, they will be like toys in our lives. But if we treat them like the power of the universe, then such will they be for us."
— Marianne Williamson

"*I'd Change My Life if I Had More Time*" is the title of one of Doreen Virtue's most recent books. To instill in her readers the essential spark, fire, and passion that brings about the realization of dreams is the goal of this prolific author and metaphysician. She believes that what we desire, what we dream of doing, is God's plan for us. "God wants us to be happy," she says. "Suffering is not natural. It's God's good pleasure for us to make our livelihood in a way that fits our natural inclinations and interests."

Doreen earned her Ph.D. in psychology with a clear purpose in mind—to gain the skill and background that would enable her to write inspirational self-help books. Back in the 1970s when she was 15, Doreen was going through teenage turmoil. Laura Huxley's book *You Are Not the Target* became her best friend and daily resource. "Laura's wisdom was a Godsend, and it helped me understand that I didn't need to be a target, that my self-consciousness didn't mean the world was out to get me," Doreen explains. "My social life changed as I changed my thoughts about myself, and I began to feel better emotionally and physically." Doreen determined right then to dedicate her life to writing self-help books. Starting out as a journalism major in college, she soon changed her major to psychology. She recalls:

> From the beginning, my Psych 101 teacher set the tone that kept me focused on my goal. Barbara treated students with utmost respect and spoke to me as if I already had a degree. She would say, "As a psychologist, you will use this information or that approach." She allowed me to try on how it would feel to be a psychologist, and I could see that the role fit me. Even when things became repetitive or depressing in later classes, I remembered Barbara's enthusiasm and love for her chosen field and her faith in me, and that kept me going until I earned a Ph.D. eight years later.

Doreen's most significant model and motivator as she grew up, and still one of her closest friends, is her mother, Joan Hannan, a third-generation metaphysician and a Christian Science Practitioner. Her mother always expected and received miracles as a natural part of life. Doreen's parents had been married for seven years but her mother still hadn't been able to conceive a child. She went to a church near their home and asked for prayer support that she might conceive and bear a child. In less than a month, she became pregnant with Doreen, and two years later her brother was born.

Doreen believes she chose to be with her family, and that she chose well. She has always appreciated the intuitive communication and the harmonious childhood she shared with her brother, and Doreen is also proud of her father, the author of 15 books and a monthly magazine column.

> My dad is an exceptionally kind, gentle, and spiritual man who always encourages and supports my writing, and we share writing frustrations and triumphs over the telephone. As we grew up, he constantly taught his children the necessity of practicing random acts of

kindness—whether through giving a smile, a kind word, or by holding a door open for a stranger—and I've never forgotten this important lesson.

While other kids put medicine and Band-Aids on their cuts and wounds, Doreen's family applied prayer to any problem that arose. Experiencing miracles in everyday life was perfectly natural for Doreen because she saw God's power come through again and again.

One day while walking home from grade school, Doreen lost a coin purse that contained a few coins, but which had no identification. The small red patent leather purse with beautiful clasps was special to her. Devastated by the loss, Doreen couldn't stop crying. Her mother took her usual metaphysical approach and said, "Well, let's pray and know the truth that nothing is lost in the world of God," and she kept repeating that over and over until Doreen's tears stopped. Finally, feeling comforted by her mother's faith, Doreen fell asleep.

When I opened my eyes the next morning, I found the purse right next to me! My mother said she didn't know how it got there, and she never lied to me. Finding that purse beside me was my first profound miracle. To this day, that kind of thing still happens, and I still consider it normal. Whenever I lose anything, I know that nothing is ever lost in the world of God, and the item does appear.

Doreen's mother, a part-time counselor for Weight Watchers, also modeled for her daughter the importance of our mental image of our body and how that perception affects health and weight. Doreen recalls that when she was a little girl, she became obsessed about her stomach and believed it was sticking out too much because a girl at school had made fun of it. Her mother taught Doreen to visualize her body as she wanted it to be and to stop thinking about what she *didn't* want. This ideal influences Doreen's thinking and behavior to this day. Her books *Constant Craving, Losing Your Pounds of Pain,* and *The Yo-Yo Diet Syndrome* address weight issues and offer strategies for creating the body and life the reader wants.

Two contemporary women authors, Louise Hay and Marianne Williamson, profoundly influence Doreen's life and writing at the present time.

Louise's first book, *Heal Your Body,* was turned down by every publisher she tried. She mimeographed copies and gave seminars to groups of as few as two people. Through all this, she never gave up faith in what she had to say. She proves that if we really believe in something and have persistence, our dreams can come true, just as they have for her. Now a bestselling author, her books and seminars help millions heal physically and spiritually. She has her own publishing house, travels worldwide, and enjoys a comfortable and elegant lifestyle. I am impressed that she did all this by herself, without leaning on others—especially some man. What a role model for women!

Marianne Williamson is another author I appreciate because she is completely unafraid to be authentically who she is in print. She doesn't hide behind what she perceives to be politically correct and safe to say. She shares the valleys as well as the peaks of her life journey. Her example helps me to "come out of the closet," so to speak, regarding my own spiritual beliefs.

Because of the climate in Doreen's neighborhood and in society as she was growing up, her mother told her children not to discuss the miracles that happened in their house because people would think the family was "kooky." They were not to reveal that they raised the cat from the dead or that they helped people heal cancer with positive thoughts. This caveat stayed with Doreen well into adulthood, and she tended to keep her spiritual beliefs under wraps unless she felt safe with a person. Marianne Williamson now models for Doreen the beauty of authenticity. Doreen explains:

I gain strength from the courage she displays in the midst of her critics. My book *"I'd Change My Life If I Had More Time"* is my most honest one yet, and I'm excited about it. That I was able to meet and interview Marianne and receive her endorsement on the cover of my book fills me with wonder.

Through her own writing, Doreen encourages people to take charge of their lives. When they tell her about their dreams, she encourages them by sharing how she is beating the odds in her own writing career. Only a small percentage of authors make their entire livelihood from writing, but she makes a very handsome living from her books and magazine articles.

She believes that Divine Direction implants desires into our hearts and minds, and if we follow that direction, we will be given enough time, money, intelligence, and talent to manifest our dreams. "I am thankful," Doreen says, "that God doesn't just go partway with us. He gives us the whole kit and caboodle!"

BEE WEICHERS
Outrageous and Autonomous

"But maybe I ought to practice a little now?
So people who know me are not too shocked
and surprised when suddenly I am old and
start to wear purple."

— Jenny Joseph

B ee Weichers lives alone in her own home high on a California mountain in a recreational area called Moose Camp. Born in 1902, she is anything but a typical turn-of-the-century woman. She has always had a zest for life, and has often embraced a license to be outrageous. That she has met her challenges, made her own choices, and lived life from her own inner set of values is indisputable.

Always beautifully coiffed and immaculately and smartly dressed, she looks much younger than her years. Described recently by her granddaughter's husband as "a 94-year-old grandmother who looks 60 and acts 20," she recently modeled clothing for a large chain store's fashion show. Life continues to be an ever-unfolding adventure for this very active and mobile lady.

Bee, born and raised on a cattle ranch in California, has seen massive changes in her lifetime. She has lived through four wars, the act of putting a man on the moon, and the birth of instantaneous worldwide communication. She started riding horses with her father when she was a young child and traveled ten miles on horseback to take music lessons. When Bee was 15, she and her father began hunting together, and she has only missed two hunting seasons since then. Even though she claims she had no female role models as she was growing up, she was obviously born a free spirit. "I was defying convention long before the bra-burning era," she chuckles.

That independent spirit led her to marry a traveling salesman 21 years her senior. He was, in her words, "a flourishing man, and I was young and easily influenced." For the first four years of her marriage, she lived out of a suitcase. They had one son, and when he was two years old, Bee took him and left, divorcing her husband. Two years later, she remarried.

Bee's zest for life has led her down diverse paths. She helped raise and harvest broom corn in West Texas during the early 1920s, and in 1937, she was the first woman in Lasson County, California, to obtain a pilot's license. She speculates that she might have been at the bottom of the ocean like Amelia Earhart because she wanted to ferry bombers during World War II. However, by that time she had two small sons—an insurmountable barrier to fulfilling such a mission in those days. From 1943 to 1944, she trained at Ft. Bragg to become an x-ray technician and then worked for 20 years in the chiropractic office of her second husband. She also became Susanville, California's first car saleslady, which included chauffeuring cars to auto dealers in Reno.

When we first met Bee back in 1981 at her son's home, she was just 80 years old. We all attended the local county fair together and were watching the rodeo from the fairground bleachers. As the rodeo was in progress, we heard an earsplitting whistle and turned to see which young kid had made the sound. Much to our amazement, this white-haired, perfectly dressed 80-year-old with her pinkies in the corners of her mouth was blasting forth! When we asked if she remembered the incident, she gave a hearty laugh. "I'll tell you one better than that, honey. I was with Wayne [her son] in a department store, and there didn't seem to be any salesclerks around. Wayne was fussing and fuming, so I said, 'Do you want me to bring them, son?' As I put my fingers to my lips, he said, 'Oh, Lord, no, mother, please don't do that!'"

Bee's zest for life is not confined to the outrageous or unconventional, however. For many years, she was part of a dance group for women over the age of 55 that traveled all around the country performing and raising money for several charitable organizations. She currently is involved in the Montgomery Creek Grange Women's Activities Club whose mission is to look after the year-round needs of the homeless, the needy, and senior citizens. The group recognizes that many people are willing to help those less fortunate at holiday time, but they also recognize the needs that exist all year long, so they involve themselves in the spirit of giving for all 12 months during the year.

In 1992 there was a large fire in Bee's mountain community, and all the houses were burned to the ground. Many of the residents were discouraged and had decided not to rebuild, but when neighbors asked Bee about her plans for the future, she firmly replied, "It's my home. I intend to rebuild." When people heard this, they began to respond by saying, "If that 90-year-old lady can do it, so can we." And that's how the community rebuilt itself. Since Moose Mountain is a recreational area, most of Bee's neighbors leave during the winter months, and she is often the only full-time dweller.

Bee's life models a "can-do" attitude for women of all generations. When asked if she had any regrets or would do anything differently, she replied, "I've done lots of unusual things, and there have been hard times and good times. But I'd not change a thing. I'd do it all over again." Her goals for the future? "To keep on living and enjoying life; I intend to go to 100 or beyond!"

JUDY WILLINGHAM
Pharmacist and Lifelong Learner

*"Let woman then go on—let her receive encourage-
ment for the proper motivation of her own power."*
— Lucretia Mott

Tall, capable, and articulate, Judy is a strong, no-nonsense woman, and there is no doubt that she can accomplish whatever she sets out to do. Presently, she is responsible for pharmacy standards in the state of Washington.

As a young girl, Judy resolved to follow a different path from that of her mother, who was agoraphobic, unable even to go to the grocery store by herself. On the other hand, her paternal grandmother was once a suffragette who taught in a one-room schoolhouse and later helped care for Judy when her mother was hospitalized. Judy's grandmother felt it was important for all women, but especially for mothers, to receive an education so they could more capably raise their children. Judy decided to follow her grandmother's example.

At the time Judy entered pharmacy school, 15 percent of the students were women; that figure is now up to 65 percent. She recounts that one of her prime motivators in school was a narrow-minded somewhat cruel professor who kept asking when she was going to drop out so that a real pharmacy student could take her place. Her anger at this treatment pushed her to constantly improve her grades each term. She vowed that she would never treat another person in such a caustic manner if she ever found herself in a position of authority.

Participating in psychology classes and sensitivity groups helped Judy understand that she had basically frozen her emotions during her growing-up years. "I couldn't count on my mother to be well, so I didn't have the opportunity to be a carefree child," Judy remembers. Seeking to be a good parent to her own children, Judy took Parent Effectiveness Training classes, which opened a new door for her. The teacher was a student of Carl Rogers, a well-known therapist, and the author of *On Becoming a Person*. One result of taking the class was that Judy begin to accept and express more of her buried emotions. Eventually, she enrolled in a residential seminar in Rogerian experience, then studied Applied Behavioral Science for two years. "There were so many teachers, fellow students, and counselors who helped me along the way. I can't get specific without writing a book!" she declares. Judy remembers her single most memorable mentor.

Margarite Villars was head of the pharmacy department at a hospital in Spokane, Washington. She was less than five feet in physical stature, warm-hearted, incredibly industrious. She commanded respect and gave respect back to others. We frequently had long discussions and often disagreed, but we were always open and respectful to each other. A few months before her scheduled retirement, Margarite was fired from her job and had to take a much less prestigious position just to survive; yet she carried no resentment.

I admired her attitude, and I learned from Margarite's experience. At the time, I was surprised and appalled that such a thing could happen. I later learned how common it is; a hospital retirement fund is too often all puff and stuff. As a result of being close to Margarite and her experience, I obtained a more stable position with the state of Washington.

Always interested in helping and educating other women, Judy enjoys talking to women's groups about their health. She reminds them to "honor your own observations concerning your bodies because you certainly have been intimately involved with them much longer than any physician."

During the past few years, Judy has monitored pharmacy standards all over the state of Washington. Although she holds a position of authority, she makes an effort to support and encourage young female pharmacists. She listens to their concerns and is pleased to see them bringing more feminine energy into the entire profession, even influencing the men they work with to relate more compassionately to patients. "I like to connect with these young female pharmacists at a deeper level than merely professional," Judy says. "I appreciate their contagious high energy and find them a joy to be around. After I retire, I hope to do more mentoring than my present position allows."

Judy feels that her real emergence is taking place on the spiritual level as she becomes increasingly committed to her spiritual growth and more involved with her church. Although her pharmacy career will soon be drawing to a close, she will certainly not retire from active involvement in the events and activities she finds important. She recently participated in a link-up day for Women of Vision and Action in her area of Washington state as part of a national link-up day for the group. "I'm trusting," Judy says, "that I will find many new opportunities to grow, to minister, and to mentor as I move into the next exciting stage of my life."

MARION WOODMAN
Jungian Analyst

"Much madness is divinest sense
To a discerning eye;
Much sense the starkest madness."
— Emily Dickinson

Making sense of her world while helping others to make sense of theirs has been a life mission for this internationally known Jungian analyst who practices in Toronto, Canada. Since she was a child, Marion has explored below the surface of "worldly" sense. She makes it clear that probing the depths has been no easier for her than for anyone else. Her own struggle has produced compassionate understanding for the often difficult and frightening processes we all must go through on our way to individuation, on our way to understanding and living from a more complete and authentic self.

For the past three years, Marion has faced one of her most difficult challenges—cancer. However, she is now doing well and beginning to lecture or lead workshops about once every two months. Most of all, she is living in the moment. She affirms:

> When I get up each morning, I appreciate the world before me. I'm delighted to be able to work in my garden. I've come through my illness with new eyes and new ears and feel a profound sense of unity with people and with nature. In mystical, crossing-time moments, I see the divine in the ordinary. Whatever hostility and anger I felt before my illness has been drawn out and replaced by love. Yes, I see my illness as a gift.

We are moved by Marion's depth of feeling, but early in her life, she experienced profound emotions and perceptions she was not encouraged to share.

> People thought I was being melodramatic, so they didn't take me seriously. I had lots of friends and was not outcast in that sense, but I knew there was a limit to what feelings I could share with them. I learned to keep deep personal emotions to myself and to express them only in my journal. Poetry was another essential outlet. Because Emily Dickinson articulated my passions and conflicts when I was in my teens and twenties, she's had a powerful effect upon my life. When I first read Emily's poetry, I shouted, "That's it!"

At that time, Marion was in rebellion against her minister father's Orthodox church and was seeking spiritual answers for herself. Marion points out that Emily Dickinson was a profound Christian outside the church, and she had to find her own way spiritually, often via agonizing routes. Marion felt a close affinity with her. She says, "I appreciated her ironic stances, her sense of humor, her connection with nature. Her capacity for the agony and ecstasy of life, particularly in relationship to men, was something she used as a way to the Christ. I understood that."

Marion's Irish mother was also a major positive influence. "She was a character," Marion smiles, her voice full of warmth as she remembers her.

> Of course, that was not the way minister's wives were supposed to be. She had a strong voice I respected very much. She was a smart

dresser and wore the clothes she wanted to, which wasn't always acceptable. She also had strong feelings about furniture and what was right for our home whether the Ladies' Aid agreed or not. She taught me, her only daughter, how to cook and care for the house, and I often accompanied her when she went out to help sick people.

I observed her uncanny intuition and saw she was very much in tune with nature and the true motivations of others. We went through some difficult times, but by the time I was 25 we were like sisters. We recognized each other's aloneness and respected it. We were very much attuned to each other.

In 1976, the year of her mother's death, Marion was a student at the C.G. Jung Institute in Zurich, Switzerland. On a visit home, Marion had an intuitive feeling that she shouldn't return to Switzerland for the next term. However, when Marion voiced her feelings, her mother insisted she return to school. "Go, Marion," she said. "If you can find freedom, go." Marion returned to Zurich but was soon called home due to her mother's illness. By the time she arrived, it was too late. Standing alone by her mother's coffin the next morning, Marion was shattered by grief and guilt and rage. "I was not there when she needed me," Marion says. "No final word was said. It took me two years to realize that in her death, she gave me birth. What an incredible gift!"

From today's perspective, Marion understands the importance of her mother's last words to her: "If you can find freedom, go." In the process of searching for her own freedom, Marion continues to help many others discover a path to theirs. She is committed to discovering deeper levels of freedom from patriarchal values and to reaching for the eternal feminine in herself and in her clients, whether men or women. She also shares her wisdom in workshops and lectures and in her books. In *Leaving My Father's House: A Journey to Conscious Femininity*, Marion and three of her women analysands tell their stories of birthing creative masculine and feminine strength. Provocative and touching, it inspires us to delve into deeper levels of understanding. She is also the author of several other books, including *The*

Pregnant Virgin, Addiction to Perfection, and *The Ravaged Bridegroom.*

A teacher of English and creative drama for 23 years before she went to Switzerland for Jungian training, Marion's career change was entirely unplanned. When she was in her forties, she was looking for a spiritual teacher, and a friend recommended one who just happened to be a Jungian analyst. Profoundly moved by his presence, she worked with him for three years, delving ever more deeply into the individuation process. Then her inner voice directed her to Switzerland.

As we speak with Marion, she makes it very clear that she sees "the eternal feminine thrusting her way into contemporary consciousness." She explains:

> I'm talking about the feminine in both genders, the feminine principle. I know many men whose feminine is more developed than that of many women. In the end, our maturity depends on a balance between the masculine and feminine in each of us, regardless of gender. In my work, I'm seeing more feminine archetypes emerging than ever before, often manifesting in dreams as a goddess.

Marion also sees the new femininity manifesting in our concern for the planetary environment and through our understanding that we must integrate nature's laws into the activities of our lives. She sees the feminine principle manifesting in the new science that uses terms and phrases such as "nonrational, synchronistic, particles and waves, and 'perceived and perceiver are one.'" She sees the emergence of feminine consciousness in the business world as well.

> They're asking such questions as, "What will feed my soul, what will give meaning to people coming in from nine to five? Can we allow people to set their own hours as long as the work gets done?" I see increased efforts toward giving value to individual work and creativity. It's a tragedy that this consciousness hasn't permeated the educational system yet!

It is also imperative, Marion believes, that we integrate more of the feminine spirit into our relationships. She points out that our culture is riddled with the loss of feeling values; too often the feeling function is an embarrassment. The more that technology, television, and computers take over, the greater the danger of our being distanced from each other, and the more the feminine principle is in jeopardy. We must reach out, particularly to other generations and to other nations. Marion explains: "It's so easy to say, 'I don't understand you!' However, we need to learn to contain opposites, really listen to each other without anger, to value our differences. I'm learning this at deeper levels with my husband, Ross, in the later years of our marriage. The beauty of our relationship is in the treasuring of otherness."

Finally, as we share our vision for this book with Marion, she is very encouraging.

It's important for women to share our stories with each other so that we will not be isolated, so that we may have a more powerful vision of ourselves as expressions of the eternal feminine. As we share stories of what it means to be women, we gain a new sense of what is possible. It's time to allow our femininity to return from banishment, time to allow it to transform our lives.

❧ PART II ❧

Weaving New Patterns of Emergence

DISTINGUISHING TRAITS OF EMERGING WOMEN...AND HOW TO UNFOLD YOUR *OWN* POTENTIAL

"What a woman needs is not as a woman to act or rule, but as a nature to grow, as an intellect to discern, as a soul to live freely and unimpeded to unfold such powers as are given to her."

— Margaret Fuller

The more we talk with and observe women who are breaking the mold and moving away from traditional roles and ways of perceiving their world, the more aware we have become that what at first seems to be a myriad of characteristics, actually falls into five broad categories. These categories are congruent with the last four of psychologist Abraham Maslow's hierarchy of basic needs. Maslow noted, however, that as people reach that last level and become autonomous and self-actualizing, some of them go even further to encompass transcendence by embracing transpersonal and global concerns. We have chosen to make the characteristics of this latter group, for the sake of clarity, into a fifth category.

As with most things, there is always some overlapping, and many of these characteristics are like a spiral, appearing in all five categories at increasingly sophisticated levels. Even though the lines we have drawn are not always clear-cut, they do provide a fairly accurate picture of some of the major traits that seem to appear repeatedly and which are pivotal to the emerging woman. The manner in which each woman embraces and uses these traits often differs according to the uniqueness of her personality and life situation, yet each profiled woman exhibits skill in nearly all of these areas:

- Self-responsibility, honestly confronts challenges (Maslow: Esteem needs—to achieve, be competent)
- A learner (Maslow: Need to know, understand, explore)
- Balance (Maslow: Need for beauty, symmetry, order)
- Strong sense of personal values, autonomy (Maslow: Need for self-actualization, self-fulfillment, realize potential, be self-governing)
- Transcendence—global concerns and/or spiritual awareness

While the emerging woman usually has all or at least several of the individual traits listed on the following pages, she is a complex person, and no simple formula defines her. If there is a universal definition, it would have to be that she is ultimately her own best friend and teacher. She listens to her own guidance and unfolds and expresses her true nature in ever-expanding ways as she learns and grows and as she gains new insights and revelations. She remains open to new possibilities and is both fluid and adaptable. She takes the responsibility for making her life work, and while she may sometimes do so in unconventional ways, she no longer allows her fear of criticism to be in control of her destiny. She is learning to be what Maslow would call a self-actualizing human; she is, indeed, an empowered woman! Let's now explore specific traits in order to discover just how we might consciously gain from one another's experiences and further enhance our own emergence.

Takes Responsibility, Confronts Challenges, Seeks Solutions

One major characteristic of the emerging woman is her willingness to take full charge of, and responsibility for, her own life. By doing so, she surrenders her victim mentality and learns to create the life she wants. She confronts her challenges honestly, looks at her options, seeks healthy solutions, and takes action to manifest what she desires.

"As long as I actively attack a problem, I am confident that the situation can be improved," says Shari Lewis, the well-known puppeteer. That statement best exemplifies the emerging women we encounter.

Linda Ellerbee, a broadcast journalist, is a prime example of a woman who has confronted her many challenges and who has looked for solutions and lessons. Among other difficulties, she has confronted both alcoholism and breast cancer and seems to have conquered both. The lessons she learned in the process have, one by one, changed her life. She says she now makes time for things she doesn't want to miss and finds more balance in her life.

Emerging women are doing more in the area of creating joyous and fulfilling lives for themselves. In our book *Women Alone: Creating a Joyous and Fulfilling Life* (Hay House, 1995), we show how women are creatively meeting the many challenges that face them in the areas of loneliness, finances, health, single parenting, aging, and so on. While the title might seem to indicate that the book applies only to single women, it really is a book that all women can benefit from reading—for ultimately we are the only ones who will never leave us. Emerging women, alone or partnered, understand that they need to complete themselves, and they recognize the futility of trying to make anyone or anything outside themselves responsible for their happiness. They are becoming what Maslow describes as self-actualizing, or autonomous.

After the recent assassination of her husband, Prime Minister Yitzhak Rabin, Leah Rabin of Israel spoke these words to her nation: "The terrible price we all paid was not in vain, for we rose from the nightmare to a different world. You are still our hope for peace and a society that will be better." Her courage in the face of such great loss reminded us of Jacqueline Kennedy and how she helped to hold our nation together in 1963 with her demonstration of strength. When their spouses became national leaders and they found themselves playing out roles in their country's destiny, both of these women exemplified indomitable will and courage.

The emerging woman finds that she has the strength and capacity to confront challenges and seek solutions to the problems she faces, and in the process, she dedicates herself to becoming proactive. The emerging woman is capable of "reframing" her perception of experiences, and her creative mind can perceive in a myriad of ways. She pursues alternatives until she finds an acceptable and workable solution. She is unwilling to be a victim or a martyr. She sees the issues and is prepared to take action to do the personal inner work necessary for her integration.

Suggestions for Unfolding Your *Own* Potential in This Area

- Look at the challenge you are facing as honestly as possible, and use a journal to note what emotions you are experiencing.
- Acknowledge to yourself and to a friend or therapist that you are not a victim of circumstances, but you are open to exploring your alternatives.
- List all the possible solutions to your challenge that you (and your friend or therapist) can think of. Try to be creative even though some solutions seem impossible. ("Impossible" may turn out to be more viable than you think.)
- Star the solutions that you *could* do, even in part, immediately.
- Commit to one step you will take within the next three days that will lead toward resolving at least one small facet of the challenge.
- Continue adding another step every three days until you have either resolved the challenge or made peace with it.
- Affirm: *"Within me is a higher power that knows the perfect solution and will support any constructive steps that I take to find the highest good in all that is happening."*

Displays Courage, Takes Risks

The emerging woman is a risk taker. Sometimes she seems to be born with a natural tendency to be daring, which some may see as being reckless. She does things that seem to be unconventional and which can cause a certain amount of consternation to those around her. Parents, siblings and friends (or even, sometimes, her own children) shake their heads and caution her or get upset by her actions, which they view as contrary to social convention and good judgment.

However, she is often impelled by an inner longing to search, to explore, and to push her own "growing edge," which often serves to stimulate those around her. As the years go by, she makes an interesting discovery: She was born too soon! As cultural shifts occur, she finds that 15 or 20 years later, everyone is doing what was considered almost blasphemous when she did it years before. Of course, by the time those earlier actions have become acceptable and mainstream, she is off doing something else that pushes everyone's edge in still another direction, and her actions are still inspiring raised eyebrows and curiosity on the part of those in her world.

For example, some of the women who have probably baffled many people by their daring pursuits include Alison Hargreaves of Great Britain, who was the first woman to reach the top of Mount Everest, an altitude of 29,028 feet. She climbed the mountain solo, without taking oxygen tanks and other equipment with her.

Monika M. is a world adventurer many times over. Traveling alone, she was stuck in Calcutta, unable to leave India and return home because her money, passport, and green card were stolen. Yet, it was not a traumatic event for this globetrotter. She has been in 41 countries and has been robbed in Madagascar, Laos, and Thailand. She has hiked for miles through deep snow in Pakistan and was once stranded in the middle of Algeria in the dead of night. She claims that nothing frightens her; she just "goes with the flow."

A petite blonde woman who stands 5'2", Monika leaves every January for a three-month trip. She doesn't take organized tours and travels very inexpensively. She prefers getting to know the people in the countries she visits and is often given bed and board by the people she meets along the way. Monika had uterine cancer when she was 28 and breast cancer in 1986; she recovered on both occasions, but these physical challenges liberated her. Discovering that she had a lot of things she wanted to do, she decided to see the world.

Author Gail Sheehy, in her book: *New Passages, Mapping Your Life Across Time,* writes that men of two or more decades ago were complaining that they had grown and their wives hadn't, but now the roles are reversed. It is more often the woman who has an expanded vision of herself and has moved toward autonomy while claiming her personal power. This has often served to frighten the men in her life.

Still other emerging women are moving ahead and taking risks but are doing so quite unobtrusively. Therefore, many of the people around them are unaware of what is happening. Eventually it may become obvious, but it doesn't usually create "waves" in its wake— at least not for a while. These women are able to keep one foot in two worlds and are more content to undertake change or personal growth in a more cautious or methodical manner. They don't wave flags, carry banners, march in protests, or do too much to draw undue attention to themselves or their activities. This type of risk taker may go back to school, start her own business, or undertake a new venture, but she usually has a support system in place so she is not out on a limb without alternatives. She is certainly moving forward, but she is proceeding on the journey in "easy pieces."

A third kind of risk taker is the woman who, while not born with a natural affinity for taking blatant risks or even led by a driving need for change, has nonetheless come to view it as a necessary step for her emotional well-being. Often circumstances that seem beyond her control become the impetus for moving her in a new and more expanded direction. She may seek a therapist to work with or a support group that can help point the way and give her courage to propel herself forward.

The risks this type of woman takes are often quite small, but include a growing awareness that she does have needs and the right to control her own destiny. She is often afraid, but she comes to the place where she is willing to take risks in spite of her fears simply because nothing can be worse than to stagnate in her existing patterns. No longer finding the role of victim comfortable or profitable, she determines to quell her trepidations enough to tentatively take personal responsibility for moving her life forward. Once she begins, no matter how minute the steps, she discovers a feeling of real personal power and finds it exhilarating. While it's not always easy, she begins to feel the momentum necessary to impel her forward, and her life begins to change dramatically with each victory. Eventually, the change in her becomes evident, and it may shake up her life and relationships as she becomes unwilling to continue to live in the ruts of the past. Seldom does the emerging woman look back with regrets.

A risk taker is defined as a woman who is willing to "get off dead center" even when she's afraid. She is willing to sacrifice safety if need be in order to live her life more fully. She might decide to give up the corporate rat race or the security of a mundane job with benefits in order to be an adventurer prepared to find a way to earn her livelihood doing what she loves.

Kari Wagler, a young divorcee with two small daughters and a degree in English, knew she couldn't count on collecting child support from an unemployed husband. Although she could have found a job teaching, that didn't appeal to her because she wanted a flexible schedule that would allow her to be more involved with her small children and to continue her own psychospiritual journey. She decided to take a career risk that would allow time for these two pursuits even though she knew it would be a struggle to support herself and two children.

Kari first took training as a hypnotherapist and opened a small office. She was a conscientious therapist, and while it was not easy, she managed to survive. As time went by, she took additional training in alternative therapies, became a workshop leader, and eventually entered a program to obtain her Master's degree in psychology while working as a counselor in private practice. Over the years, she has been increasingly successful and has raised her children to young adulthood. She is now in a position to continue living life "her way." She has put in long, hard hours, but her goals have been unwavering and are always worth working toward.

We remember Kari's early years. At times she was scared and often at the brink financially, but her persistence and willingness to risk has brought her to the place she envisioned. Without being willing to take the chances she did, her life would have been much less satisfying.

We (Julie and Ione) both left tenured teaching jobs to move our lives in newer and more exciting directions. Each of us gave up financial security and good benefits, yet neither of us regrets our decision to work at what we love to do rather than remain in positions that were no longer soul-satisfying to us.

It has been said that all the great changes in the world have been made not by popular opinion, but by brave souls with the courage to risk, lead the way, and stand up against the criticism leveled by the majority. However, once the change has transpired, it is usually accepted by increasing numbers of people until it is more fully embraced.

We have seen many such positive and humane social changes gain increasing acceptance in the last two decades. For example, women no longer need to lie about the date of their marriage if they find themselves pregnant. In earlier decades, wedding pictures would appear in the newspaper saying the ceremony had taken place secretly a few months earlier in order to coincide with the necessary gestation time. Everyone knew, or at least suspected and gossiped about the situation, but it was the accepted way to do things. This may still happen occasionally, but for the most part, even if tongues click, it's being acknowledged that women sometimes conceive children before weddings, and even bear and keep them with about being married at all.

In earlier generations, women who were unmarried during pregnancy were often sent away without any close family support, and they had to bear the child alone in disgrace. Some claimed they were married in another state to a man they divorced and then kept their children. But, more often than not, those women were forced to give the child up for adoption and spend the rest of their life in silent shame or grief. Certainly, while we recognize the immense advantages of a loving two-parent family, it is still wonderful that many of us can view the single mother with more compassion and understanding than we did in previous generations. Certain Hollywood actresses became catalysts for change when they decided to take the risk of single parenthood. They are no longer willing to play societal games to mask their chosen behavior.

How *You* Can Learn to Take More Risks

- This week observe and record all the things you *think* about doing but tend to retreat from. Objectively evaluate all of these withdrawals. Do they contain elements of fear? Note your bodily reactions when you think about each one. (How does your stomach feel? Does your body stiffen? How does your breathing change?)
- Choose one situation to act on, completely or in part, next week.
- Role-play what you want to do or say. Solicit a supportive friend to help you, and report back to that person with the results. Often the support, as well as a verbal statement of intention, helps increase courage.
- Continue to observe and record these areas, and commit to at least one or two risks (large or small) each week.
- Keep a journal, and record your feelings about each experience. Even those risks you attempt and don't complete can give you valuable information, so be sure to record those as well.
- It's important to remember that each person may be at a slightly different "risk-taking level," so don't compare yourself to anyone else. Just be conscious about your own growing edge.
- Affirm: *"I am surrounded by the love, light, and protection of Divine Spirit, and I step forward boldly and with courage to live life fully, courageously, lovingly, and peacefully."*

Makes Her Own Choices and Is Assertive

Emerging women are assertive and make their own choices. For some women, this may mean more involvement with the world; for others it may mean less. There is no one *right* way that best serves everyone. Taking responsibility for weighing their individual needs, women are determining their own values and making the personal choices that best honor their own inner truth. Willing to reconsider and recreate their lives as they pass through the various phases and circumstances of their existence, they become adept at listening to their own rhythms.

Betty D. is a good example of an assertive woman who has a firm conviction that people should have choices about their lives and that those choices should extend to the very end. She has faced death in its various forms and has made grief presentations to discussion groups, and she was politically active in Washington state's death-with-dignity Initiative 119. She found that people want to come to terms with their own mortality and make decisions about their own death process. She is quoted as saying, "Control over one's dying is an honorable extension of living. The business of living is making choices, especially the last one." Betty puts her energy into helping secure that freedom of choice not only for herself, but for others as well.

At age 53, Marilyn M. received her degree 35 years after her college career had begun at Portland State University in Oregon. Quitting college to marry and raise a family, she focused on the traditional role model of her time. As her daughters reached adulthood and she and her husband separated, the focus and meaning of her life was gone, and she found herself in a deep depression. Mandated by necessity to enter the work force, she was encouraged to begin taking some college courses. Taking care of herself for the first time in many years and thoroughly enjoying her new adventure, she has been renewed. Looking toward the future, she sees vast new choices, and she intends to savor each one as she moves toward her immediate goal of an advanced degree in social work.

In Bangladesh, women who have been under extreme oppression

rallied to protest Islamic clerics' attacks on female education and employment. The women, 100,000 strong, converged outside Parliament. They had arrived by train and bus, and some had even hitchhiked. The rally was sponsored by the Association of Development Agencies in Bangladesh, which promotes jobs, literacy, family planning, and health care for women, and it has been the target of a campaign by Muslim clerics who seek to discredit its goals. In spite of the fact that there could be harsh repercussions, these women made a clear choice to be assertive, to find strength in numbers, and to make their collective voices heard.

These are but a few examples of the vast number of women who are awakening to their right to make choices concerning their own lives. Whatever their choices may be, emerging women insist on making their own and are willing to take the responsibility for them. Nothing boosts self-esteem and a sense of confidence more than being able to make decisions and take charge of one's life.

Developing Skill in Making Your Own Choices

- Begin by going to the library or to a bookstore to find a good book on Assertiveness Training. Learn the difference between being assertive and being aggressive. Aggressive communication accuses and blames and usually begins with "you make me feel...," whereas, assertive communication does not blame or accuse, but attempts to express personal responsibility and feelings and generally begins with "I feel...."

- Observe and record in a journal each time you back away from a personal choice because you either fear conflict or are acting out of a sense of guilt that you might "hurt someone." Begin to distinguish between what is really harmful to another and what may just be your fear of conflict. (As you evaluate, remember that in most cases, people make the choice as to how they perceive a situation. It is *not* unlov-

≈ 309

ing to be true to oneself in spite of how another may choose to view it—especially if the other person isn't getting his or her own way.)

- Begin testing your capability to be assertive. Kindly send back the food you've ordered if it isn't prepared as you asked, or graciously refuse to do a favor when it impinges on previous commitments to others or yourself.

- When you make choices, ask yourself the following questions: "Is this something I really want to do, or am I allowing someone else to make this choice for me? Am I doing this because I'll feel guilty if I don't do as I'm asked? Am I doing it because I fear the conflict that might result if I say no?"

- Observe how many times you resent doing something, but feel you have no choice in the matter. Rethink it! You have far more choice than you've allowed yourself to acknowledge.

- Affirm: *"I make my own responsible and healthy choices regarding the right use of my time and resources. I am constantly guided by an inner sense of what is right and perfect for me."*

Perpetually Learning

The new woman emerging into 21st-century American culture is more conscious than the vast majority of women in previous centuries. No longer living in a predominantly survivalist society, she is inundated by the media with new insights and opportunities for personal growth, interesting health-care alternatives, and shifting paradigms for women. She knows that she, and she alone, must take the responsibility for creating the life she wants. She is coming (or has already come) to the realization that no person or no-*thing* can complete her or be the giver of all that she needs and desires. In short, she is learning to make her own opportunities and to fulfill her own desires by taking action and creating the fertile soil for growing her own soul. This awareness is, ironically enough, a state of freedom as well as one of responsibility. It permits her to search for options and decide on a course of constructive action. No longer a pawn in someone else's hands—or a victim of fate—she is empowered to find new meaning and direction.

Thus, the emerging woman rapidly becomes an avid seeker and learner. She is open to expanding both her mind and thinking patterns through reading and other forms of information retrieval, yet she judiciously selects from the plethora of materials, as her inner guidance and wisdom direct. As she gains knowledge and skill in living out expanding and changing belief systems, she finds life—even in times of challenge—more understandable, more rewarding, and more manageable. She is, indeed, emerging from her cocoonlike existence, where she might once have lain curled up and immobile, into the world of butterflies where she tests her wings. Her emergence is a thing of beauty, and seldom would she opt to return to her former state and relinquish her freedom to fly.

When a woman is pushed into personal growth through outer circumstances—for example, if her spouse asks her for a divorce, she may find the growth shift so dramatic that she will never be the same. Should the couple get together again a few weeks or months later, the woman who has emerged during this process does not re-enter the relationship at the same level. As one woman stated, "When my husband asked to try it again, I insisted we begin all over with a period of dating and getting acquainted. I warned him that I was not, nor would I ever be again, the same woman he was previously married to or the same woman he left. He needed time to see if he really wanted me as I'd become, and I needed time to see if I could find enough commonality between us to even consider trying again."

The woman asserted that this statement did not come from a place of anger or an attempt to get even; rather, it was an honest acceptance of her own growth and self-esteem and reflected her uncertainty about whether the "new" her would find the relationship worth redeeming. She added that she would have exactly the same attitude toward any new relationship. No longer "needing" someone else to complete her or make her happy, and loving her expanding lifestyle and freedom, she would not lightly or unconsciously enter into any relationship.

The emerging woman has come to enjoy exploration into new worlds and is hooked on learning about a myriad of subjects. The increase in the number of self-help books, support groups, workshops, seminars, and lectures attest to the importance being placed on learning. An ever-increasing number of women are also attending adult learning centers and going back to college—often after their children are in school or grown—and forming spiritual support and healing circles.

Other women travel the globe as never before and are doing things only rarely accomplished by women of previous generations. Margaret De Croff Millsap, 68, of Spokane, Washington, is a perfect example. She jumped at the chance to bicycle through the Netherlands. She went alone and pedaled 796 miles, visiting all 12 provinces, staying at bed-and-breakfast inns, and sometimes riding in 90-degree weather. She loved it!

From 1985 to 1988, we (Julie and Ione) traveled the entire United States and supported ourselves by giving workshops wherever we went. It was a wonderful time of adventure, and we were both teachers and students simultaneously. We often had people raise their eyebrows and ask how we managed on the road—two middle-aged women driving a motor home alone. And yet, in many of those voices there was as much envy as there was surprise.

Whatever learning mode she chooses, the emerging woman is interested in finding answers and understanding both herself and her world in-depth. She has become a perpetual learner.

Suggestions for Satisfying Your Thirst for Knowledge

- Look in your local community college catalogs for courses

that might appeal to you, and register for one class.

- Peruse the community column of your local newspaper where lectures, workshops, and seminars are listed, and commit yourself to attending at least one every two or three months.

- Search the self-help or spiritual shelves of your local library or bookstore and find at least one book to read each month. (Some excellent selections are listed in the back of this book.)

- Scan your local newspaper for places or projects that appeal to your sense of personal values, and commit yourself to do something that reaches out to touch the lives of others. (Sometimes it is best to make a one-time or brief commitment to a project until you ascertain if it is a meaningful activity for you.) You might explore causes such as Habitat for Humanity, helping out in your local school, participating in local clean-up or environmental projects, working in your local Meals-on-Wheels-type program, volunteering for the campaign of someone running for office whose values you admire, joining the Women of Vision and Action Network, forming a women's healing circle, or becoming involved in any other project that appeals to you.

- Affirm:*"My mind and heart are open to the expanded learning and understanding of things physical, emotional, mental, and spiritual. The right opportunities are presenting themselves to me on a daily basis, and I am always divinely guided to my highest good."*

Interested in Self-Knowledge, Self-Observation

The emerging woman seeks to become more aware of what energies motivate her actions and control her daily life. Through self-help groups, healing circles, therapeutic work, reading, meditation, dream work, or a combination of techniques, she is gaining insight and understanding into what often compels her reactions. Through this insight into her inner life and thought processes, she can gradually move from unconscious reactions to conscious responses and from being compelled to being impelled. There is a vast difference between being a responder versus being a reactor. The more she understands herself, the more she understands the wide range of possible motivations that lie behind the behavior of others. With increased understanding comes compassion—both for herself and for others. Much of what appears as chaos on our planet is a result of our failure to understand our own motives or those that underlie the behavior of our fellow humans. We forget that we are, indeed, all *one*.

The emerging woman becomes an astute self-observer. She often begins this process by looking for the areas of her life that are unproductive and asking herself, "Why?" She is not afraid to look at her unvarnished self, nor is she afraid to seek answers and understanding. She does not berate herself when she observes her own inappropriate reactions; she has long since learned that every event provides a growth opportunity. However, she does take detached note of it in order to explore what may have precipitated her behavior in that particular moment. Under those conditions, she will be more likely be a "responder" the next time a similar situation occurs.

Older people often engage in a life review of sorts and look back over their lives to try and make sense of it all. They will often attempt to complete any "unfinished business" and resolve any conflicts or emotions that have created separation between themselves and those they love. However, the real beauty of the emerging woman is that she is no longer waiting for the last stage of life to look back and make sense of it all. Instead, she is using her powers of observation to comprehend events as they unfold before her. She finds her lessons and resolutions moment by moment, which keeps her life current. Looking at life honestly and making its daily lessons her "temple and her religion," as the philosopher Kahlil Gibran so aptly advises, becomes a vital part of her spiritual practice and journey. She fully realizes that having a peaceful world is contingent on first finding peace within herself.

Ione once observed herself having negative feelings each time she looked at a certain person in one of her classes. Since she'd had no personal contact with this individual that could have precipitated such emotions, she began to explore the root cause of her reaction. In doing so, she discovered that this particular person looked like and had similar mannerisms to a woman she had known several years earlier. This earlier acquaintance—a religious fundamentalist with deep fears— was frightened of Ione and her expanded belief system and had spread ugly and untrue rumors about her. Ione discovered that she was unconsciously projecting that past unpleasantness on the innocent woman in her class. Only through honest self-observation could she change her thought patterns and project love instead.

Of course, the opposite reaction is also true. Have you ever found yourself immediately drawn to a stranger who reminds you of someone you admire or love? Observing ourselves carefully throughout the day is a real eye-opener and provides an interesting glimpse into the vast number of ways we act out of deep internal energies. Self-observation gives the emerging woman special opportunities to learn about herself and to acquire skill in living life more consciously and, ultimately, more powerfully. Self-observation is, without a doubt, the single most important way of allowing true transformation to evolve.

Developing Techniques of Self-Observation

- Begin to develop the capacity to step back and observe the dynamics of situations happening around you. How are you feeling about them? How is your body reacting? What is happening to those around you? Is anyone able to respond thoughtfully, or is everyone reacting?

- Write your thoughts down in a journal after the situation is over. Record your observations, including your own reactions or lack of response.

- After you have completed writing about the particular situation, ask yourself these questions: "If I could do it over, how could I have handled it differently? What did I observe and learn about myself?" (It's important not to flagellate yourself; remain the objective observer and know that you are learning about yourself as well as your possible choices for responding.)
- Observe if your reaction to the situation triggers any memories of other times or places where similar circumstances and reactions have occurred. Ask yourself if there is any indication that you may need some inner healing (inner child) work to resolve any old issues. If the answer is yes, you may wish to seek outside help in finding some resolution.
- Practice being mindful of your emotions and reactions as they are happening.
- Review the day's events before going to bed each night, and gently observe your role in each one.
- Affirm: *"I am a living, breathing, expanding human being, and I am learning to respond creatively and positively to all people and to all situations."*

Recognizes the Need for Balance

The emerging woman recognizes the need for balance and constantly tries to find and maintain that delicate line between the various facets of her life. She wants to be sensitive and caring *but* not overly sensitive and taken advantage of; she seeks both a rich inner *and* rich outer life; she wants to be strong *yet* gentle; involved *but also* independent (with time for solitude); she seeks to value inner truth *while* staying open to other opinions; she needs to express her feminine side *while* rejecting female stereotypes and role expectations; she has to have time to develop her own interests or career *and* have time for home and family. These are but a sampling of the issues women struggle to balance.

Depending on age and other considerations, the balancing issues women face are both universal and individual. However, unlike earlier generations, the struggle between job or career versus home and family has never been greater, and women are finding that an assessment of individual circumstances and personality are the only criteria for judging which is best in any given situation. According to a study by Louis Harris and Associates, many women understand that both career and family are essential, and a majority of American women wouldn't give up either the nurturer or provider role. According to Ellen Galinsky, project director of the study, "Most women feel they are providing for *and* nurturing their families. They do have too much to do, but they see it as a weighed scale and not one that's tipping."

Anna Quindlen, already the recipient of a Pulitzer Prize, left her job at the *New York Times* to write fiction from her home office. She was widely thought to be the first woman likely to break through the top ranks of that esteemed newspaper, but she relinquished that possibility in order to obtain more balance in her life. Having lost her own mother to ovarian cancer when she was still a teenager, Quindlen wants more than just quality time with her children; she wants quantity time as well. However, she was balancing that act long before she chose to resign her job as op-editor for the *New York Times*; she also wanted time to write novels. Anna asserts that real power comes from being able to balance her life, to do what she wants, and to make it pay!

Seeking balance in a world sometimes severely out of balance is a top priority for most emerging women. Many are making time to plant a garden, take a yoga class, write in a journal, work on dreams, meditate, or sip a leisurely cup of tea with a friend; they are valuing simplicity, inner harmony, and contentment. Often women find that while they must financially support themselves or help support their family, they want to make their life count for something greater than just acquiring material possessions. They aspire to work in fields that give meaning to their existence and that promote a gentler and kinder world. No longer content to focus solely on "me and mine," they move to expand their creativity, and endeavor to be more inclusive and concerned about others in both their thinking and actions.

We both find that as writers, seminar leaders, and counselors, our work goes much more smoothly when we carefully monitor our lives to include a healthy balance of activities. We normally begin our days with meditation, journaling, and dream work, and then when we're at home, we divide our remaining hours into segments for writing, errands, household chores, appointments and meetings, and for relaxation and entertainment, either alone or with friends. We are a part of a women's healing circle that meets regularly for prayer, spiritual growth experiences, and to discuss planetary concerns. Our life, on the whole, is a balance between inner- and outer-directed activities— with both giving out and taking in. When we are on the road, we sometimes find it harder to stay balanced, but we are committed to finding the delicate point that allows us to remain centered wherever we happen to be.

We are usually able to balance our lives and vary our activities in a very healthy manner, but we must stay conscious about it, for the tendency and temptation to overextend is ever-present. When any one of the three of us who shares our home here at the Holo Center starts to get irritable, it is a definite warning, and one that calls for examination of where our balance has gone awry. It is almost always an overload in one area or another that calls for an immediate adjustment.

Learning How to Develop a Balanced Lifestyle

- Define and list the "push/pulls" in your life—things such as: work/play, involvement/solitude, career/family, rest/activity, and so on.
- Observe which side of the "push/pull" polarities gets the most attention from you. Begin to explore some of the ways that you can begin to equalize them a little better.
- Determine which areas can be better equalized on a daily, weekly, monthly, or yearly basis. (If you work all week,

you may have to equalize by taking one weekend a month for a mini-vacation away from home; or if your employment is seasonal, you may work longer hours for six months of the year and create more personal time the other six months.)

- Honestly look at all the things you do, and determine how many of them are truly necessary. Think about eliminating some of the unnecessary or less important activities.

- In all areas of your life where others are involved, decide if responsibilities are equally shared. If not, insist on a more equitable division of labor.

- Affirm: *"Balance brings more order, productivity, and health into my life. I deserve time to be all that I truly am and to enjoy all that I do. A healthy balance is my divine right, and from this moment on, I am attaining that balance in my life."*

Independent, Autonomous, Self-Actualizing, Self-Governing

The emerging woman develops a capacity for deep introspection in order to find her own inner truth and integrity. It is within herself that she discovers what she values, and it may not necessarily come from the prevailing societal standards. Maslow found in his studies that self-actualizing people accept what is good about the American system and reject what isn't. The emerging woman also lives from the center of her own being rather than adhering strictly to the shifting winds of acceptability. She is not prone to yield to peer pressure or other people's opinions unless they resonate with her own deep inner sense of truth.

As we spoke with a woman who was a part of the counter-culture movement of the 1960s, she made some vital statements concerning her emerging self:

When I "dropped out" in the '60s, I thought I disdained wealth and embraced its polar opposite. So for a time I lived a nomad life of poverty, and perhaps that was necessary in order to shed the culture's programmed worship of material goods. However, as the years went by and I matured, the realization dawned that it was not money per se that I was spurning. In my youthful exuberance, I had mistaken it for what was really bothering me. What I valued was independence, the freedom to explore my world and to live in a manner that was different from my parents and the world I grew up in. It was freedom and simplicity that I was seeking; I didn't want to be tied down to the care, protection, and support of possessions.

As I gained experience in unfolding my own talents and passions, I eventually found that I could make a decent living doing what I loved. I didn't have to hate what I was doing—as my parents had—just to make money. It was a wonderful revelation to discover that I could make a good income by freelancing and working at what I loved. I probably labor as hard as my parents did, and often put in longer hours, but the difference is loving what I do! And, while I'm also able to earn a healthy income, I use it differently than did my family of origin.

My home is simple, and furnished with comfortable and easy-to-care-for things. There are the necessities, but I place no emphasis on accumulating. I love to travel and explore different cultures, and I enjoy contributing to causes that make the planet a better and safer place for my children. I value in-depth and long-lasting connections with people, and I shun the artificial roles and games my parents played in order to get and stay ahead in the jobs they hated. I'm not willing to play games; I want to be as authentic and honest as I'm capable of being in any given moment. I don't want to perpetuate a lie about who I am either to myself or anyone else.

I'm happy with the path I've chosen, and while I would never feel comfortable trying to impose my way on another human being, I'm always being told by someone that they envy me. Friends tell me they admire my courage for taking the risks I took in my early years in order to evolve to my present state of being. I guess if I were someone else, I would envy me, too, because I'm exactly where I want to be even though I'll always be learning, growing, and expanding my consciousness. I feel confident enough to make changes in my life at any time I choose, and possibly that has become my most treasured gift!

In developing and retaining her personal sense of power, the emerging woman is also learning to tear down her walls. In other words, the more secure she becomes in who she is, the less she feels any need to defend herself. She is able to state her convictions and let the chips fall where they may. This is done neither out of rebellion nor out of a need to shock. It comes from a place of inner integrity and honesty; it is done out of a need to express her true nature. Whether others agree with her or not is less important than the desire to be authentic. The emerging woman is developing strong and healthy ego boundaries, expressing them with clarity and firmly maintaining them despite outside demands.

Ione's mother used to say, "If you love me, you'll show it by doing as I ask." This is both a manipulation and a common distortion of the meaning of love. It took Ione almost four decades to realize that *love* does not necessarily give others what they demand or want. Since she desired to be a loving person, she had figured that love meant always doing what others wanted; when she didn't, she felt unloving and demeaned herself. She finally realized that *love* means being true to the course of one's own soul and allowing others to do likewise; it means being kind even when saying no without compromise. When someone levels the accusation that we are being selfish, it's usually because we are not doing what they "selfishly" want us to do, and if we will remember this, we can guide our life without feeling defensive.

The emerging woman cuts her co-dependent ties with her own parents, with her own children, and with others who would try to tie her into guilt. This does not mean that she doesn't listen to the opinions and ideas presented by others, nor does she deliberately refuse to learn or refuse to respectfully weigh calm well-presented viewpoints. It does mean that she is not a puppet on someone else's emotional string, and she carefully weighs what another is asking or demanding in light of her self-understanding. Since she has already released her need to be liked or accepted, she can come from a place of inner security and make a solid decision about what she feels is right for her to do. She does not need to be defensive because she is coming to thoroughly accept her own power and embrace the evolution of her own soul.

Developing Values to Live By

- Work toward clarifying your values. Record these values in your journal, and refine them over a period of several weeks or months. It's a good idea to review your values at least once or twice a year—updating as you reprogram and reweave your life.

- Once your set of basic values has been clearly defined, observe how frequently you make your decisions and responses in accordance with what you value. Record in your journal both your successes and failures.

- When you have made a choice contrary to one of your basic values, evaluate whether you did so from outside pressure, fear, guilt, etc. (Perhaps someone is making derogatory, prejudiced, or uncomplimentary statements about another person in your presence and you have laughed or kept silent even when you value being free of prejudice.)

- Play that choice over and see how many other ways you might have responded that would better reflect what you value. Role-play it with a friend, and collaborate on an appropriate response the next time a similar situation occurs.

- Affirm: *"I honor those things that I value, and I make my decisions and live my life according to my core beliefs. I am a strong, multifaceted, and autonomous woman, able to act on what I believe to be right. I am a positive influence in my world."*

Strong Sense of Self, Refuses to Accept Limitations

The emerging woman works on maintaining her trust and faith in herself. Even when she makes mistakes, she knows it is an opportunity to learn, and since she neither thinks of herself as incapable nor infallible, she is learning to take it all in stride. She is fully aware of her strengths, as well as her lack of expertise or skill in other areas, so while constantly trying to improve or expand her abilities and learn more about her "shadows" and unconscious motives, she nonetheless has a realistic understanding of who she is.

With this strong sense of self, emerging women are aware of their androgynous nature and are no longer willing to only play out the traditional roles assigned to them. They ask for the opportunities that allow them to unfold their potential and use every talent and ability they possess. This often means moving into occupations traditionally filled by men, and women are accomplishing this in many different fields. They want to be acknowledged for their talents and not suppressed because of gender issues.

The Women's Auto Clinic in Newport News, Virginia; and My Favorite Mechanic, in Atlanta, Georgia, are just two of a growing number of garages that are owned and operated by women. Janet Brown, an older woman who founded the Women's Auto Clinic, feels that more women's garages will be opened. Women still only comprise a small percentage of the total number of auto mechanics, but the numbers are growing, and more women are entering the field. Margie Seals, owner of My Favorite Mechanic, says her business has been successful since day one.

Women once took their identity, and thus their value and worth, from their husband's role in the world, and if he left, so did their sense of self. No longer content to live out a vicarious identity, women are not only seeking employment outside the home, but they are becoming the employers as well. According to a recent study by the National Foundation for Women Business Owners and Dun & Bradstreet, women-owned businesses are not only flourishing, but are more likely to succeed than the average American company.

According to this study, women employ about a third more workers in the United States than the Fortune 500 companies do worldwide.

With a strong sense of their personal value and ability, women are a strong proactive force. They are stepping in to do things that need to be done and that have been long overlooked. They have created women's resource centers and battered women's shelters, they have brought child-abuse issues to the foreground, and they have been active in forcing legislation to guarantee the rights of women and children. While the job is not finished yet, they are a diligent bunch, and with patience and fortitude, they keep hammering away at the issues.

And what has become obvious throughout many of the profiles in this book is that women are the peacemakers, too. They are not only nurturers for their immediate families, but they are striving to nurture new concepts, give birth to new ideas and paradigms, and to be visionaries of a global transformation. The ability to accomplish these tasks arises out of a soul that does the inner work necessary to make the outer action productive and powerful. With a strong sense of who and what we are as women and as individuals, there is no limit to what can collectively be accomplished.

<u>Some Practical Steps for Overcoming Limitations</u>

- Note in a journal those things you think you'd like to do (for yourself or in the world) if....
- Record what you view as the limitations that prevent you from fulfilling these desires.
- Go over the list you have just made and honestly determine how many limitations are imposed by the culture and how many are self-imposed or seem impossible due to personal circumstances.
- Look at the limitations that seem to come from the culture, and determine whether or not you want to fulfill your

desires enough to buck the system and other people's opinions in order to accomplish your dreams.

- Determine which limitations are self-imposed or seem to come from your personal circumstances. How many of your goals could be accomplished in some measure with a little planning and reorganizing of your life and/or finances?

- Choose one item from your list of desires, and despite all outer appearances of limitation, begin to take steps to make it happen. Refuse to allow negative opinions to deter you, but instead, as in the children's book *The Little Engine That Could,* repeat to yourself: "I think I can, I think I can, I think I can." With each success, your sense of self increases.

- Call on a Higher Power, according to your personal belief system, to help open doors and give you the courage to forge ahead. (Remember how Rama Vernon, without personal resources, received all the airline tickets she needed for her many trips to Russia? This type of story is not at all uncommon for those asking for the help that comes from a greater source.)

- Affirm: *"I am free, I am unlimited, I am victorious over all circumstances and am able to accomplish my deepest desires. I know that my path is already laid out before me, and the energy of the Holy Spirit draws to me my highest good."*

Thoughtfully Ascertains Values and Sets Goals

The emerging woman has deeply held values and tries to live her life in alignment with what she believes. She is also able to set whatever goals are necessary to live according to those principles. Many women feel that a good education for their children is a core value, and they set a goal of making regular contributions to a savings plan in order to be certain that their daughters receive the same opportunities as their sons. Many emerging women believe that in order to demonstrate a female's worth to their daughters, they must set self-improvement goals and model behaviors that portray a sense of self-esteem and competence. It may mean modeling the role of a woman who is active in the world, expressing concern for local and global issues, and working in her way to help give birth to a new consciousness—both personally and universally.

Women are emerging and creating evolutionary changes in almost every facet of life and defining their values by looking deep inside themselves. They are not willing to follow a tradition that no longer makes sense. Margaret MacCurtain, an Irish Catholic nun, is preaching that the Roman Catholic hierarchy is wrong and that divorce is a decision that rightfully belongs to the individual.

Rebecca Nappi (profiled earlier in this book), an editor for the *Spokesman Review* in Spokane, Washington, wrote an editorial that stated in part: "Janet Reno is in trouble for being, as some call her, 'chief of the federal thugs,' and Joycelyn Elders got in so much trouble she lost her job." Rebecca concludes that it's a wonderful thing when women get into trouble, and says, "Our society should celebrate each time a high-profile woman gets in trouble for the right reasons. For sticking to her guns. For refusing to apologize if she's right. For admitting a mistake. For telling the truth, even if the truth is painful."

According to Nappi, "Women have truly arrived when they are in trouble for their ideas and convictions, and not because they have strayed from our culture's opinion about what women ought to be and do." She feels that "young girls should see and know that women troublemakers blaze the way for change." Truly, all of us as women have the opportunity to be conscious role models, motivators, and mentors, and we certainly can be the agents of change and create a new paradigm for the young women of our world.

Not all emerging women have exactly the same values and goals, even though many seem to be very similar, but most are certain about their personal belief systems and work to live in accordance with what they have ascertained to be important. One of the more interesting discoveries we made as we researched the shifting roles of women in today's world was that even when women play out what appears to be traditional roles, there is often more than meets the eye. For some women, "mothering" is a definite value and career choice.

Beth, a professionally trained woman and wife of a busy physician with ample financial resources, has chosen to stay home and make children her career while they are still of preschool age. "The children are small for such a short time, and I am the one who can best model the values I wish to instill in them," she declares. An intelligent, active woman who will one day resume a career, she is, for the present, immersed in raising her small children, and is obviously enjoying every moment of it.

Women who value child-rearing as a top priority are very clear about the importance of their role, and while they may be involved in volunteer work or are even willing to take on limited work assignments, they have no doubt about their personal values and priorities. They have carefully considered their choices, and many have arrived at the conclusion that they are not willing to sacrifice families for corporate benefits. These women have often consciously chosen to bear children, and they want to be a primary influence in their youngsters' life; they have begun to value nonmaterial gain over acquisition of material goods.

These women, unlike their earlier sisters who often retreated from the work force and stayed home because it was expected, love to be productive and engaged in life while being deeply involved with home and family. For them, it is neither a dull nor thankless job, but a role they find stimulating and rewarding. It can also allow a certain amount of freedom to pursue other interests, such as additional education, freelance work, or social reform.

Some women are taking on the tremendous responsibility of home-schooling their children for periods of time. The reasons for doing so are varied, but in each case the mothers are convinced they can offer their children more than the outside world provides. Strong convictions and a belief in the values they wish to impart impel women to become at least part-time teachers and orchestrators of their children's education.

One woman was chagrined that the educational system was so restrictive due to pressures from fundamentalist-oriented parents. She wanted her children to be empowered through exposure to a wide variety of processes that included visualization, open exploration of all issues, and the use of various creative and innovative techniques. After trying unsuccessfully to encourage the local school system to implement a more expansive program, and thwarted by a fearful school board, she decided to leave full-time university teaching to educate her children according to her understanding of what good education should be. She firmly adhered to the concept that education, at its best, consists of opening minds to rich possibilities and helping children learn how to question, explore, and theorize.

Sometimes empowered women decide, for a myriad of reasons, that they want more quality time for their families, and yet, they place a high value on their careers and their own need for individuation, so they remain in their jobs or careers at a less involved level. Others, while valuing their families deeply, feel the need or desire to remain fully involved in their jobs or professions. And there are among us those emerging women who have such an overwhelming passion and deep sense of mission for the greater good of humanity that they choose to remain child free or model for their families a different kind of commitment. The common denominator in any of these circumstances is reduced to one simple fact—emerging women make their choices after thoughtful consideration of their own unique situations, and then, with the courage of their convictions, they carry through their decisions in a way uniquely appropriate for them.

Strategies for Developing Goals

- Under the section entitled *Independent, Autonomous, Self-Actualizing, Self-Governing*, there are suggestions for clarifying your values. If you have not already completed this step, it is important to do so now. In order to ascertain what goals are worth obtaining, you need to know what you value.

- As you look at what you value, take your journal and begin to form some immediate goals. (If you value time for spiritual activities, you might set a goal of meditating for 10 minutes twice a day.)

- On a separate page of your journal, determine your long-term goals and begin to break them down into attainable pieces. (If you value advanced education and want a degree, you may have to set an overall goal for the number of years you feel it will take to reach it. Then you may set smaller goals concerning the number of credits you want to take each year.)

- On still another page, jot down future goals. Since you do not want to overwhelm yourself and be unrealistic in what is possible, you can set some goals aside for later. However, it is a good idea to always have new ideas ready as circumstances change, so it doesn't hurt to have dreams ready!

- As suggested in the section on values, review your goals every few months to be certain you are on target with them. If they are inadequate, revise them, or if they are no longer viable, revamp them to fit your ever-changing, growing lifestyle.

- Affirm: *"I create my life by the goals I set and attain. I am committed to accomplishing those objectives that are important to me, and I have the will and self-discipline to reach my highest good. I fully participate with Spirit in unfolding my perfect path, and I give thanks that it is manifesting now."*

Possesses a Zest for Life, a License to Be Outrageous

Emerging women have a zest for living. While all may not take out a license to be outrageous, they certainly exude a certain quality of enthusiasm, hope, and faith in what they are doing and in their life's purpose.

Without fail, when each woman profiled was asked to describe what she was currently involved in, her voice took on a vibrancy and enthusiasm that was exciting to hear. Each one expressed a deep passion for her chosen work and has faith in and commitment to the mission she is pursuing! The emerging woman certainly believes her life is important and her energies will make a difference. She has a zest for life, and no obstacle holds her back; she views challenges merely as opportunities to learn or as reasons to creatively explore a different path to achieve the end result. She is alive, and her obvious involvement with what she is doing is truly contagious.

Fritz Perls (the father of Gestalt therapy) said that everyone should be born with a license to be outrageous, and many emerging women allow themselves to occasionally indulge in a bit of outrageousness. As Norman Cousins demonstrated in his book, *The Anatomy of an Illness,* humor and fun are essential parts of healing and wholeness. As serious as our tasks and passions may be, we all need the balance of humor to keep things in perspective. We both love to observe people in the act of being outrageous, and we have a tendency to cheer them on a bit. We once watched a woman at a concert in California whose full-length coat was totally covered with buttons containing every conceivable message. It was obvious she was having a wonderful time strutting through the crowd looking much like a peddler.

Elizabeth Schuett, a teacher and writer from Ohio, tells of a time she and a friend were in Cannon Beach, Oregon, and she was sprawled out on a floor sorting through a mass of earrings while her friend tried on toe rings. She said that between them they had lived 114 years and raised three children. They were, in her words "acting as through we barely had good sense and loving every minute of it."

We have often mused that we take life so much less seriously, have much more fun, and do far more daring things than we did when we were younger. Having shed some of the programming from our past and no longer concerned about "what the neighbors might think," we often delight in being outrageous. Laughter is a universal language, and it's hard to hate someone with whom you've just shared a deep belly laugh!

A Few Suggestions for Developing a Zest for Living

- Observe how you feel about the activities that comprise your waking hours. Do you enjoy them? Do they stimulate you? Are they creative? Do they provide you with a deep sense of satisfaction? Do they lead you into new avenues of self-discovery? Do they convey a sense of purpose and meaning beyond the personal self?

- If you find that you have an overabundance of meaningless duty-type activities, begin to sort out which ones are necessary and which are not. Begin to eliminate those that have just become habitual and unproductive. (Don't worry what other people think you "should" do— make your own conscious choices.)

- Look at those tasks that are necessary but do not give you pleasure. Are there some ways you can spice them up? (Two sisters in Iowa used to do their ironing together one night a week. The husbands bowled in a league on Friday evenings, so the sisters got together, and while their children played, they talked and caught up on one another's week and accomplished what each considered to be an otherwise boring task.)

- If you find that you have too few activities that bring you deep satisfaction or a sense of buoyancy and excitement while doing them, you probably haven't found your passion. Begin looking for at least one or two things that you can really immerse yourself in and love doing. There are plenty of opportunities to explore various avenues of expression until you find those that speak deeply to you. These may include both personal and/or service projects. Remember, it's important to your health and well-being to maintain an excitement about life.

- Allow yourself occasional indulgences in harmless acts of outrageousness. Gather a group of friends for an evening of fun and laughter. Provide some props (such as masks, puppets, etc.), and put on some impromptu performances.
- During a warm summer's downpour, allow yourself to go out and dance in the rain—it's okay to get drenched!
- Observe when those instantaneous impulses hit to do or say something outrageous. Instead of repressing the desire, allow yourself to look ridiculous for a spontaneous moment of harmless fun and laughter. (One evening in downtown San Francisco, a friend flung her scarf over her shoulder and sashayed across the intersection singing, "Hello, Dolly" a la Carol Channing.)
- Affirm: *"My enthusiasm for life, my zest for living, and my ability for harmless and sometimes outrageous behavior is a divine gift. I revel in the excitement and joy of living life to its fullest extent. I am blessed."*

Expresses Sexuality in a Healthful Way

Emerging women do not fear their own sexuality. They are fully aware that it cannot be contained in neat little boxes tied with a bow, nor can it always wear a definitive label. For generations, women have been coerced into conforming to the limited and prevailing cultural norms regarding their more sensual natures. This has often meant either denial and repression of certain aspects of their sexuality, or taking the risk of being given uncomplimentary labels. Since the 1960s, many women have been freeing themselves to explore the heights and depths of their sexuality and are often surprised to find that it is a multifaceted exploration. They find that human sexuality is not always, if ever, a simple matter, but rather, it is a rich tapestry woven in threads of many textures, hues, and patterns.

Traditionally, women have not been taught that they deserve fulfillment in a sexual relationship. Rarely have mothers in past generations offered their daughters advice on what kind of sensual or sexual fulfillment they have a right to seek or expect. As women, many of us (especially those over 40) received instructions from our mothers, probably the night before our wedding, which went something like this: (1) Keep him happy in the bedroom and he won't go looking for other women, and (2) give "it" to him when he wants it; it will be over in a few minutes.

All too many women have been taught to view their sexuality in this manner, and while more open sexual attitudes have brought up some other issues to be resolved (venereal disease, AIDS, and so on), it has also helped women to realize that procreation might not be the only function of their sexuality.

As women embrace their sexual nature and explore all its various facets either consciously or through material revealed in dreams, they seldom find it to be a clear-cut issue. When they bravely confront the honest facts and feelings, many often go through a state of confusion wondering whether they may be homosexual, heterosexual, bisexual, or just plain promiscuous. (It was reported in a recent television documentary that the anthropologist Margaret Mead believed bisexuality is the natural condition.) While some cultures are more accepting of varying sexual expressions, our country has been so homophobic that it has not been willing to honestly confront the issues surrounding human sexual desires. We have been in such deep cultural denial about sexuality in general and about homoerotic feelings, specifically, that we have failed to recognize that almost every human being experiences them at some point in time. We have found over the years that as we work deeply with people and their dreams, they often discover many aspects of their sexuality for the first time.

Emerging women, however, know they are free to make choices

about how they will or will not express their sensual natures and are, therefore, not afraid to own all aspects of their sexuality—whether it be a strong inclination or merely a fleeting thought. Some women discover their attraction to other women as they grow older and after they have considered themselves to be heterosexual for most of their adult lives. Some choose to experiment with this aspect and find deep and long-lasting satisfaction in these new relationships. Author Gail Sheehy, in her book *New Passages: Mapping Your Life Across Time*, says that many women over the age of 50, and "particularly those who have lived with traditional men for most of their adult lives, are starving for intimacy." Sheehy maintains that a growing number of these women are "opening up to the possibilities of same-sex intimacy." She goes on to say, "Clinical experience suggests that the number of women who were previously heterosexual and who are choosing or exploring gay lifestyles in middle life is growing and may well be above 50 percent. The psychological literature reports, 'They describe finding intimacy with women at levels and depths they have never before imagined or experienced.'" Still other women find that even though they have expressed themselves solely as lesbians, they have a heterosexual side longing to be defined. An acquaintance of ours who had always considered herself in homosexual terms called recently to say that at age 40 she had recently married and was loving that experience, too.

Whether women are choosing to express themselves as heterosexuals or homosexuals, many are realizing the bisexual possibilities within them. Two friends of ours, Sue and Kate, told us that as young women of the '60s, they had experienced a variety of sexual relationships, and both women confessed that they could easily have gone either way in a long-term committed relationship. They explained that they had each made a conscious choice while in their late twenties to go in the direction of their heterosexuality because they wanted children, and they felt the children would benefit by having a balance of male and female energy during their childhood. The women were happy with their choice, but they honored the validity of both sides of their sexuality even though they had also made a conscious choice to be monogamous. Other women conclude that the sexuality they have always expressed, whether homosexual or heterosexual, is, indeed, their more natural expression, but they do not fear owning up to the other possibilities if those feelings should arise.

And, finally, some emerging women find that they need either a short- or long-term period of celibacy. Being able to embrace that course of action and allow themselves space from all sexual activity is another powerful position. It is a conscious choice that can allow energy for a variety of pursuits and creative activity that might otherwise be diverted.

This new view of sexuality allows emerging women to know and understand aspects of themselves that may have been, heretofore, largely unconscious. With awareness comes a wide range of possibilities and options. Albeit difficult to "buck" social norms and familial expectations, women now have the opportunity to select from a wide range of choices. Since emerging women are learning to be risk takers in many areas of their lives, they are likely to begin opening some of these more nontraditional doors.

Perhaps the most obvious example of an emerging woman who, with personal honesty and integrity, made the decision to challenge conventional mores and live her life according to her inner sense of truth, is Margarethe Cammermeyer. She is the highest-ranking officer in the military to be discharged for being gay. While answering questions to gain top-secret clearance in the Washington National Guard in 1989, she simply said she was a lesbian when asked about homosexuality. A colonel with 27 years of outstanding military service, she was discharged in 1992 for no offense except her sexual orientation. Even though married for 15 years and the mother of four sons, Margarethe has embraced her lesbian sexuality and built a life with another woman. Cammermeyer, a decorated Vietnam veteran, says that coming out was very difficult, but she can vouch for the freedom she has found as a result.

Through the willingness to look at all the possibilities inherent within their sexual or sensual nature, some women are, essentially, "touching the forbidden." But according to the last levels of

335

Maslow's hierarchy, whenever anyone achieves autonomy and self-actualization, the values and the rules by which they govern their lives come not necessarily from society, but from looking deep inside themselves. Emerging women are doing just that.

Developing Healthy Attitudes Toward Your Sexuality

- Thoughtfully write down your early impressions regarding sexuality in general and your own, specifically.
- Explore how many of those ideas still permeate your consciousness and imprint your current view. Are they healthy concepts? Have they served you well?
- If the answer to those last two questions is no, ask yourself how those early attitudes have impacted your life. How would you like it to be different?
- Begin by learning to love your own body—just as it is. Indulge yourself in sensual pleasures such as bubble baths with candlelight, special bath oils, or luxurious lotions.
- Open your mind and read some of the many new and enlightening books concerning human sexuality—you can find them in libraries and bookstores. (There is an abundance of books on relationships and sexuality that are written from a very spiritual perspective. Seek and you shall find!)
- Replace those old attitudes through working with your inner child in individual therapy or with a support group. Support groups abound, so check your local newspaper, 12-step programs, metaphysical bookstores, or health food stores for information or notices about time and place.
- Affirm: *"I am a loving, sensual human being entitled to joy, love, and intimacy. I express myself in deeply meaningful and satisfying ways. I am a divine spirit clothed in an earth suit, and as such, my sexuality expressed through love in its myriad forms is a pure form of prayer."*

Accepts Change as a Part of Life

The emerging woman understands that change can be a positive experience. She may have preferences as to the way she would like things to be, but she has learned not to be addicted to outcomes. Even when she has given her best to any situation, she realizes that releasing her attachment to the final outcome is important to her peace of mind. Changes can be "grist for her mill" and can reflect things that she may need to learn about herself or others.

One trait that permeates throughout the emerging women we have observed or interviewed for this book, is they all seem to be "response—able," responders to life (not reactors) and are learning to flow with changing conditions; they are striving to become flexible even while deeply engaged in life and its various activities. Many interviewees assured us that, in retrospect, often the changes they resisted the most when they occurred are the very ones they now look back on as blessings. These situations ended up being the catalysts for bringing them into an expanded experience that couldn't have otherwise occurred. Most of us can probably look back at something we resisted and see how it ultimately benefited us; we just weren't able to see the long-range results at the time.

"Don't push the river, it flows best all by itself" is a familiar quotation. This is certainly not to say that emerging women are content to sit back and not do what they can to make a difference. They are, however, able to sense how, when, and where their energies are most likely to succeed in creating necessary change and are able to build new pathways to achieve a goal when that becomes necessary.

The only certainty is change! Things are always changing—evolution is always happening, and to stay stuck in one place mourning the past reduces the likelihood of being able to enjoy other rich and rewarding experiences. Aging is an ongoing process, and to try to escape is to no avail. Women certainly go through many stages of evolution as the years go by, but they also take useful lessons and other elements from each stage along with them.

We recently took note of three articles on the issue of aging gracefully. One was written by a woman who had just celebrated her 30th birthday and found herself "advancing to a different phase of life." She commented on the enormous shifts that had occurred in her life during the past decade, and while she bemoaned some of the physical changes, she admitted to loving the emotional ones—the maturity and the new and evolving relationship with herself. The second article focused on a book by Erica Jong, *Fear of Fifty: A Midlife Memoir,* and the third was entitled "Older Can Be Better" written by a 60-year-old. In each of these offerings, despite a three-decade age difference among the authors, it was evident that the women were flowing with the changes that age offered and were finding richness in spite of a cultural belief that aging is to be avoided. Wisdom and self-assurance were prevalent common denominators.

All change offers opportunities to learn and to expand our horizons. It challenges us to bring our full creative capacity to bear upon whatever circumstances seem to dictate. Nowhere is this better demonstrated than in the profile of Judith Billings, Washington State Superintendent of Schools. Change is accepted by emerging women, whether or not it is what they would choose or prefer to have happen. They have learned to be adaptable even while engaged in altering the change itself or the results it has engendered.

Ways of Embracing the Challenges of Change

- Look honestly at your resistance. Is the change really destructive, or is your reluctance to accept it based on fear? (For example: A woman's husband leaves her, and even if it may be better for everyone concerned, she may resist because she is afraid of being alone, afraid that she can't make it on her own, or afraid it may appear that she has "failed.")

- If resistance is based on fear, investigate your feelings and look at your options. You will find that once you confront fear, it begins to lose its power over you. More than one person has said that the end of one phase of life has opened up into a far greater opportunity.

- You may be able to make some changes in smaller pieces. If you want to make a job change, begin to look at new alternatives, and see how you might be able to work at something more rewarding and create a whole new niche for yourself. (You may even be able to start a new endeavor while still working at your current job.) Don't be afraid to be creative!

- Seek the support of someone you trust. Often change does not loom so large when someone cares and is willing to listen and help you sort it out.

- If a sudden change occurs, give yourself time to adjust, and then learn all you can about your new status. If an unwanted change is thrust on you suddenly, as in a death, divorce, or job loss, join a support group and find out what other women are doing under similar circumstances. (Our book, *Women Alone: Creating a Joyous and Fulfilling Life,* is a good resource under these circumstances.)

- Recognize your progress each time you find yourself resisting less and accepting more. You might even eventually begin to look for the "gift" that might be hiding behind the guise of change. At that point, you will have joined the ranks of the true emerging woman!

- Affirm: *"I embrace the ebb and flow of events in my life. I understand that everything is ultimately working together for my highest good, and I rest in that divine concept."*

Is Open-minded, Seeks Win/Win Solutions

Emerging women are open-minded and willing to look at all sides of an issue. Receptive to new information and possibilities, they are active listeners, more interested in cooperation than in competition. While no longer willing to be doormats, neither do they achieve their goals at someone else's expense. All challenges are viewed as opportunities to find workable solutions that benefit the whole. Their commitment is to making their immediate environment (and often the global environment) a more peaceful, loving, and healing place. Emerging women are thoughtful and carefully weigh the various facets of any given situation. They tend to see things from a higher perspective and are aware of the impact on others, as well as how an individual might be affected. They generally believe in communicating to the point of mutual understanding whenever possible and are willing to listen actively in order to gain that perspective. They work hard to lay aside preconceived notions or past programming in order to allow synergy to take place.

As emerging women enter into the highest level of Maslow's hierarchy, it is interesting to note that he felt these characteristics appeared only in the healthiest of people. Only emotionally healthy individuals are able to be self-actualizing and to follow their calling into the higher realms of consciousness. The women we've interviewed in these pages all exhibit the capabilities and, to one extent or another, the qualities necessary to be models, motivators, and mentors for their 21st-century counterparts.

Developing Skill in Negotiating Win/Win Situations

- Carefully observe the judgments you make. Are they based on fact? On someone else's opinion? On first impressions? On a projection or mirror image out of your own ego?
- When you catch yourself in the act of judging, stop for a moment and say to yourself, "I could choose to see this differently." Then, allow yourself to explore the other ways in which you might perceive the situation. For example, instead of saying, "She didn't speak to me; she's a snob," one might say, "Perhaps she doesn't have her glasses on," or "She might be preoccupied with a problem." You can

even choose to perceive this situation as a reflection of the times you have ignored or discounted someone else and make a resolve to be more considerate now that you know how it feels. Thus, you have just turned your act of judging into a gift of learning.

- Make a resolution to remain open to new ideas and perceptions. You don't have to accept them all, but at least be open to them. Most emerging women can reflect back and see how their thinking has changed in the past 20 years, and if they are honest, they'll have to admit that they fought those changes in the beginning, which now seem so obviously right.

- When conflicts arise, try to find win/win solutions. Most issues are not so clear-cut that there is no room for a solution that is beneficial to all concerned. It does take time, energy, and the willingness to listen and communicate.

- Once you have gained expertise in creating win/win situations in your personal life, start applying this practice on a larger scale at work, church, or in other outside activities. This is the beginning of conflict resolution skills that will allow us to honor and defuse our differences and help us create a more unconditionally loving and peaceful world.

- Affirm: *"I am a loving, expanding soul, and I am learning to observe my world with an open mind and through the eyes of Divine Spirit. I am able to see loving solutions in all situations, and I am bringing this wisdom into my dealings with all people at all times. I am a vehicle for the pure expression of LOVE."*

Explores Universal Connections and Is a Visionary and Transcender

Maslow found two types of self-actualizing people in his studies: those who transcend and those who do not. Both types are wonderful human beings, but they are distinctly different. The nontranscenders operate within their personal scope of reality and in the realm of a linear time frame. Those who transcend move toward a more spiritual view, a multidimensional concept, are visionaries, and are in touch with a larger reality. These women have transcended personal perceptions for a transpersonal point of view. Both categories of self-actualizers act responsibly in the world even though they may not always conform to societal norms, and each has learned to honor an inner sense of right action.

Of the women interviewed for this book, most seemed to have a connection to a concept or source much larger than themselves. Either they spoke of a spiritual energy that they called by various names, or they spoke of the oneness of all life. For the most part, there was an acute awareness that the inhabitants of planet Earth are a global family, and it was felt we must embrace our universal unity if we are to survive. This sense of the oneness of *all* life seems to be a pervading belief in most of the emerging women we spoke with.

Many women are already actively involved in making a difference at the global level, while others are "blooming where they're planted" and making a difference at local, state, and national levels. These women believe they are part of some larger destiny, and almost universally, turns to something higher than their conscious minds for sustenance. As self-actualizing women, they take many different pathways to this higher concept, but most have spiritual beliefs or practices that provide them with inner strength. They seem to have a firm conviction that we each can make a difference in bringing about greater universal understanding and tolerance. With a keen sense of responsibility, they are committed to doing their part. Without such a belief, most of these women would not have the heart or energy to continue their time-consuming tasks. If *Love* is the answer, then these women are providing plenty of answers.

It has been a commonly held notion that being "called" applied only to those entering the religious life. That is certainly not true. All of us, if we would only listen, have an inner passion, a yearning, a soul purpose, and that is our calling. Growing into what we were meant to be is risky business. It often requires life-altering changes and the surrender of many earlier programmed patterns that dictate what we "should" be as women. It takes real courage to transcend those messages in order to find out who we truly are at the very core of our being, and then to follow "the small, still voice within." But this is the journey for the widening stream of emerging women—it is a road to self-discovery, self-actualization and, finally, transcendence.

How to Live a More Expanded Life

- There are a vast number of books available that will stretch your mind and spirit. (A partial listing can be found at the back of this one.) Many of these books contain helpful exercises to expand your awareness, so try them. Make this a part of your daily practice even if only for a few minutes each day.
- Try some form of daily meditation.
- Write in a personal journal on a daily basis.
- Listen to your dreams and your intuitive thoughts. Listen for the "still, small voice" within, and take note of the synchronicity of events in your life.
- Join or create a women's healing circle. (*The Feminine Face of God*, by Sherry Ruth Anderson and Patricia Hopkins is an excellent resource guide for this activity.)
- Listen and do the exercises on Jean Houston's tapes on *Awakening the Body, Awakening the Brain,* and *Awakening Creativity* (these are available from Hay House).
- Join The Women of Vision and Action Network or some other group that works on a global level and espouses the oneness of all humanity/creation.
- Keep your eyes and ears open for the things going on around you, and participate to the degree that you can.

Look in the resource section at the back of this book for additional information on some terrific options.

- Affirm: *"I am a universal and transcendent being in the physical universe. I am constantly awakening to my real transcendent, multidimensional nature; I am at one with all life energies, and I am evolving toward total awareness of my status as co-creator of the future.*

CONCLUSION:
Womanspirit Rising

"What are the buried bones of my life?
When was the last time I ran free?
How do I make life come alive again?"
— Clarissa Pinkola Estes

While so much of the global community is in seeming chaos, increasing numbers of women and men are passionately determined to reorder and to rebuild it. Jungian Marion Woodman reports that many sensitive men are seeking, embracing, and expressing more of their feminine nature, while strong women are seeking, embracing, and expressing more of the masculine principle as they each strive for balance. Attaining balance between the intellect and the emotions, between the right brain and the left brain, we are more fully equipped to solve the complex problems continually presented to us.

In pre-history, in the time of "her-story," Mother Earth was called Gaia, and the feminine face of God was revered. Beginning as early as 4500 B.C., the pendulum slowly began to swing from herstory to history. Thus, the pattern of existence on earth changed from a gentle reverence for nature to a pattern of violence and conquest. For thousands of years, the more negative aspects of the masculine principle have overpowered the feminine. Now the pendulum is swinging back again, and we are being presented with an opportunity to find a balance between the two polarities. We are being challenged to move from confrontative modes to cooperative ones that are more likely to allow for our survival on this planet. Womanspirit is beginning to rise up into equal status and equal responsibility with the masculine spirit. Like the Phoenix bird that was apparently destroyed by burning but then rose from the ashes, Womanspirit is rising after thousands of years, alive and strong, and ready to assume full partnership in the evolution of "our-story."

We see today's emerging woman choosing to evolve into a new freedom and power, choosing to create and to live in a new paradigm. She is making changes in whatever arena she happens to find herself. She loves and cooperates with the men in her life, but in a more healthy partnership. She is no longer satisfied with less than full respect and equal responsibility. As author Betty Friedan said, "Who knows what women can be when they are finally free to become themselves?"

As the new emerging woman frees herself, she is no longer intimidated by male-dominated institutions. Entering these inner sanctums in increasing numbers, women are demystifying them and discovering the underlying issues and problems. Jean Houston points out in *A Mythic Life* that "when thinking and doing are largely linear, analytic, hierarchical, and lacking in the feminine dimension, and when the self that does the thinking and doing is insular, fearful, manipulative, and overly masculine, our best intentions in problem solving become a crazy-quilt patchwork of Band-Aids." Wise enough to refuse to imitate masculine methods, the emerging woman instead brings her own unique perspective to the tasks at hand and trusts her own approach.

Unfortunately, some women allow themselves to become caught up in the masculine modus operandi. This happens in all areas and at all levels, and it may take awhile for older, unproductive competitive patterns and Queen Bee syndromes to fade away. Mary Collins Shields, a former businesswoman and now a women's counselor, says, "We've had to spend so much time learning to relate to men that many of us don't know how to relate to women."

A commonly told story illustrates an important point about change: Scientists were studying the behavior of monkeys on a small group of south sea islands. The monkeys' usual routine was to eat the abundant breadfruit just as it was, usually covered with sand. Then on one island, one monkey began to wash its breadfruit before eating it. Another monkey observed this and began doing the same. This behavior began to spread as more and more monkeys got the idea. When approximately 10 percent of the monkeys on this island began washing their breadfruit before eating it, the monkeys on a neighboring island began to wash theirs in the same manner, even though there was so much water between the islands that the monkeys had no physical contact with each other!

This simple story shows that when change reaches a certain point, it not only accelerates, but makes a quantum leap that profoundly affects *everything*. We see this critical mass being reached by emerging women all over the world who refuse to retreat back into the old paradigm, no matter how severe the consequences. As Margaret Mead reminded Jean Houston, "You can't turn around the social order of thousands of years in a few decades without expecting a backlash."

Visible women leaders of the past few decades too often suffered the sting of backlash, and some continue to do so. Margaret Sanger, the outspoken proponent of birth control, had to leave the country for a while to avoid being arrested; Betty Friedan and Gloria Steinem were ridiculed in the earlier days of the women's movement; historically, any president's wife who seems to be an individual and have a mind of her own is disparaged. Eleanor Roosevelt drew particularly cruel and caustic criticism but still managed to withstand it, thus providing a model for future First Ladies such as Hillary Rodham Clinton. The words of Eleanor, spoken from the perspective of her own difficulties, can inspire any woman whose goal is to be true to herself as she uses her gifts to serve humanity in spite of personal attacks: "If our desire is to serve humanity, we will be crushed and broken-hearted. But if our desire is to serve God, then no amount of ingratitude can keep us from serving our fellow human beings."

Throughout history, strong women have been determined to lead and to serve humanity, beginning with Old Testament biblical figures such as Esther and Ruth, and continuing with strong rulers such as Queen Elizabeth I, Catherine the Great, and Indira Gandhi. In fact, inspired and strong women have made valuable contributions in art, religion, science, and in virtually every area of endeavor. However, the stream of women *allowed* to make a difference in patriarchal societies has been relatively narrow compared to the stream of men who traditionally have been *encouraged* to make a difference.

Now, the push for equal opportunity that began earlier in this century is giving women a wider window of opportunity and influence. The numbers of women, just in the last half of the '90s, who are doing the equivalent of washing their breadfruit and showing others how to do the same, is expanding into a wider and wider stream. These are the emerging women who are breaking the old patterns, smashing the old molds, finding their life purpose, fashioning a more satisfying life for themselves, and working to make our planet a more hospitable place for all humankind.

In the process, women are reaching out to one another in increasing numbers as they discover the life-enhancing power of mutual support and encouragement. For example, Mary Collins Shields was the busy CEO of a successful Colorado Springs real estate agency, but felt she was dying inside. A turning point came when she attended a seminar for women who were open to exploring their feelings and their identities. As Mary shared with others in her small circle, she determined to make a life change. She went back to college, studied psychology, and opened a counseling practice. She made the decision to "follow her bliss," and her passion for life quickly returned. Because the women's circle was such a dramatic and profound change agent for her, Mary utilizes the small-circle format in her own practice. She sees women transforming their lives and functioning at a higher level as a result of their participation. She believes that something magical happens when women get together, and we too witness that magic wherever we present our *Emerging Women* workshops.

As individual women blossom in nourishing environments, they are empowered to engineer richer more balanced lives for themselves. They are then ready to join with other women to improve the quality of life for everyone. Certainly, the Women of Vision and Action Network is a prime example of the positive changes that groups of women are capable of making. These emerging women and many others like them are becoming what Jean Houston calls "social artists."

Social artists, male and female, are found in every area of endeavor. They may be teachers, learners, parents, children, philosophers; they are engaged in every profession and occupation. Fully involved and refusing to sleepwalk through life, a social artist asks questions and participates in creative solutions. A social artist is a community builder on a local and a planetary scale.

Once a woman's growth process begins to accelerate, she is primed to become a social artist, and the universe rejoices and cooperates with her. Old patterns fade quickly as she embraces her new-found wisdom and power. When Barbara Marx Hubbard began to expand her life in new ways, her daughter said, "Mother, you have transformed from a cave-age lady to a space-age lady in one year!"

That kind of Womanspirit is rising everywhere, and we women are now emerging from our long dormancy. Enlightened and empowered, we have reached critical mass; we are becoming part of the widening stream of women ready to accept full partnership with men in giving birth to the new Universal Human. We claim our full power as embodiments and expressions of the Creative Force of the universe. We are emerging into the role we were assigned from the beginning of time. We are waking up. The time has come for the birthing of "our-story," and it cannot be held back. Standing together, we face our challenges with courage and compassion and bless the strength and wisdom we gain from them. We embrace and support one another in love and joy as we take our place in the widening stream of emerging women, empowered and committed to social artistry as we build a new world!

Appendix

RECOMMENDED READING

Alicia—My Story, Alicia Appleman-Jurman. New York:
Bantam, 1988.

Awakening the Heroes Within, Carol S. Pearson. San Francisco, CA:
HarperCollins, 1991.

Constant Craving, Doreen Virtue, Ph.D., Carlsbad, CA:
Hay House, 1995.

A Course in Love, Joan Gattuso. San Francisco, CA:
HarperCollins, 1996.

Elegant Choices, Healing Choices, Marsha Sinetar. Mahwah, NJ:
Paulist Press, 1988.

Empowering Women: Every Woman's Guide to Successful Living,
Louise L. Hay, Carlsbad, CA: Hay House, 1997.

The Feminine Face of God, Sherry Ruth Anderson and Patricia
Hopkins. New York: Bantam, 1991.

Goddess in Everywoman, Jean Shinoda Bolen. New York:
Harper, 1984.

Herland, Charlotte Perkins Gilman. New York:
Pantheon Books, 1979.

The Hunger of Eve, Barbara Marx Hubbard. Harrisburg, PA:
Stackpole Books, 1976.

Illuminata, Marianne Williamson. New York:
Random House, 1994.

It Takes a Village, Hillary Rodham Clinton. New York:
Simon and Schuster, 1996.

Joycelyn Elders, M.D., Joycelyn Elders, M.D. New York:
William Morrow, 1996.

Leaving My Father's House, Marion Woodman. Boston:
Shambala, 1992.

Life! Reflections on Your Journey, Louise L. Hay, Carlsbad, CA:
Hay House, 1995.

*Losing Your Pounds of Pain—Breaking the Link Between Abuse,
Stress, and Overeating.* Doreen Virtue, Ph.D. Carlsbad, CA:
Hay House, 1994.

Moving Beyond Words, Gloria Steinem. New York:
Simon and Schuster, 1994.

A Mythic Life, Jean Houston. San Francisco, CA:
HarperCollins, 1996.

The Other Side of Death, Jan Price. New York: Fawcett, 1996.

The Possible Human, Jean Houston. Los Angeles, CA:
Tarcher, 1982.

The Power of the Mind to Heal, Joan Borysenko, Ph.D. and
Miroslav Borysenko, Ph.D. Carlsbad, CA: Hay House, 1994.

Quest—The Life of Elisabeth Kübler-Ross. Derek Gill. New York:
Ballantine, 1980.

Revelation, Barbara Marx Hubbard. Mill Valley, CA:
Nataraj, 1995.

Revolution from Within, Gloria Steinem. Boston:
Little, Brown, 1992.

The Way of All Women, Esther Harding. New York: Harper, 1970.

When God Was a Woman, Merlin Stone. New York:
Harcourt, Brace, Jovanovich, 1976.

Where the Girls Are, Susan J. Douglas. New York:
Random House, 1994

Womanspirit, Hallie Iglehart. New York: Harper and Row, 1983.

Women Alone: Creating a Joyous and Fulfilling Life,
Julie Keene and Ione Jenson. Carlsbad, CA: Hay House, 1995.

Women Who Run with the Wolves, Clarissa Pinkola Estes, Ph.D.
New York: Ballantine, 1992.

You Can Heal Your Life, Louise L. Hay. Carlsbad, CA:
Hay House, 1984.

GENERAL RESOURCES

The Age of the Great Goddess (2 audiocassettes—140 minutes) with archeologist Maria Gimbutas. $18.95. Available from Sounds True Catalog. (800) 333-9185.

Foundation for Conscious Evolution (Barbara Marx Hubbard). P.O. Box 6397, San Rafael, CA 94903-0397. (415) 454-8191 Fax: (415) 454-8805. E-mail: fce@hooked.net. Website: http://www.co-creation.com. Evolutionary Circle Guides: $75; shipping; $6 US; $15 foreign.

Health Wisdom for Women Newsletter, Christiane Northrup, M.D. Phillips Publishing, 7811 Montrose Rd., Potomac, MD 20854. (800) 705-5559.

Holo Center (Ione Jenson, Julie Keene, Masil Hulse). E. 955 Grand Tour Drive, Hayden, Idaho 83835. Holo brochure with stamped self-addressed business envelope. To order *From Soap Opera to Symphony* by Julie Keene, send $16 (includes postage) to Julie at the above address.

International New Thought Alliance. 5003 E. Broadway Rd., Mesa, AZ 85206. (602) 830- 2461. *New Thought Journal* (4 issues a year, $12).

The Quartus Foundation (Jan and John Price). P.O. Box 1768, Boerne, TX 78006-6768. (210) 249-3985.

Society for the Universal Human. Living Enrichment Center, 29500 SW Graham's Ferry Rd., Wilsonville, OR 97979. (800) 893-1000.

A Unifying Movement (Rev. Susan Michaels). 9055 E. Catalina Way, #4204, Tuscon, AZ 85743.

Women of Vision and Action (Rama Vernon, Eleanor LeCain, and Barbara Marx Hubbard). For more information, call: (800) 909-WOVA (9682), or write: P.O. Box 550, Bowie, MD 20718 for brochure.

SELF-HELP RESOURCES

The following list of resources can be used for more information about recovery options for issues surrounding addictions, health concerns, death and bereavement, or problems related to dysfunctional families. The addresses and telephone numbers listed are for the national headquarters; look in your local yellow pages under "Community Services" for resources closer to your area.

In addition to the following groups, other self-help organizations may be available in your area to assist your healing and recovery for a particular life crisis not listed here. Consult your telephone directory, call a counseling center or help line near you, or contact:

American Self-Help Clearinghouse
St. Clares-Riverside Medical Center
Denville, NJ 07834
(201) 625-7101

National Self-Help Clearinghouse
25 West 43rd St., Room 620
New York, NY 10036
(212) 642-2944

♫ ♫ ♫

AIDS

AIDS Hotline
(800) 342-2437

Children with AIDS Project of America
4020 N. 20th St., Ste. 101
Phoenix, AZ 85016
(602) 265-4859
Hotline:
(602) 843-8654

The Names Project— AIDS Quilt
(800) 872-6263

National AIDS Network
(800) 342-2437

Project Inform
19655 Market St., Ste. 220
San Francisco, CA 94103
(415) 558-8669

PWA Coalition
50 W. 17th St.
New York, NY 10011

Spanish AIDS Hotline
(800) 344-7432

**TDD (Hearing Impaired)
AIDS Hotline**
(800) 243-7889

ക ക ക

ALCOHOL ABUSE

Al-Anon Family Headquarters
200 Park Ave. South
New York, NY 10003
(804) 563-1600

Alcoholics Anonymous (AA)
General Service Office
475 Riverside Dr.
New York, NY 10115
(212) 870-3400

**Children of Alcoholics
Foundation**
P.O. Box 4185
Grand Central Station
New York, NY 10163-4185
(212) 754-0656
(800) 359-COAF

Meridian Council, Inc.
Administrative Offices
4 Elmcrest Terrace
Norwalk, CT 06850

**National Association of
Children of Alcoholics
(NACOA)**
11426 Rockville Pike, Ste. 100
Rockville, MD 20852
(301) 468-0985

**National Clearinghouse for
Alcohol and Drug Information
(NCADI)**
P.O. Box 234
Rockville, MD 20852
(301) 468-2600

**National Council on
Alcoholism and Drug
Dependency (NCADD)**
12 West 21st St.
New York, NY 10010
(212) 206-6770

ക ക ക

ANOREXIA/BULIMIA

**American Anorexia/Bulimia
Association, Inc.**
293 Central Park West, Ste. 1R
New York, NY 10024
(212) 501-8351

Eating Disorder Organization
1925 East Dublin Granville Rd.
Columbus, OH 43229-3517
(918) 481-4044

♫ ♫ ♫

CANCER

National Cancer Institute
(800) 4-CANCER

ECAP (Exceptional Cancer Patients)
Bernie S. Siegel, M.D.
300 Plaza Middlesex
Middletown, CT 06457
(860) 343-5950

♫ ♫ ♫

CHILDREN'S ISSUES

<u>Child Molestation</u>

Adults Molested As Children United (AMACU)
232 East Gish Rd.
San Jose, CA 95112
(800) 422-4453

National Committee for Prevention of Child Abuse
332 South Michigan Ave.,
    Ste. 1600
Chicago, IL 60604
(312) 663-3520

<u>Children's and Teens' Crisis Intervention</u>

Boy's Town Crisis Hotline
(800) 448-3000

Covenant House Hotline
(800) 999-9999

Kid Save
(800) 543-7283

National Runaway and Suicide Hotline
(800) 621-4000

♫ ♫ ♫

<u>Missing Children</u>
Missing Children-Help Center
410 Ware Blvd., Ste. 400
Tampa, FL 33619
(800) USA-KIDS

National Center for Missing and Exploited Children
1835 K St. NW
Washington, DC 20006
(800) 843-5678

♫ ♫ ♫

Seriously Ill Children (fulfilling wishes)

Brass Ring Society
(918) 743-3232

❦ ❦ ❦

CO-DEPENDENCY

Co-Dependents Anonymous
60 E. Richards Way
Sparks, NV 89431
(602) 277-7991

❦ ❦ ❦

DEATH/GRIEVING/ SUICIDE

Grief Recovery Helpline
(800) 445-4808

Grief Recovery Institute
8306 Wilshire Blvd., Ste. 21A
Beverly Hills, CA 90211
(213) 650-1234

Mothers Against Drunk Driving (MADD)
(817) 690-6233

National Hospice Organization (NHO)
1901 Moore St. #901
Arlington, VA 22209
(703) 243-5900

National Sudden Infant Death Syndrome
Two Metro Plaza, Ste. 205
Landover, MD 20785
(800) 221-SIDS

Seasons: Suicide Bereavement
4777 Naniola Dr.
Salt Lake City, UT 84117

❦ ❦ ❦

DEBTS

Debtors Anonymous
General Service Office
P.O. Box 400
Grand Central Station
New York, NY 10163-0400
(212) 642-8220

❦ ❦ ❦

DIABETES

American Diabetes Association
(800) 232-3472

   

DRUG ABUSE

Cocaine Anonymous
(800) 347-8998

National Cocaine-Abuse Hotline
(800) 262-2463
(800) COCAINE

National Institute of Drug Abuse (NIDA)
Parklawn Building
5600 Fishers Lane,
    Room 10A-39
Rockville, MD 20852
(301) 443-6245
    (for information)
(800) 662-4357 (for help)

World Service Office (CA)
3740 Overland Ave. Suite C
Los Angeles, CA 90034-6337
(310) 559-5833

   

EATING DISORDERS

Eating Disorder Organization
1925 East Dublin Granville Rd.
Columbus, OH 43229-3517
(918) 481-4044

Overeaters Anonymous
National Office
Rio Rancho, NM
(505) 891-2664

   

GAMBLING

Gamblers Anonymous
National Council on Compulsive
    Gambling
444 West 59th St., Room 1521
New York, NY 10019
(212) 903-4400

   

HEALTH ISSUES

Alzheimer's Disease Information
(800) 621-0379

American Chronic Pain Association
P.O. Box 850
Rocklin, CA 95677
(916) 632-0922

American Foundation of Traditional Chinese Medicine
1280 Columbus Ave., Ste. 302
San Francisco, CA 94133
(415) 776-0502

American Holistic Health Association
P.O. Box 17400
Anaheim, CA 92817
(714) 779-6152

Chopra Center for Well-Being
Deepak Chopra, M.D.
7630 Fay Ave.
La Jolla, CA 92037
(619) 551-7788

The Fetzer Institute
9292 West KL Ave.
Kalamazoo, MI 49009
(616) 375-2000

Hippocrates Health Institute
1443 Palmdale Court
West Palm Beach, FL 33411
(407) 471-8876

Hospicelink
(800) 331-1620

Institute for Noetic Sciences
P.O. Box 909, Dept. M
Sausalito, CA 94966-0909
(800) 383-1394

The Mind-Body Medical Institute
185 Pilgrim Rd.
Boston, MA 02215
(617) 632-9525

National Health Information Center
P.O. Box 1133
Washington, DC 20013-1133
(800) 336-4797

Optimum Health Care Institute
6970 Central Ave.
Lemon Grove, CA 91945
(619) 464-3346

Preventive Medicine Research Institute
Dean Ornish, M.D.
900 Bridgeway, Ste. 2
Sausalito, CA 94965
(415) 332-2525

World Research Foundation
20501 Ventura Blvd., Ste. 100
Woodland Hills, CA 91364
(818) 999-5483

～ ～ ～

IMPOTENCE

Impotency Institute of America
10400 Patuzent Pkwy, Ste. 485
Washington, DC 20006
(800) 669-1603

～ ～ ～

INCEST

Incest Survivors Resource Network International, Inc.
P.O. Box 7375
Las Cruces, NM 88006-7375
(505) 521-4260

～ ～ ～

COURSE IN MIRACLES COUNSELORS

Miracle Distribution Center
1141 East Ash Ave.
Fullerton, CA 92631
(714) 738-8380
(800) 359-2246

～ ～ ～

PET BEREAVEMENT

Bide-A-Wee Foundation
New York, NY
(212) 532-6395

The Animal Medical Center
510 E. 62nd St.
New York, NY 10021
(212) 838-8100

Holistic Animal Consulting Center
29 Lyman Ave.
Staten Island, NY 10305
(718) 720-5548

～ ～ ～

RAPE

Austin Rape Crisis Center
1824 East Oltorf
Austin, TX 78741
(512) 440-7273

～ ～ ～

SEX ADDICTIONS

National Council on Sexual Addictions
P.O. Box 652
Azle, TX 76098-0652
(800) 321-2066

SMOKING ABUSE

Nicotine Anonymous
2118 Greenwich St.
San Francisco, CA 94123
(415) 750-0328

ॐ ॐ ॐ

SPOUSAL ABUSE

**National Coalition Against
Domestic Violence**
P.O. Box 34103
Washington, DC 20043-4103
(202) 638-6388

**National Domestic Violence
Hotline**
(800) 799-SAFE

ॐ ॐ ॐ

STRESS REDUCTION

**The Biofeedback &
Psychophysiology Clinic**
The Menninger Clinic
P.O. Box 829
Topeka, KS 66601-0829
(913) 350-5000

New York Open Center
(In-depth workshops to
invigorate the spirit)
83 Spring St.
New York, NY 10012
(212) 219-2527

Omega Institute
(A healing, spiritual retreat
community)
260 Lake Dr.
Rhinebeck, NY 12572-3212
(914) 266-4444 (info)
(800) 944-1001 (to enroll)

Rise Institute
P.O. Box 2733
Petaluma, CA 94973
(707) 765-2758

The Stress Reduction Clinic
Jon Kabat-Zinn, Ph.D.
University of Massachusetts
Medical Center
55 Lake Ave. North
Worcester, MA 01655
(508) 856-1616
(508) 856-2656

ABOUT THE AUTHORS

Ione Jenson is a counselor, dream therapist, and teacher who holds degrees in education, psychology, and counseling. She is the co-author (with Julie Keene) of *Women Alone: Creating a Joyous and Fulfilling Life*. She is also the author of the self-published book, *Empowering the Child from Within: Education and Parenting for the Twenty-first Century*. For the past several years, Ione has been conducting workshops and doing private spiritual counseling. She is co-founder of The Holo Center, a retreat community in Hayden Lake, Idaho.

Julie Keene was formerly a professor at Ferris State University in Michigan, then went on to serve as a minister in Unity churches throughout the country. She is the co-author (with Ione Jenson) of *Women Alone: Creating a Joyous and Fulfilling Life*, and has also authored an autobiographical work called *From Soap Opera to Symphony*. She now works and lives at The Holo Center, a retreat community in Hayden Lake, Idaho, where she conducts workshops with a focus on spiritual and psychological growth.

Masil Hulse, the artist who painted the lovely work on the front cover of this book, is available for private commissions, and prints of her existing works are also available. You may contact her by calling The Holo Center in Idaho: (208) 772-2816.

We hope you enjoyed this Hay House book.
If you would like to receive a free catalog featuring
additional Hay House books and products,
or if you would like information about the
Hay Foundation, please contact:

Hay House, Inc.
P.O. Box 5100
Carlsbad, CA 92018-5100

(800) 654-5126 • (800) 650-5115 (fax)

Please visit the Hay House Website at: **http://www.hayhouse.com**